THE IRRESISTIBLE GROWTH ENTERPRISE

Breakthrough Gains from Unstoppable Change

Donald Mitchell and Carol Coles

ILLUSTRATIONS BY *Tobi Kahn*

Sty/us

STERLING, VIRGINIA

Published in 2000 by

Stylus Publishing, LLC
22883 Quicksilver Drive
Sterling, Virginia 20166

Library of Congress Cataloging-in-Publication Data

Mitchell, Donald, 1946–
    The irresistible growth enterprise : breakthrough gains from
      unstoppable change /
        Donald Mitchell and Carol Coles ; illustrations by Tobi Kahn—
      1st ed.
        p. cm.
    Includes bibliographical references.
    ISBN 1-57922-026-6 (alk. paper)
    1. Industrial management. 2. Organizational change. 3. Corporations—
Growth. I. Coles, Carol. II. Title

HD31.M476 2000
658.4'062—dc21   00-055712

First edition, 2000
Hard cover ISBN: 1–57922–026–6

Printed in the United States of America

Printed on acid free paper

10 9 8 7 6 5 4 3 2 1

*This book is dedicated to Peter F. Drucker for his
pioneering work in developing the practice
of management and his unstinting encouragement
of our efforts to share our ideas.*

CONTENTS

ACKNOWLEDGMENTS

The Irresistible Growth Enterprise was improved by assistance from hundreds of people, and space doesn't permit us to thank each of you individually here. We hope you will know we appreciate and care about you, and are indebted to you for what you did for this book. Thank you!

We acknowledge the following people for their special contributions:

- Mitchell and Company's clients over the past twenty-two years deserve first mention and thanks because they provided the opportunity to develop the insights in the book. In many cases, they also served as examples, usually anonymously. We thank them for providing for our firm's success, as well, so that we had the time and resources to devote to this project. Many dozens of client executives also took time to provide helpful comments that were used in revisions of the manuscript.

- Some of the members of the Twenty Times Progress Steering Committee went out of their way to provide useful comments and guidance that proved critical to our final result. We want to especially recognize the assistance we received from Timothy D. Althof, Neil H. Bruckner, Richard E. Koch, and Michael A. Sharp.

- During the drafting of the book, many executives and academics took the time to consider our words. The comments and ideas we received from the following people proved to be essential to the final version of the book: Norman R. Augustine, chairman of the executive committee, Lockheed Martin; Michael J. Birck, chairman and CEO of Tellabs; Arie de Geus, former head of planning at Shell; Professor Peter F. Drucker; Alan G. Hassenfeld, chairman and CEO of Hasbro; H. William Lichtenberger, chairman of Praxair; Robert Rock, chairman and publisher of *Directors & Boards;* Glenn Schaeffer, president of Mandalay Resort Group; Jerre Stead, former chairman and CEO of Ingram Micro; and Hicks B. Waldron, former chairman and CEO of Avon.

- Tobi Kahn worked for months on dozens of potential images for this book based on his careful study of the book's content. He was tireless in helping us at a time when his own successful career was placing unprecedented demands upon him. Thank you, Tobi!

- We want to thank Irene Majuk for suggesting the term "ideal best practice" to replace our earlier formulation of "theoretical best practice."

- Pam Ellsworth was wonderful with her many useful comments, questions, research, fact checking, and aid in locating and obtaining permissions for illustrations. We could not have completed the project without her.

- At Mitchell and Company, Phyllis Smalls helped in many ways, too numerous to mention.

- We were indeed fortunate to have a perceptive, hard-working, and ever-helpful publisher in John von Knorring of Stylus Publishing. John added many wonderful improvements to the book, and has been a pleasure to work with. His enthusiasm for the project was an important source of inspiration for us.

- Bernice Pettinato of Beehive Production Services provided invaluable guidance with the structure and editing of this book. We are very grateful for her tireless and valuable assistance. She made the editing process a joy!

- Finally, as coauthors, we would like to acknowledge and thank each other for the great support and many contributions provided to each other. We could not have had this wonderful adventure without the two of us.

That having been said, we want to emphasize that the responsibility for any errors or missed opportunities to improve the book is ours alone.

This illustration shows you two paths that diverge to the left and right from a central pathway that begins at the bottom left. Imagine yourself at the crossroads now. Which path should you take? If you follow the path to the left, you will find yourself following a route that becomes more and more narrow, probably providing few choices. If you follow the path at the right, the route and the opportunities soon expand. By first exploring down both paths a little, you can make the right choice. In the same way, this book will help you improve your decisions. You will learn how to understand better the future consequences of your current decisions so that you will always choose the better path.

THE MISSING ELEMENT

A single idea, if it is right, saves us the labor of an infinity of experiences.

—Jacques Maritain, philosopher

The fundamental premise of this book is that no matter how successful you and your organization are, you are performing at a modest level compared to the potential you can unleash through adopting the irresistible growth enterprise perspective described in this book. If your organization is typical, it's spending a lot of time and resources struggling to offset the negative effects of externally-driven irresistible forces (like technological development, new ways of working, customer preferences and business conditions) on its current direction. You should, instead, be changing your strategic orientation to use those forces to your advantage. That idea is the missing element needed for achieving breakthrough gains that will deliver irresistible growth.

To make the irresistible growth adjustment requires a revolutionary shift in focus that is difficult to accomplish. Indeed, the barrier to irresistible growth is not unstoppable, uncontrollable external change, but fixed (and frequently unexamined) ideas of how to respond to those changes. *The Irresistible Growth Enterprise* is your how-to-change manual. In it you can learn how to build your enterprise faster with an integrated bottom-to-top shift in how you operate that includes an improved leadership style; a powerful vision for the future that every enterprise needs regardless of its mission; a strategy to execute that vision; tactics and an organizational structure to implement that strategy; and a management process for executing the tactics, as well as the best way for everyone in your operation to learn and apply this operating concept.

The Challenging, Changing Environment for Your Organization

John Kenneth Galbraith, the economist, noted that "The enemy of the conventional wisdom is not ideas but the march of events." And the tide of expected future change in our society is now rapid and breathtaking to most—whether we consider irresistible forces like the advent of the Knowledge Age (with knowledge doubling in many fields within a few years, months, or even days); the electronic improvements in communication choices (the potential number of ways for you to receive or send a message will continue to grow rapidly for many more years); shifts in work activities (from routine fulfilling of standard tasks to Peter Drucker's knowledge work) and stability (as a result of downsizing and a "free agent" work force); demographic-driven social changes (ever older populations in the developed countries and younger ones everywhere else); weather volatility (both in temperatures and storms); the movements of currencies and markets; social mores of the moment (fads get shorter and shorter); or personal styles of the young teenagers (differentiating them from older teenagers, not just from adults).

There is no doubt that today the world has become much more complicated and interconnected. For businesses, globalization means that the number and distance of customers, suppliers, and competitors have grown geometrically. Such interconnectedness also means that what affects one can quickly spread and affect all, like the rapid expansions of computer and human viruses. These connections mean that economic and financial adjustments, especially in prices and currency values, travel faster and further than before. Your irresistible growth enterprise must be agile in adapting to these changes. We believe that making quick and best use of rapid changes in powerful conditions no one can control is the key to becoming an irresistible growth enterprise.

When asked in the 1950s about how much control they had over their business's success, U.S. CEOs felt they had a great deal. By the start of the 1990s, CEOs often felt that irresistible forces had more impact on the company's success than the employees did. You only have to look at charts measuring events over the past 100 years to see that the volatility of many irresistible forces is also growing. In the past 30 years alone, this volatility has included an unprecedented success by a commodity cartel (the Arab oil embargo); the fall of a major political system around the world (communism); extraordinary growth in U.S. stock prices; fluctuations in interest rates from more than 20 percent to as low as the single digits in North America (and more widely elsewhere); and diversion of the resources of the burgeoning service economy (of stores and local brokerage offices) into creating an information-based economy.

As these examples suggest, the degree and speed of change are both accelerating. At one time, corporate leaders could conduct leisurely studies of such changing phenomena after they began to occur, thoughtfully select the right actions, and then experiment with the best way to proceed. Today, the time involved to deliberately study its choices often costs a company its biggest opportunities and can even lead to failure. Consider Barnes & Noble, the leader in bricks-and-mortar bookstores. Before launching its electronic commerce business, it decided to first watch what happened with Amazon.com as it studied its options. By the time it was ready to act, Amazon.com had built a commanding electronic lead that will be very difficult to overcome.

Naturally, it's nice to be able to find one trend and ride it for a long time, like McDonald's did. The company's premise is based on customers' desires for dependable, inexpensive food, served quickly and effectively in convenient, clean locations. From its beginnings as a single hamburger stand in the 1930s in San Bernardino, California, it has become a global giant today. But even McDonald's has had to learn to adapt to the irresistible force of consumer food preferences as it moved beyond North America. The familiar hamburger, fries and soft drink menu has had to be expanded to offer curry in England and a glass of wine in Paris.

Today's enterprises will find such long-term rides to be the exception to the rule. Consider how Microsoft flirted with disaster in the 1990s by missing the early significance of providing Internet software and services, or how Intel, originally a memory chip manufacturer, shifted into microprocessors as its primary business somewhat by accident. Indeed, the world is full of shuttered stores that failed to meet customer needs. Their boarded-up windows are mute testimony to the necessity of shifting with the changing trends.

Many of the most significant irresistible forces (such as new technologies, improved communications, the weather, demographics, user preferences, and economic conditions) have grown much more volatile and unpredictable in just the past five to ten years. Analysts suggest that this trend will accelerate due to the "chaos" effects of how a small change in one place in the world can cause an enormous change elsewhere. For example, in computer-based weather simulations, the equivalent of a butterfly's flapping in one continent can produce a killer storm in another. This multiplier effect will increasingly happen with all irresistible forces, and this is the key insight upon which you must act now! While most organizations will react to such forces and their changes only when it is impossible not to (out of self-preservation or fear), the irresistible growth enterprise will see its primary tasks as the creation of broad unstoppable change, the accurate anticipation of such changes, and the steady beneficial harnessing of such changes to achieve its purposes.

Only a relative few have made significant, successful adjustments to changing conditions. Simply consider all of the changes that Jack Welch went through to turn General Electric from a slow-growing industrial goods manufacturer into a financial services powerhouse with high-margin manufacturing specialties. Any one of these changes would have overwhelmed most organizations, yet Welch has succeeded with several. How well the company fares under Welch's successor will reveal a lot about the difficulties of continuing as an irresistible growth enterprise. There is, perhaps, no more interesting example of such success than Berkshire Hathaway, which started as an owner of a failing textile mill that eventually did go out of business. Warren Buffett, Berkshire's founder, has successfully navigated the changing tides of business and financial markets over the years to build one of the most successful companies ever. Unlike Microsoft and Intel, which had relatively few important shifts in irresistible forces, Berkshire Hathaway has weathered several by redirecting its resources and energies into new, more promising directions. After having been primarily a portfolio manager of a handful of common stocks for many years, the company has recently shifted again to emphasize purchasing and operating companies. By utilizing the processes presented in this book, you can learn to catch the full benefit of today's volatile and rapidly changing forces, and spur your enterprise on to greater and more rapid growth than ever before.

Being in the Right Position to Optimize Opportunity

Many businesspeople are fond of saying, "I'd rather be lucky than smart." Anyone who has experienced the exhilaration of an unexpected boost from favorable circumstances certainly would like it to happen more often. Applying the concepts from *The Irresistible Growth Enterprise* will enable you to create your own good fortune.

When asked why he scored so many goals in hockey, NHL scoring champion Wayne Gretzky replied that he always skated to where he thought the puck would be going. That strategy gave him an important edge because most other skaters go toward where the puck is already. But it isn't enough to just be in the right place at the right time. The tightrope walker working outdoors in the wind prefers that the wind be at her back because a side wind could more easily knock her off balance. Setting up the tight rope to make the breeze's direction favorable can provide the necessary advantage for her. She can further improve security by using a balance pole. To help you achieve irresistible growth, this book shows you how to choose actions that will put you in the right place with the right resources to benefit from powerful trends, regardless of their source or direction.

To move your enterprise from its current position to a better one takes hard work. It's like the tightrope walker finding the wind coming from the wrong direction and demanding that the tightrope be repositioned before she performs. Then, the equipment handlers have a lot of hard work to undo and redo. That's the bad news about getting into the right position. The good news is that once your company has reached its ideal position, its subsequent need to change will be less. Like the Olympic wrestler who fights his way to a position securely on top of his opponent, you'll be able to seize advantageous positions no matter how your competitors react and your business environment changes. Most organizations today are, unfortunately, like the winning wrestler's opponent, operating subject to the whims of powerful competitors and the vagaries of circumstances as their noses are ground into the smelly, dirty mat. Is yours one of them?

If your enterprise is like most, it operates according to a plan. Your business now pays attention to executing that plan. When things go wrong, most people in your organization will try to protect their self-interest and their chances for achieving the plan's goals. If things get really bad, they'll be stunned into inaction. These behaviors reflect some of the many faulty thinking patterns you need to abolish and replace in order to achieve a winning position in an increasingly volatile and unpredictable organizational environment.

You need to focus on getting the most benefit from your enterprise's irresistible forces, the powerful factors beyond your control that fundamentally shape your opportunities. Most people see such forces as random factors or inconveniences, but *The Irresistible Growth Enterprise* will show you how to use all those forces instead of trying to avoid some of them.

Every change in irresistible forces provides new opportunities to those who have learned to see them that way. For very cyclical businesses, when demand is strong, you can sell high-cost facilities and obtain long-term relationships with attractive customers. When demand is weak, you can buy low-cost facilities, repurchase your own stock, negotiate lower prices from suppliers and get complementary competitors interested in merging with you. Optimal opportunities for gaining important advantages from your business's environment always exist; you just have to be able to recognize them.

Once an opportunity is recognized, you need to be properly prepared to take the right actions at the right time. You have to have the flexibility to take advantage of rapid and extreme changes in irresistible forces. Such flexibility can be developed through the use of planning extreme scenarios—what we refer to in this book as Nth-degree searches—that greatly exaggerate the future impact of forces to clarify opportunities. This requires using an improved kind of scenario planning for possible future circumstances, most of which will never occur. You'll learn how to understand more about what causes your irresistible forces so you can better appreciate their potential. Your enterprise will then locate and be ready to implement its "Always-Win, No-Lose" opportunities, that minimize the down side, while leaving the up side open-ended, regardless of the irresistible forces.

The Irresistible Growth Enterprise also shows you a breakthrough way to focus and simplify your company's implementation of its best opportunities. This new paradigm replaces the costs and delays that arise from learning primarily through broad-scale trial and error (as Maritain's quotation at the beginning of the Introduction suggests). As a result, you'll be able to make best use of your opportunities to be in the right place, with the right resources, and taking the right actions in a timely manner. Irresistible force management is the missing element that will make this possible.

Adaptability Models

A more flexible and proactive approach for your organization will usually serve your purposes better. Nature provides an intriguing example of how individual adaptability expands success chances for larger groups of individuals in an organization. According to John Tyler Bonner in the December 1984 issue of *Science '81,* a type of amoebas, known as cellular slime molds, displays some very valuable characteristics in the face of daunting circumstances that affect their survival, their irresistible forces.

Normally these amoebas live individually on the forest floor and are limited in their potential to grow and prosper by the local supply of food they can reach in a fixed position. The size and location of the food supply serves as an irresistible force for the amoebas. For most organisms that are essentially stationary, high death rates follow the exhaustion of food sources.

When food sources are scarce, these particular amoebas have the capability to group together as slime molds to move to where there is more food. These temporary clumps of amoebas creep across the forest floor to warmer, sunnier areas where food supplies are more plentiful—something they cannot do individually.

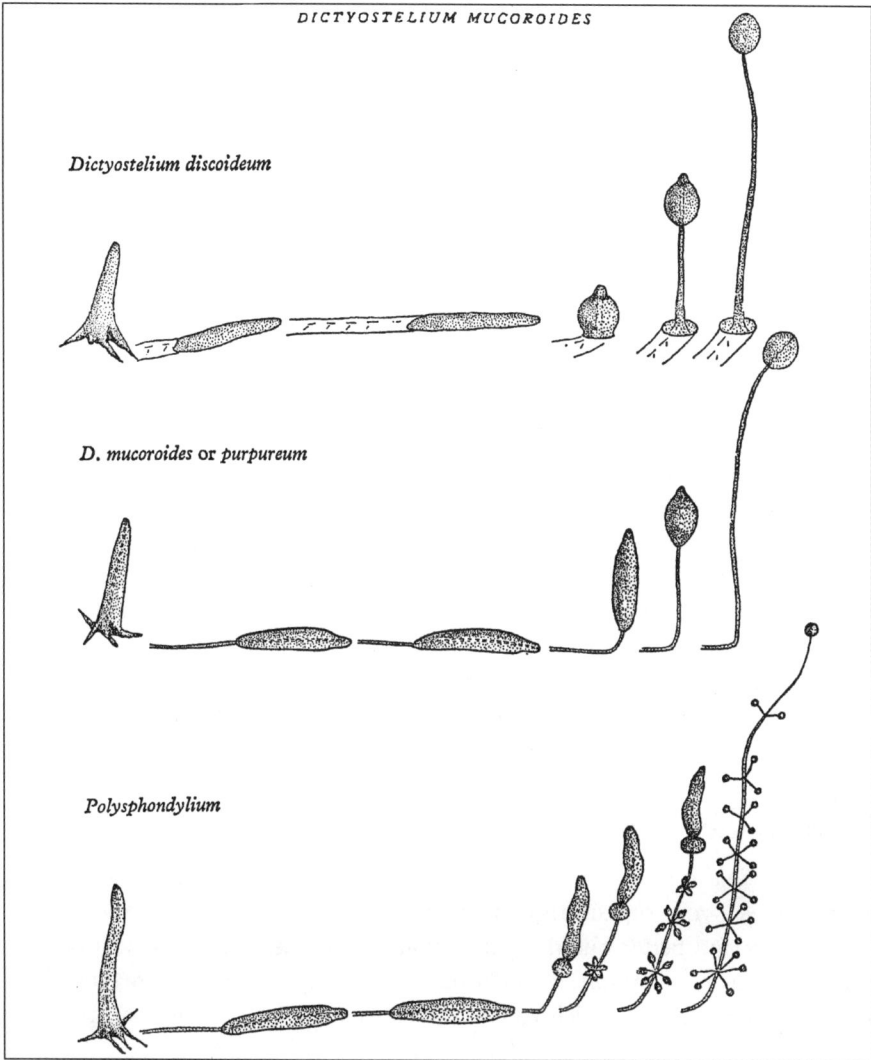

DICTYOSTELIUM MUCOROIDES

Dictyostelium discoideum

D. mucoroides or purpureum

Polysphondylium

Slime mold amoebas have the ability to cluster together when food is scarce, and move to new locations. They can also develop spore sacs that attach themselves to animals to allow the amoeba strain to travel greater distances. Such amoebas can serve as a model for effective adaptability to irresistible forces. This illustration shows how three different types of slime mold amoebas adapt. (Bonner, John T., *The Cellular Structure of Slime Molds*, Copyright © 1959, revised edition 1967 by Princeton University Press. Reprinted by permission of Princeton University Press.)

In time, some of these clumps will undergo additional physical changes and create a multicelled stalk culminating in a spore sac filled with dormant spores. When animals and people brush against the sac, the dormant spores attach themselves and are carried to other new locations beyond the range of movement for the clump. By the cooperation they employ, organized slime molds are much more successful as a species in survival and growth than individual amoebas are. Imagine how your organization would have to change in order to have the same ability to adapt successfully to irresistible forces, and how much more would be accomplished if that were the case.

Human beings can do better than slime molds because we have the physiological and psychological agility to take advantage of even unpredictable change. We are far ahead of all but a few of the most sophisticated biological adaptations. For centuries, people have relied on windmills to generate power. Originally, windmills were built to face in only one direction. If the wind blew in the right direction, great results occurred. If not, either little or no power was generated. That's the way it is with many organizations: If things do not go just as planned, we simply get no benefit from our resources, time and effort.

Windmill inventors got the message about the benefits of planning for perfect, timely use of the unpredictable and went on to develop the pivoting windmill. This wonderful invention serves to turn the face of the windmill into the wind so that the greatest amount of power is produced, regardless of which direction brings that wind. We now want to you make a similar adjustment to give your organization the same ability to generate and use power from shifting winds.

How to Get the Most Out of This Book

The Irresistible Growth Enterprise has a serious and important purpose: to make you and your organization much more successful by having you ask and answer new and better questions than you've been using to analyze and plan your activities. For example, consider the following questions that are crucial for your company's future, which you will learn to answer by reading this book:

1. Do you understand what irresistible forces are affecting organizations?

2. Do you comprehend how dependent your organization's success is on the existing conditions caused by current irresistible forces?

3. What irresistible forces affect your organization today to your benefit or detriment?

4. What are the irresistible forces likely to affect your organization tomorrow?

The pivoting windmill is a good example of how human enterprises can be even more adaptable than nature in capturing all of the benefits of irresistible forces. By using a vane, the windmills constantly rotate to face into the wind so that they will turn with the greatest velocity regardless of the wind's direction. (© Kevin Fleming/CORBIS)

5. Which of your current solutions for dealing with irresistible forces are actually barriers to better performance, by causing you to resist rather than co-opt the irresistible forces?

6. Where are your faulty irresistible force solutions (in 5 above) costing you the most in terms of what you could accomplish?

7. How can you more quickly and accurately identify, measure, anticipate, and create the irresistible forces that will affect your enterprise?

8. How can you use an improved understanding of your company's irresistible forces to be more successful than you are now?

The contents of this book will help you understand the importance of such questions. You will also discover how to achieve 2,000 percent solutions (getting 20 times better or faster results from the same or fewer resources) for harnessing irresistible forces that can propel your organization to greater growth and success.

What You'll Find in This Book

Unlike many business books, in *The Irresistible Growth Enterprise* we focus on *what new things to do* rather than on how to improve existing practices. This book will not tell you about chaos theory, complexity science, data mining, learning facilitation, and other important cutting-edge analytical concepts per se that you may or may not be using now. Instead, this book shows you how to harness the key lessons of these and other useful concepts and tools in one integrated process that will improve your performance across a broad range of activities from creating a vision, to leadership, to implementation.

To do this, we draw your attention to important questions and actions that your enterprise should be, but is probably not, addressing now. To that end, we've made the book easy and fun to read, with many more anecdotes and stories than most business books to trigger your own thinking about how to improve your own future.

When you read the examples, you may be surprised sometimes to see different conclusions reached and new details provided than have been reported in the business press. The authors have drawn on their access to top executives over many years to provide you with an inside and more accurate view of what happened. Where the company is unnamed, the experience probably comes from a consulting assignment with a client to whom confidentiality is owed. Where the organization is named, the information may have come from publicly available sources, a competitor, industry expert, or a current or former executive of that organization.

Throughout the book, we will stress the importance of establishing more effective bonds of mutual cooperation within and outside your organization—with employees, customers, suppliers, partners, shareholders, and the communities in which you operate—as a key element of irresistible force management. You'll learn a totally new way of thinking about how a company should relate to its operating environment, a way of thinking that can be applied to just about any issue that arises in your organization. The lessons found in *The Irresistible Growth Enterprise* should be practiced at every level of your enterprise. These principles should guide all of your organization's thinking and communications systems if you are to achieve the potential growth from unstoppable change.

How to Use This Book

In the first part of the book, you can learn about habits that cause organizations to make the mistake of resisting irresistible forces rather than embracing them. We call these harmful habits "stalls." Stalls are the downside of our memories. We learn to do things in a certain way that works reasonably well. Pretty soon this repeated action becomes such a confirmed habit that we aren't even aware of our patterns of behavior and thinking. An example of this kind of routine thinking is the reaction that some have in hiding problems. They hope that no one will find out that they are having poor results because of an irresistible force before conditions improve. Those who supervise rogue commodity and securities traders often seem to operate on this assumption, appearing to look the other way as the traders report gains while actually piling up ever-larger losses. They may smell a deception, but they'll hold their noses. The supervisors are comfortable with this approach because of the great results the traders are sending to the bookkeepers. Although the accounting alarms may be signaling a problem, the phony "profits" that are being booked provide for handsome promotions and bonuses all around. If the problem stays hidden long enough, the supervisors believe that all negative consequences will disappear. However, the end result is often that losses are magnified beyond what would have otherwise occurred, simply because the tide is running against the traders.

Each chapter in Part One presents personal and organizational examples of stalls (thinking habits that delay progress), sample solutions (stall erasers), and questions (or stallbusting action guides) to help you become a stallbuster. Chapter 1 defines the key concepts employed in *The Irresistible Growth Enterprise*. Chapters 2 through 10 cover the stall mind-set and the stalls most commonly experienced that harm an organization's ability to adapt to changing irresistible forces.

Read each chapter in Part One as an individual lesson in dealing with a specific stall. You may want to first read the chapters that seem related to your most important issues. But be sure to read the other chapters as well because they may describe stalls that you're experiencing but haven't understood as such. Overcoming stalls that you don't yet recognize you have is one of the primary benefits of reading this book.

Having eliminated or reduced harmful thinking, you can learn in the second part of the book a new set of thinking habits and questions that will steer you safely down the path you need to follow to relate well to *your* irresistible forces. Part Two (chapters 11 through 18) covers an eight-step process that describes how to identify and align yourself with irresistible forces to maximum advantage.

Read these chapters as soon as possible to get the most benefit from this book and reread them on a regular basis for the ultimate benefit. Although these chapters make sense as individual lessons, it is far more advantageous to read and use chapters 11 through 18 together. The ideas, questions, and actions provided in the chapters build on one another to provide a multiplier effect for your results.

The Epilogue rounds out the discussion and explains how you can start creating your irresistible force organization. It also includes instructions for getting a handy copy of the key ideas covered in this book that you should keep nearby to share with others and reinforce your new learning. You'll also find out how to keep in touch with our new research about working with irresistible forces, and how to contact us to discuss applying these principles to your organization's irresistible forces.

Appendix One addresses how irresistible force management applies to your personal life and family circumstances. And because many see the Internet's development as a monumental irresistible force, we've included Appendix Two that will help you reframe your thoughts about that form of electronic communication as an example of the book's concepts.

To emphasize the key points of each chapter, you'll find a few sentences printed in sans serif type like this at the beginning of each chapter. You can quickly get an overview of the entire book by taking a few minutes to read just those summaries. By doing that, you'll have a context for a more detailed reading of *The Irresistible Growth Enterprise*.

❖ ❖ ❖

You can use this book to change your life in positive ways. Teaching others what you learn will help you be sure you understand what you have read. In addition, you'll help your organization make much faster progress as you increase the number of people thinking about and acting on the issues. If you expand this new understanding to your customers, partners, distributors, suppliers, shareholders and the communities you serve, even greater benefits will occur. Ultimately, when many companies begin to use the ideas found in this book, you'll receive even more benefit because the overall effectiveness of the business community you operate in will greatly improve as well.

And be sure to have fun using this book. You'll learn faster, and come up with better answers and more benefits!

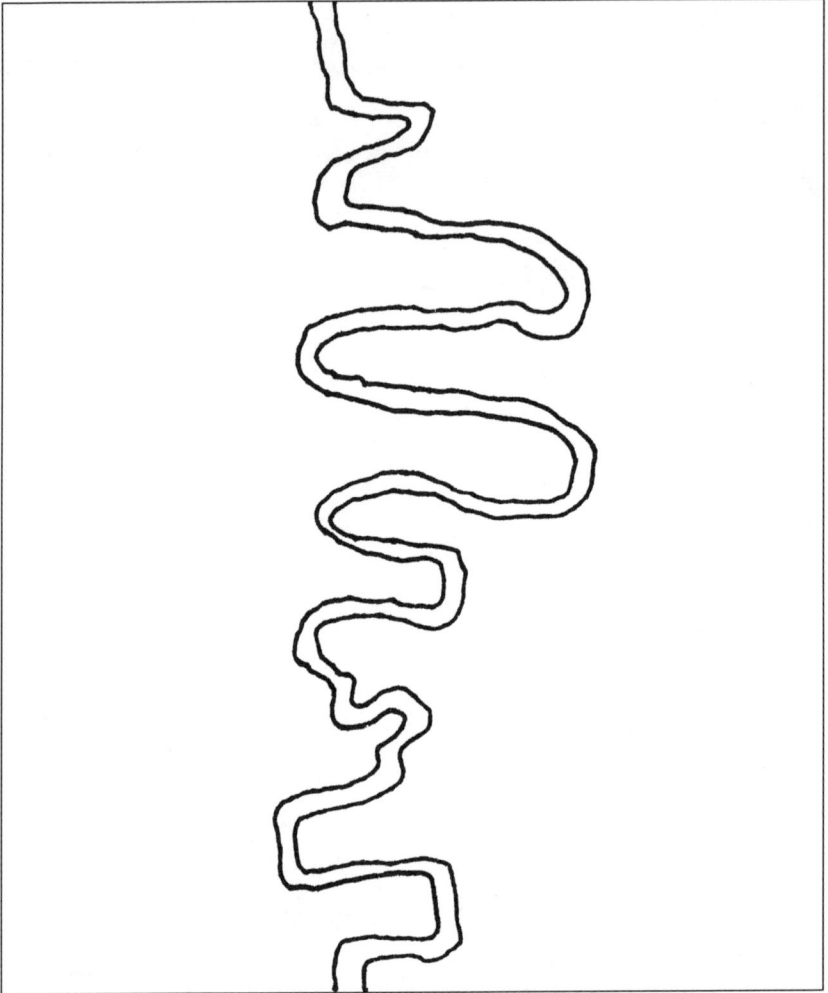

Many enterprises reach their goals by very circuitous routes. This progress normally requires a lot of trial and error. These diversions mean that your progress is slower and more costly than if you were able to move straight toward your goal. The usual result is similar to taking a narrow, winding byway rather than following a wide, straight road with a high speed limit. While on the byway, you also run a risk of missing a curve you don't anticipate and having an accident. That result can delay your arrival at your goal even more.

PART ONE

IRRESISTIBLE FORCE STALLS—CAUSES AND SOLUTIONS

May the Force be with you.

—George Lucas

The toy business is full of hits and misses as well as fad toys that quickly come and go. Witness, then, the wonder of Barbie's durability, having been a top toy and head of a top line of related dolls and merchandise for many years. Although all toy makers would like to create long-term toys, only a few have succeeded in overcoming the irresistible force of the changing tastes of children (and their parents) to experience such on-going success as have Barbie and her doll friends. In this part of *The Irresistible Growth Enterprise,* you can learn how to overcome the behavior in your organization that keeps you from creating the kind of continuing irresistible growth compared to competitors that Mattel has achieved with Barbie.

Irresistible forces are unstoppable events and factors that shape our opportunities and challenges. In a physical sense, they include things we cannot change like the tides, winds, and powerful storms. In a human sense, they include the emotional patterns that almost all of us follow, such as feeling sad at the loss of a loved one or elated by winning. In an organizational sense, irresistible forces include difficulties in communicating in a foreign language, lack of knowledge among new employees about how your organization does things, and conflicts of interest among those who are looking out for themselves ahead of customers' needs. In businesses, irresistible forces include trends in the development of technology, globalization, shifts in buying power of consumers in local markets, and increasingly demanding customers. Interestingly, each enterprise is subject to the irresistible forces in different ways. No one prescription will suffice for all, as a result.

Sometimes we initiate irresistible forces, such as when we encourage a new fad, but we usually have little impact on them after they begin. Irresistible forces are so powerful and so important to use as resources for success, that you must avoid both opposing and being buffeted by these forces. Bad thinking habits, or stalls, of individuals in organizational settings are the primary reason that enterprises succumb to irresistible forces, rather than turn them into powerful allies and tools for faster, more profitable growth.

The dangers from and opportunities provided by irresistible forces are growing and will probably continue to do so. Evidence of this pattern is the rapidly decreasing amount of time it takes for a start-up organization to reach a billion dollars in revenues (as measured in constant buying power). Once this achievement required decades (without acquisitions). Now companies can do it in months by making good use of a rapidly growing means of communication, the Internet. Within a few decades, the same will be accomplished in days, or even possibly in hours.

Therefore, overcoming irresistible force stalls is one of the most important management skills needed for ascertaining the opportunities and responding positively to them now and in the future in a timely way. Even an organization that starts out in perfect alignment with irresistible forces will need to be agile in adapting to changes in those forces and the arrival of new forces over time. With the help of this part of *The Irresistible Growth Enterprise,* you'll learn how to identify the most common and dangerous stalls vis-à-vis irresistible forces. You will also develop skill in quickly eliminating these stalls by changing your thinking habits through the use of new questions, so that you and your enterprise can not only survive, but enjoy irresistible growth.

The concepts presented in Part One will be easiest to understand and apply if you focus first on one important area where irresistible forces are proving to be headwinds (retarding your growth) or cross winds (pushing you off target from where you want to go) for your organization. Then reread the material with a second irresistible force issue in mind and continue reviewing the material for other issues until the application of this material becomes a new habit for you.

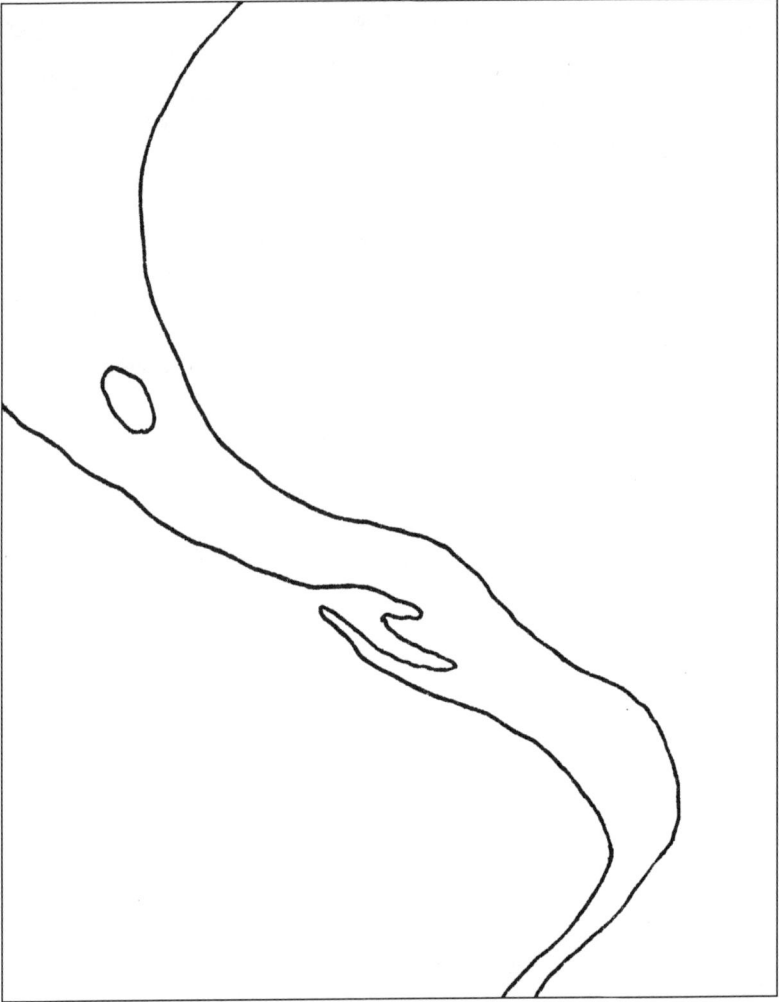

You can travel down a river with the current behind you faster than you can travel upstream against the current. That strong current is an irresistible force that you cannot ignore. To speed your progress the most, you must pick the part of the river where the current is fastest on the downstream trip while going where it is slowest on the upstream journey. In this illustration, the current runs from the bottom to the top. At the same time, you have to beware that you do not let the current cause you to lose control of your ship. If you do, you may be driven into a side channel like the small one on the left. Such a side channel can stall your progress by making it hard to return to the mainstream route you want to take. In this book, you will learn how to locate such "stalls" well in advance so that you can avoid them.

THE LIGHT AT THE END OF THE TUNNEL

Key Concepts

If you can see the light at the end of the tunnel,
you are looking the wrong way.

—Barry Commoner

Chapter 1 provides the definitions and explanations of key concepts used throughout the book: "irresistible forces," "stalls," "stallbusting," "2,000 percent solutions," and the "irresistible growth enterprise." Understanding these concepts is essential for you to get the most benefit from the rest of the book. Building on these concepts, you will find out how to achieve the most outstanding growth and results for your organization, now and in the future.

Have you ever had your plans delayed or put on hold indefinitely by a change in your organization's operating environment? Perhaps fashion suddenly shifted, and few wanted the kinds of products or services you provide. Possibly the laws changed to make what you were planning to do no longer compliant. Or maybe raw material costs suddenly dropped for an old-fashioned version of what you make, and customers flocked to the now cheaper alternative. Maybe even a change in the weather meant that new winter coats weren't needed in December due to unusual warmth. If any of this sounds familiar, then you will benefit greatly from reading this book and acting on its lessons.

Shine the Light on Opportunities to Avoid Tunnel Vision

Most people are at least a little claustrophobic when they find themselves in a dark, confined space, like a tunnel. Whatever source of light first promises an escape route will attract attention, much as the flame attracts the moth. Similarly, people in tight circumstances due to factors beyond their control will often quickly take any way out that they see. In a business that is starved for cash, for example, this sense of urgency can mean committing to the first offer of funding rather than the best one.

If you look only at the proverbial "light at the end of the tunnel," you will often be making a mistake. The tunnel itself may be full of better opportunities, such as valuable minerals or other natural resources. You may also be better off inside than out due to danger from some natural force such as an avalanche. Be sure to always consider all of your options before reacting to the light at the end of the tunnel.

This book can help keep you from "looking the wrong way" by being a guiding light, like a powerful search light in a tunnel, that you can use to find the best and most enduring opportunities in the face of forces and trends beyond your control. By learning the lessons we offer here, you'll be able to spotlight the opportunities for anticipating those forces and trends and position yourself so that these forces work in your favor.

Let's consider, for example, how two organizations dealt with a powerful trend in electronic technology in different ways. One was proactive and successfully highlighted and utilized advantages from the trend. The other organization reactively focused on the light at the end of the tunnel, and found itself pummeled by the trend in a way that led to major losses.

Moore's Law states that semiconductor effectiveness will double every 18 months at a more or less constant price. Computer manufacturers have used this law for decades as an irresistible force that permits them to anticipate the technological changes needed to design their new machines. A new opportunity has been grasped in recent years by people who understand the law well. They expand its application beyond computer hardware to upset the competitive dynamics of other industries.

In the 1990s, Microsoft began offering an encyclopedia product named *Encarta* as part of a bundled package of software to computer manufacturers, or as an add-on to consumers for less than $100. In comparison, traditional encyclopedias cost many hundreds of dollars. Soon, *Encarta* was the best-selling encyclopedia in the world, and it was wildly profitable because its sales grew rapidly while its production costs were very low. The original version of

Encarta was based on a printed encyclopedia sold in retail stores, so development costs were low, and creating electronic copies was almost costless.

By choosing the electronic form for this product, Microsoft ensured that it would continue to have the irresistible force of Moore's Law on its side as it competed with traditionally printed encyclopedias. Improved semiconductors will lower the price of personal computers, which, in turn, will increase the size of the market. A larger personal computer market means more chances to sell electronic encyclopedias. In addition, better semiconductors will make it faster and easier to use electronic encyclopedias, so more people will want to have and use them. A larger electronic encyclopedia market will reduce the development and production costs of each electronic encyclopedia sold. Finally, as the market leader, Microsoft will get almost all of the benefit from the technological trend because computer manufacturers are unlikely to offer more than one electronic encyclopedia as part of their preloaded software packages. This product is an example of a 2,000 percent solution because Microsoft achieved more than 20 times the growth and profitability that a traditional new entrant into the encyclopedia business would have experienced.

Now consider the reactions of printed encyclopedia publishers. They also developed electronic encyclopedias, but, not wanting to displace their printed offerings, generally charged higher prices than Microsoft did for their electronic versions. Caught in an almost-always lose and seldom-win situation, their sales and profits naturally declined. Had they preempted Microsoft's *Encarta* strategy, the traditional encyclopedia publishers could also have been wildly profitable by selling two highly differentiated product lines. Most of the profits would have come from the low-end electronic product, which could then have helped to make up for the loss of sales and profits from the high-end printed products. Not having adopted this strategy is an example of "stalled" thinking, or seeing the world in a constant way while in the midst of dynamic change.

Like Microsoft with its *Encarta* product, the irresistible growth enterprise seeks to illuminate the benefits of powerful trends beyond its control by overcoming stalled thinking and creating 2,000 percent solutions. In this chapter, you will learn more about these important concepts as a springboard for becoming adept at applying them in your organization.

Irresistible Forces and Their Benefits: Headwinds and Cross Winds Become Tailwinds

To illustrate what an irresistible force is, imagine that you are planning to take a plane trip around the world. If you think about the jet stream, a powerful wind that flows generally from west to east at flight altitudes, you will have identified an irresistible force that will have a large impact on your journey. If you travel from west to east, the jet stream will be a tailwind and help you forward. If you travel from east to west, it will be a headwind and slow you down. Of course, if you travel from south to north, the jet stream will also delay your journey somewhat by pushing you off course and forcing you to fight off some of its effects as a cross wind.

The existence of the International Date Line can similarly affect your travels. When you go from west to east, you will gain a day when you cross that line. Traveling in the other direction, you will lose a day instead. So, for a trip around the world, careful alignment with the two irresistible forces of the jet stream and date conventions can save you more than two calendar days and a lot of time in the air.

Despite these substantial advantages, many people will choose to travel from east to west because airlines tend to schedule these longer flights during the daytime while making the shorter west to east flights at night. The desire to avoid the "red-eye" flights will make these travelers miss the opportunity to save lots of time. By focusing on the end of the tunnel, the airline schedules, they are blind to the opportunities for doing the trip in the fastest way.

While the term "irresistible force" conjures up images of overwhelming power—like the jet stream, a tornado or an earthquake—that often suggest conflict or annihilation, it can also mean something that is so alluring that we are drawn to it despite our will. In the *Odyssey*, for example, Odysseus had to be bound to the mast of his ship so that he could resist the songs of sirens as he sailed past their island. In this book, an irresistible force can have either attribute. It can be so strong that it overwhelms you physically, as in a force of nature, or it can be so attractive that it is hard to resist psychologically, as in a temporarily low interest rate that leads you to borrow excessively.

In business, irresistible forces are powerful trends that can significantly affect the direction of your enterprise. Such forces abound. Customer needs and the circumstances that create those needs, costs that are hard to control, government regulation, taxes, trends in the development of technology, globalization, the weather, physical limits, and human behavior are some examples. An irresistible force is simply anything that is mostly beyond the control of you and your organization in influencing your business.

As an example, consider a company that provides accessories for sport utility vehicles (SUVs). When the demand for SUVs is high, the accessory manufacturer is busy trying to make enough products to keep up with the demand. As newer and better models of SUVs come out, the demand for accessories shifts in new and unpredictable ways. Similarly, when SUVs lose their popularity—because of higher insurance premiums, revelations of overhyped safety or capability for driving in snow, decreased family size, or objections to airborne emissions—the accessory maker has a hard time selling accessories even if they are vastly improved and offered at a low price. Thus, the accessory business can be buffeted by irresistible forces in different directions and in unpredictable ways, going rapidly from enormous growth to potential free-fall.

What Is a Stall? If It Was Good Enough for Grandma, Let's *Not* Leave Well Enough Alone

All enterprises are subject to many and potentially changeable forces. Unfortunately, the powers that be in many organizations convince themselves that the status quo will remain in place forever. They create a business model that keeps them focused on fine tuning their current state of affairs. All that is well and good, until the irresistible forces shift in such a way that they encourage your customer to join instead with your toughest competitor.

Such a shift is inevitable in most businesses if for no other reason than demographics. People change their consumption patterns as they age, and the number of people in various age groups changes as well. Such changes have meant, for example, that the latest needs of baby boomers have driven the U.S. economy in fundamental ways since the 1950s and will continue to do so for quite some time.

Remember the diaper services that did so well in the late 1940s? Freshly laundered cloth diapers were delivered to the home and soiled diapers were sent out to be washed. That business was eventually subjected to many irresistible forces that changed its profitability. As women began to work outside the home in increasing numbers and better birth control allowed for increased family planning, births declined and fewer diapers were needed. By the time the first baby boomers were having children, disposable diapers were introduced and quickly became the rage. Diaper services saw their business disappear into the sewers and landfills of America. They became victims of a "stall," a complacent frame of mind and way of thinking that cause bad organizational habits that impede progress and the achievement of an enterprise's full success potential.

Suppose the owner of a diaper service recognized the irresistible forces of the changing demographics and the disposable diaper? He could capitalize on the disposable diaper trend by providing the convenience of both disposing of and delivering the bulky items. And if he touted ecologically appropriate disposal, wouldn't his service appeal to even those consumers who care about conservation and are otherwise inclined to buy and dispose of the diapers themselves?

For the enterprise to achieve irresistible growth it is necessary that it recognize and overcome the stalls that delay positive action in dealing with irresistible forces.

What Is Stallbusting? Rethink Your Position

Before Muhammad Ali (born Cassius Clay) entered the arena, heavyweight fighting was usually a brawl in which two fighters unmercifully pounded each other until one fell bloodied, bruised, and battered to the canvas for the ten count. But Ali, acting on the realization that getting near a hard-hitting heavyweight fighter in the ring is a dangerous thing to do, changed the sport forever. He got into top shape aerobically and danced all around his opponents. He could quickly reach in and flick a punch, and then retreat before the other fighter could react. In fact, the late counterpunch that caught only air helped Ali by tiring out his opponent. Ali's motto was: "Float like a butterfly, sting like a bee."

With his strategy of being outside the range of the irresistible force of the other fighter's fists, Ali is a classic example of taking a stallbusting approach: using conscious thought to challenge old habits. He realized that getting hit didn't make you a successful boxer, that success could be achieved by being constantly on the move to be where you could hit but not be hit.

Similarly, consider the prospects for a poor artist at the beginning of the twentieth century. The avant garde styles were changing from Impressionism to Expressionism, while traditional collectors ignored both in favor of polished realism. Clearly, tastes would range from the classic to the most avant garde in the rest of the century. How could an unknown succeed?

Viewed in this light, the career of Pablo Picasso shows that he was a champion stallbuster, as well as one of the century's great artists. He was a master of technique who easily succeeded with any style and genre he chose, producing works in virtually every known style in almost every major medium. In addition, he added his own inventions, such as cubism and collage. Consequently, there was always a type of Picasso to appeal to almost everyone, and his lifetime income was many times larger than those of his contemporaries. By using a stallbusting approach to the changing art milieu, he found a 2,000 percent solution to being an outstanding artist who was well appreciated and well paid during his lifetime.

What Is a 2,000 Percent Solution? Drive the Windmills with Your Mind

Most organizations see their plans and preferred ways of operating as unchangeable best ways to do something. This attitude is like having a windmill that is fixed to face in only one direction. When the wind blows in just that direction, the windmill generates lots of energy. When the wind blows in any other direction, the windmill is idle. The person who figured out how to make a windmill that turned on its axis so it would always be facing the wind came up with a 2,000 percent solution. Such a windmill generates maximum energy over all 360 degrees of the compass, rather than only over a range of 15 degrees or so. As a result, with a wind blowing randomly from all directions, it creates 20 times more power than a fixed-facing windmill. The beauty of such a solution is that it makes a virtue of uncertainty rather than taking the risk of a narrow view of where the wind will come from in the future.

A 2,000 percent solution can be a way to do something that provides 20 times or more benefit from the same or similar level of resources (such as a pivoting windmill) than when applying the usual or 100 percent solution (a fixed-facing windmill). It can also be a way to do something 20 times faster to get the same benefit from the same or similar level of resources. A pivoting windmill also exemplifies this feature because it will generate the same amount of power as the fixed-facing windmill in less than 5 percent of the time in locations where the wind blows randomly from all directions.

In some situations you can have 2,000 percent solutions that provide improved methods and increased speed simultaneously for a combined 4,000,000 percent benefit (2,000 percent times 2,000 percent equals 4,000,000 percent). This circumstance is most likely to occur when having the benefits sooner is worth vastly more than having the same benefits stretched out over time. It occurs routinely when the benefits of one 2,000 percent solution produce skill, time, and resources to add new 2,000 percent solutions to other areas of practice. This transferred advantage means that time and resources are constantly being used more efficiently across the whole organization.

For simplicity, in this book we refer to any solution that has at least 20 times the benefit or speed of a current conventional solution as a 2,000 percent solution, even if the benefits are much greater than that. And when irresistible forces are in play, the benefits are likely to bloom way beyond the 2,000 percent level because those forces create enormous momentum for the first organization that responds appropriately, leaving other organizations in the dust.*

---

*For more information on creating 2,000 percent solutions independent of using irresistible forces as a growth engine, please see *The 2,000 Percent Solution* (AMACOM Books, 1999) by the authors and their co-author, Robert Metz. Excerpts from that book are available at <www.2000percentsolution.com>.

Consider Amazon.com and its pioneering entry into selling books and music on the Internet. Shortly after going public and within months of being started, the company had achieved a market capitalization for its stock that was far larger than that of all its conventional competitors combined. As a result, the company was able to pay for even faster development of its position on the Internet, which made its future growth and profit potential expand much sooner as well. While it was still losing money selling each book, Amazon.com stock had a multiple of more than 20 times the total price of each book the company sold. This high stock price was used indirectly to allow the company access to vast resources for the book business and to enter other electronic commerce markets. Now that's stallbusting your way to a 2,000 percent solution involving irresistible forces!

What Is an Irresistible Growth Enterprise? Not Just Survival, Geometrically-Growing Success!

Have you ever watched someone use judo to defend against an attack from a larger, more powerful person? The judo user can employ the strength and inertia of the attacker to make self-defense easier. If the attacker throws a punch, the judo defender may grab the wrist of the attacker's extended arm as it speeds forward and pull the attacker to the ground by tripping her or him at the same time. Of course, without the judo, the results could be quite different. Properly harnessed, irresistible forces (even threatening ones) can be used successfully to create irresistible growth for your enterprise.

In this book we generally refer to irresistible forces, stalls and stallbusting, and 2,000 percent solutions in connection with commercial business examples and problems. However the lessons we present are equally applicable to any other type of organization or group, from a charitable organization depending on volunteers and contributions, to government departments, to educational institutions. We chose the word "enterprise" to describe such organizations because it captures the sense of being proactive, energetic, and effective. We want you to think in those terms as you learn how to transform your organization into an irresistible growth enterprise.

An irresistible growth enterprise is simply any organization that can routinely utilize the momentum of irresistible forces as tailwinds for creating and implementing 2,000 percent solutions, thus assuring increased success in today's rapidly evolving organizational environment.

Using Microsoft as an example again, we can see how this company has often used irresistible forces to create advantages for itself in various areas of its business. One of the truisms of the computer business is that users are reluctant to change operating systems, because doing so requires changing the application programs on which the user relies. The difficulty of making that change usually more than offsets the total user benefits from a new operating system. In fact, loyalty to a computer operating system supplier is one of the strongest repeat buying patterns ever measured. Microsoft realized early on that becoming the standard for IBM's new personal computer would eventually make it the standard for computing. Since most people used IBM mainframe computers in the early stages of the personal computer industry, Microsoft did whatever it could to get the operating system business for the IBM PC. Most personal computers in large businesses were originally linked to uses in IBM mainframes, so the operating systems needed to be compatible. Thus, an IBM mainframe sale translated into a Microsoft operating system sale for all of the linked-use PCs in the same organization.

When IBM later introduced its OS/2 operating system for personal computers, Microsoft perceived the threat to its position and encouraged software applications writers to create products that would work only on its DOS operating system. As a result, IBM's OS/2 system never did very well due to a limited application library.

In another arena, many people preferred Apple's operating system, but wanted IBM-compatible equipment so they could work smoothly with IBM mainframes. Microsoft eventually created the Windows software to employ some of the best elements of Apple's software. The result was to further discourage computer users from buying Apple machines. The Windows software would still run all the old DOS applications software, so users had a dual incentive to upgrade with Microsoft's product rather than switching to OS/2 or Apple.

On yet another front, when the Internet took off, Bill Gates realized that Microsoft had missed an important irresistible force. He quickly refocused the company to create a browser and online services, and the company was soon among the leaders in these areas as well. In this case, Metcalfe's Law came into play, which says that the more people who are in a community, the more valuable the community is to each person. With so many users already in Microsoft's community, the pull on new Internet-using customers to use Microsoft's browser and network is nearly overwhelming.

By aligning with irresistible forces, Microsoft was able to create large, profitable businesses. Then it was able to use those business strengths to make the establishment of the next alignment with other irresistible forces less costly, more easily achieved, and even more valuable. As a consequence, the company was able to go from being a start-up to the world's most valuable enterprise in about 25 years—a definitive irresistible growth enterprise.

Looking Ahead for the Opportunity

Regardless of the activities you are engaged in, creating an irresistible growth enterprise is an exceptional opportunity. Many people now see unlimited opportunities in establishing electronic commerce on the Internet. That area is very promising because there are so many irresistible forces to be harnessed, including rapid improvements in the technology, costs, speed, size of the markets, and valuations in the financial markets. Irresistible forces are moving strongly throughout almost every market, every activity, and every enterprise. The challenge is to identify, anticipate, adapt to, and create the irresistible forces; learn to align yourself with them in a flexibly effective way; and build the capability of the people you're working with for expanding the enterprise's ability to do these things. By doing so, you'll always be in a position to use the wind to your advantage.

2

"WHAT'S GOING ON HERE?"—LACK OF UNDERSTANDING CAN CAUSE INAPPROPRIATE ACTIONS OR INACTION

IRRESISTIBLE FORCE STALLS AND THEIR CAUSES

It is better to know some of the questions than all of the answers.

—James Thurber

This chapter explains how irresistible forces adversely affect enterprises, often stalling progress and success in those organizations. When an irresistible force triggers strong emotional reactions, such as fear or paralyzing denial, incorrect actions or inappropriate inaction often follow. If these responses occur routinely, bad habits develop that make the situation worse. This discussion also includes a preview of the most harmful and common stalls that arise in enterprises due to irresistible forces. In this chapter you can begin to learn how to overcome these stalls so that your organization can use irresistible forces to achieve irresistible growth instead.

A Scenario: Weather Knots Opportunity

Anyone who travels by air has surely suffered a delay because of inclement weather. The following story describes an unusual experience that the authors had in traveling from Boston to a city in the U.S. Midwest. It may seem incredible, but keep in mind that the truth is often stranger than fiction. If you read and consider the whole story as though it is happening to you, you'll be rewarded for your perseverance with some interesting insights. You may even be able to use some of the maneuvers described here if you ever find yourself in similar circumstances.

Imagine yourself in a situation where you and your organization find the irresistible force of changing weather affecting your plans. You and your colleagues have planned and prepared carefully for the most important presentation your organization has ever made, a presentation that may establish a relationship that will lift your organization to future success (you hope) beyond everyone's wildest dreams. You are justifiably excited and are looking forward very much to the meeting. Although the presentation is not scheduled until 11 A.M. on Wednesday, you take no chances and plan to fly to the far-away city early the preceding Tuesday afternoon. You have carefully watched the weather reports and see no reason to expect any difficulties. In fact, the weather forecast is a good one, for unseasonably warm temperatures.

The whole team leaves for the airport only 12 miles away an hour early on Tuesday, in the bright sunshine. You arrive to discover a blinding fog enveloping the airport, something that occasionally happens during spring when warm air passes over the cold ocean water located next to the airport. Feeling a little concerned, you check the airline's monitors and see that all flights for the rest of the day have already been canceled. With wide eyes, you rush toward the ticket counter to find hundreds of people already in line.

Seeing no hope there, you quickly call your travel agent to find out what your alternatives are. Bad news! The fog is getting worse and is expected to last through Wednesday. What to do?

No problem, you think. You can drive to another airport and fly from there. More bad news! All major airports but one within 300 miles are also fogged in (they are all located near the water in similar weather conditions). Every flight for days has by now been booked from that one open airport. What do you do?

Well, you can handle that. You'll just drive to an airport 500 miles away and get a plane there. It'll take most of the night, but that's all right. Then you encounter still more bad news: There are no flights from that airport that will get you to the meeting before 6 P.M. on Wednesday. The situation is starting to get a little tougher. What next?

You and your colleagues decide to charter a plane to get you to the meeting. You find the Yellow Pages and start calling every charter company listed. Too late! Many people have called before you, and the closest plane that is available is 1,600 miles away. Plus, it has to find someplace to land in order to pick you up and then to take you where you want to go. What now?

You decide to just call the people you're meeting with, explain what happened, and offer to reschedule. They're reasonable people. They'll understand. Worse news! They can't meet again for several weeks, and that is too late for them to work with you. Even more disturbing to you is knowing that they may be meeting with some of your key competitors in the next few days. There must be something you can do. What?

How about a video conference or a teleconference instead? No good. Their video conference facilities are tied up and they don't want to go to a public facility. They think a teleconference is a bad idea. They implore you to get there on Wednesday, and they will stay as late on Wednesday as needed in order to meet with you.

Wow! You have to do something! What do you do now?

You call back that air charter outfit that had one plane left to see if they'll fly to the one open airport 100 miles away. If they will, you can then fly down early on Wednesday morning and still be in town before the day is over. Awful news! The plane has to get a crew first, which will take several hours, before the flight can start out toward that airport. And there is a bad rainstorm in their area that may delay takeoff for additional hours. There is a curfew on the airport where you want the plane to pick you up, so they may not be able to arrive before tomorrow morning. By then, the flight crew could be over its allotted flight time that the government allows and not be able to leave on Wednesday.

What the heck, it's only money! You tell them to get the plane to the airport and bring an extra flight crew if necessary, and you take your team to the car rental counter to get a car to take you to the other airport. No luck. You call ahead and find that there are also no hotels with available rooms near that airport. You all decide to go home and drive to the other airport early the next morning in your own cars. In the meantime, you'll stay in touch with the charter outfit and your potential strategic partner to keep both informed of your progress and plans.

The next day, you turn on the television and find out that the fog is gone at the airport. What good luck! You can fly down on a regular flight this morning. You head with your team to the airport. Oh, no! You can't believe your eyes; all the flights are canceled this morning, too. But the weather is perfect. You finally learn why: There are no planes! Before the fog closed in, the airlines took off with every plane they had (planes can take off in fog conditions that don't permit landing). The first flights will arrive around 11:00 A.M. and thousands of people are standing by for these flights. You have no reasonable hope of getting a commercial flight until Thursday. That will be too late! You quickly call the charter outfit, who agrees to divert your plane to this airport so at least you don't have to drive an extra 100 miles.

You head over to the charter terminal. Time passes slowly. You keep getting updates assuring you that the plane will arrive at 11:15 A.M. But 11:30 comes and goes, then 11:45. Now it's noon. You keep calling your potential partners. They say, "We'll wait for you." Finally, the plane lands at 1:15 P.M. You start to rush out. The pilot stops you. "We have to refuel, first." Finally, the fuel truck arrives, you refuel, receive a long air traffic control delay, and eventually take off at 2:30 P.M.

You call your potential partners and tell them that you are about to take off and will arrive in their city at 4:00 P.M. local time. They agree to hold the meeting as soon as you arrive at the offices, around 5:00 P.M.

The charter pilot is very helpful and asks you if you want to have a taxi waiting when you land. There is a good catered lunch on board. It's a beautiful day for flying. You are grateful. Life is looking better.

You arrive at the potential partners' office at 4:45 P.M., and they are not quite ready for you. At 5:15 P.M., they troop in and thank you for getting there. They seem quite amazed by your story, as well as somewhat skeptical. However, the meeting goes well. They promise you a reaction in a few days.

On the following Tuesday, your contact calls to tell you that everything has gone through smoothly. Hooray!!!! He then says that they had decided to check into your travel story and were able to confirm that you had indeed gone through everything you'd said on behalf of their company. In fact, it was your response to the situation that impressed them the most and allowed you to be a bigger winner with them than you would otherwise have been.

Although it seemed that the irresistible force of the weather was impeding your progress (and it had certainly been delaying your flight), it actually provided you with an opportunity to show what you can do as a resource. Many people would have simply given up because the situation seemed hopeless or overwhelming. You resisted stalled thinking and persisted in turning the irresistible force into your tailwind.

Action and Reaction: To React Is Human, to React Positively Is Divine

Irresistible forces drive enterprises in directions that are usually unanticipated and unplanned. The organization can become disoriented, as sometimes happened to sailing ships rounding Cape Horn during monster electrical storms with gale winds and towering seas. Shock, amazement, curiosity, smugness, groundless optimism, defensiveness, distrust, reckless risk-taking, and confusion are among the reactions that can result in the face of such forces. However, positive reactions can turn the power of irresistible forces to your advantage, as the travel scenario shows. Confronting your very human (and usually inappropriate) reactions to irresistible forces is the beginning of helping your enterprise to deliberately use irresistible forces for achieving better results.

Most irresistible forces don't create as much short-term frustration as did the weather in the travel scenario, but dealing with any irresistible forces can be equally time consuming and emotionally demanding. While reading the story, you may have felt many strong emotions, just like the authors did when they went through the experience. Those strong emotions can easily distract you from acting in the ways necessary to turn the irresistible forces to your favor. When the emotions divert you from pursuing your own or your organization's best interests, you have just experienced a stall.*

Psychologically, irresistible forces tend to take us back to our childhood, when almost every aspect of our lives seemed to be controlled by someone or something other than ourselves. Resisting the temptation to become an enraged two-year-old shouting "No!" to a seemingly hostile universe is important for progress. While unthinking habits of any kind can stall progress, these behaviors become much more harmful when they arise because of strong emotions. The magnitude of irresistible force effects will often cloud clear thinking by creating negative emotional reactions in those who lead and manage. And the danger is increased by the tendency of the individual or organization to be immobilized by the potential danger involved when first perceiving the irresistible force, a little like the victim who stayed, entranced by a cobra and failed to retreat to safety.

---

*For more background on stalls in general, their causes, and how to overcome common ones, see Part One of *The 2,000 Percent Solution: Free Your Organization from "Stalled" Thinking to Achieve Exponential Success* (AMACOM Books, 1999) by Donald Mitchell, Carol Coles, and Robert Metz. You can read excerpts about stalls and how to overcome them at www.2000percentsolution.com.

In addition, organizations often view irresistible forces as temporary aberrations that must simply be overcome for the time being. The usual approach is to cut costs and work longer and harder, which can be like trying to keep the *Titanic* afloat by bailing water by hand.

The foundations for irresistible growth breakthroughs are understanding that irresistible forces must be dealt with from a long-term viewpoint, being aware of the dangers, and recognizing the stalls that are likely to result in harmful responses to irresistible forces.

Recognizing Common Stalls: No More Tilting at Windmills

There are just a few stalls that are almost always responsible for causing inappropriate reactions to irresistible forces. The worst stall is to be unsure of your enterprise's purpose and direction when facing irresistible force headwinds. The effect of the irresistible force can leave everyone confused because the organization finds itself constantly shifting in new directions with remarkably different choices and opportunities. This circumstance especially arises when a business performs so poorly due to irresistible forces that its leadership is constantly being changed. Each new management team has a different idea of what needs to be done, and less and less idea of what works for this type of business. Confusion reigns amid continuing frantic activity. The situation is like being knocked off your feet by a large wave while wading and finding yourself lost underwater, wondering which way is up.

Others may experience the stall of trying to discount the irresistible force, preferring to believe in a friendly future that matches their preferences for the organization's environment. As is well known in the business world, that viewpoint is held by most paper companies, despite their having suffered from poor profitability for decades. (You will learn more about how to use these poor conditions to your advantage in chapter 4.) Still others may simply feel overwhelmed and be stuck on the spot, immobile, as though Super Glue had been applied to the soles of their feet. Many retailers with physical stores reacted this way to the first inroads from Internet-based competitors.

Some organizations may react primarily by withdrawing and turning inward. This response can take the form of simply trying to limit the harm of the irresistible force rather than turning it into a benefit. Department stores have often taken this approach when confronted with discount specialty retailers who provide more variety at a better price. Or the organization may choose to try to adapt solely with its own people and knowledge, something that will provide less flexibility than using a variety of resources. IBM, for example, initially fell behind in developing the first personal computer until it overcame this stall through outsourcing. Other organizations may become entranced by the plans they are pursuing and that fixation can render them inflexible to the actual business or organizational environment. General Motors' tremendous loss of market share in the 1990s was influenced in part by this sort of stall.

One of the most negative of responses to irresistible forces is to try to pretend that nothing adverse is happening and to cover up any damage so that no one else knows the damage has occurred. Many of the larger Japanese companies took this route during the 1990s, delaying their eventual adjustment to a changed competitive environment for their island nation. This understandable human response leaves the organization at risk for greater damage and can even destroy the enterprise.

Even if the enterprise decides to adapt to irresistible forces in positive ways, these forces are very powerful and can shift rapidly. Riding the trend may be like staying on a bucking Brahma bull. You have to match your organization's approach to irresistible forces by considering their strength and volatility compared to your peoples' ability to work with such forces. Initially faced with irresistible forces in both retailing and financial services, Sears probably made the right decision by trimming down to focus its attention solely on retailing issues.

These various responses to irresistible forces are dealt with in detail in chapters 3 through 10 and are designated as the following stalls:

"Where Are We Going and How Do We Get There?"—The Directionless Stall (chapter 3)
Many organizations drift in a set direction and then find themselves lost when an irresistible force suddenly pushes them at high speed in a new direction toward a different destination. By not knowing whether they want to go to that new destination, they leave themselves open to inaction and indecision.

Borders' slow commitment to online commerce is an example of this problem. The company had been trailing Barnes & Noble in the area of large retail book and audio stores. Consequently, its management was occupied with opening new stores and adding financial resources. Published reports suggest that Borders' management was unsure about adding online commerce as a business. By waiting until both Amazon.com and Barnesandnoble.com were operating before opening its own Internet site, Borders increased the likelihood that its cost of acquiring customers would vastly exceed those of its two key competitors.

"But That's Not the Way I Thought It Would Be!"—The Wishful Thinking Stall (chapter 4) Most enterprises act as if they can anticipate the future with a great deal of accuracy. When an incorrect assumption is made, actions become inappropriate for the real situation. Acting on this viewpoint is like following an out-of-date road map that doesn't show road closures, new roads and junctions. You may find yourself diverted in unexpected directions.

Consider that computer makers for many years believed that their profits would primarily come from selling the hardware. As a result, they would not make their software available to those who purchased other hardware. They waited for the world to beat a path to their doors, and the world went elsewhere. Apple Computer is a good example. The company had an operating system for its Mac products that was years ahead of what Microsoft had available. Apple chose not to make this software available to those with IBM personal computers and their clones. Based on the recent stock market values of Microsoft and Apple, this was an expensive error, costing Apple shareholders hundreds of billions of dollars.

"What Do We Do Now?"—The Helplessness Stall (chapter 5) When the familiar and predictable environment becomes hostile and unfamiliar, those responsible for an enterprise's progress often feel unable to regain control. They become hamstrung as a result of feeling overwhelmed by events.

For example, an auto parts supplier grew mightily during the automobile boom leading up to the second oil shock (the one that almost destroyed Chrysler). When the price of gas soared and demand for cars plunged, colleagues reported that the CEO spent day after day sitting frozen at his desk, unable to make decisions. Fortunately, they seized the reins temporarily and made the necessary adjustments to survive before it was too late. However, millions were unnecessarily lost in the meantime.

"Circle the Wagons!"—The Defensiveness Stall (chapter 6) Although some organizations avoid being left helpless by irresistible forces, they may still be harmed by introversion and focus on creating bulwarks against the impact of the irresistible force. By focusing on a defensive posture, they delay adapting to the new conditions and risk falling behind or even not surviving at all.

Many companies whose stock prices carry low price-earnings valuations will proudly describe what they are doing as a "value-improving" strategy. When asked about the fact that investors are deserting this strategy in droves, the CFO will often confidently reply that it will all turn out well in the end. On further inspection, the strategy's consequence is more often being taken over by another company at a bargain price. The new owner will immediately initiate a better strategy that does translate into significant, sustained stock-price growth. Usually, this improved strategy is one that the earlier management could also have done.

"We Can Do It All!" — The Independence Stall (chapter 7)   When new irresistible forces arrive or existing ones change their impact, enterprises may find themselves compelled by the need to adapt as quickly as possible. In their rush to respond, the organization's leaders may tend to rely on people or practices that have worked successfully in the past. They may not stop to consider whether the enterprise has the right resources to accomplish the now-required tasks.

Many Internet start-ups, for example, have a sound marketing and customer value model, but do not yet understand how that model has to be supported with effective sourcing, supply, and service. Soon they find themselves falling further and further behind in meeting customer expectations with no clear idea about how to solve the mountain of fulfillment problems.

"How Can We Miss?" — The Overoptimism Stall (chapter 8)   A sense of certainty about success or that an enterprise is well prepared for the future, or simply viewing the world through rose-colored glasses, can result in rigid commitment down the wrong path. Successful enterprises are most likely to become subject to this stall, which is one reason why they often have such a hard time anticipating and adapting to new circumstances. Everyone in the company assumes success and is slow to perceive that progress is not occurring from the organization's new initiatives.

Digital Equipment's decline illustrates the consequences of this stall quite well. Press reports indicated that Digital Equipment founder and CEO, Ken Olsen, had little regard for the potential of personal computers, likening them to toys that would never be serious tools for engineers. During this time, Digital dominated the market for minicomputers and had been successful in replacing mainframe computers in many applications. The same forces that allowed the company to prosper as a minicomputer specialist doomed the company to being replaced by competitors making smaller, cheaper machines with the same functionality. A few years after Olsen was replaced by the board, the company was sold to Compaq Computer, one of the producers of those smaller, cheaper machines. Compaq, in turn, had problems with wishful thinking, and as a result had trouble integrating the two companies and keeping up with Dell Computer's build-to-order business. Compaq's CEO soon lost his job as profits and market share faltered.

"Throw Me a Towel"—The Cover-Up Stall (chapter 9)   It isn't unusual for apparent failures or setbacks to receive the so-called mushroom treatment (put it in a dark place). Yet unexpected problems and successes often contain the seeds of opportunity to build on the power of irresistible forces. Too many organizations treat these circumstances as though something shameful has just happened, which would be better off left alone and not talked about.

Think about what happened when Monsanto used secrecy to achieve a competitive edge in the genetically engineered food market. Monsanto had been a leader in the development of these new technologies. In the late 1990s, European consumers grew concerned about the safety of the new foods, provoking a widespread backlash against these products. As the company, in many cases, had even kept the use of its products a secret from consumers in the United States, it obviously had hoped that concerns about the safety of these products would just go away if it kept a low profile. The opposite result seemed to have occurred, because the secrecy was interpreted by some as meaning that the company had something dangerous to hide from consumers.

"Let's Take a Chance"—The Underestimation Stall (chapter 10)
Organizations sometimes should take on the most extreme irresistible forces because their great volatility can provide competitive insulation, as long as a uniquely dependable method is applied for dealing with the volatility. Ignoring or underestimating that volatility, however, can result in disaster.

Only a handful of companies specialize in putting out petroleum fires. In case you're unfamiliar with this business, the best way to extinguish such a fire is to walk into the middle of the inferno carrying explosives and then to detonate them from a safe distance. This explosion uses up the oxygen that the fire needs, and the fire often goes out. If not, another explosion may do the trick. When the Kuwait oil fields were set aflame by the retreating Iraqi armies, these companies had little to be concerned about from new firefighting entrants. Few people had the skill and courage to take on that irresistible force. This same challenging opportunity could easily have proven disastrous for others who were less capable.

These stalls occur and persist in enterprises because human psychology often fosters a knee-jerk response to irresistible forces. By becoming a stall-buster, you'll learn to use irresistible forces to create breakthrough gains and success for yourself and your enterprise.

Stallbusting: Get the Better
of Those Bad Thinking Habits

Because we are all human, stalls exist in both your personal life and your organization. Stalls are basically bad thinking habits. If you become aware of and can recognize these habits, then you can begin to consciously challenge them. Eventually you can change them into habits better suited for the irresistible growth enterprise.

What Are Your Bad Habits
When You Confront Irresistible Forces?

You need to be aware of your own habits before you can fully comprehend the habits that your organization has. An organization has more bad habits than any single individual in it because the bad habits of each person are multiplied by the combined effect of the bad habits of other people. For example, in the early days of Dell Computer, Michael Dell had not yet recruited strong, experienced executives who had dealt successfully before with large, irresistible forces in fast-growth situations. As a result, many important issues about irresistible forces were not addressed until they became painfully large, as occurred when Dell first developed an unsuccessful line of portable computers in 1993. The bad habit was that Dell Computer was relying too much on Michael Dell at that point.

Now try some self-examination. Ask yourself the following questions:

How would you have reacted to the travel challenges described at the beginning of this chapter as you sought to meet with the other company? In considering your reactions, you'll learn more if you write down your thoughts. Begin by listing all the emotions that you felt strongly at different points in the story. Then, consider how those emotions might have affected your behavior. For example, think about these reactions in terms of what would have happened at your negative emotional peak. At what point would you have become irritable? At what point would you have become angry? At what point would you have gotten frustrated? At what point would you have given up? At what point would you have become stubbornly determined to go ahead?

What irresistible forces have you encountered in the past while working in your enterprise? Having seen quite a few examples by now, you should be able to identify some in your own situation. If you are having trouble finding any, here are some questions that can generate clues:

- What is working much better than you expected? Why did that occur?

- What is working much worse than you expected? Why?

- Where are demands or prices for your products or services fluctuating?

- Do you expect demand or prices to be more elastic or inelastic? What are the underlying causes?

How have you personally reacted to irresistible forces that affected your organization in the past? With regard to this question, you'll learn the most if you pick the most painful and difficult experiences you have had, especially the ones that you would like to forget about. A real lesson for you will be to locate the circumstances under which you have made the worst errors, driven by negative or positive emotions. Be sure also to give yourself credit for what you did well. You can build on that success in the future.

How could you improve your ability to stay calm, open-minded, and effective in similar circumstances in the future? One answer to this question is to give yourself some emotional space when a situation first arises. Then while you are suspending judgment about how you choose to react, you can try to step outside yourself and examine yourself as a third person would. That perspective should help you become more objective about your situation. You may find it especially helpful if you imagine different types of people in that third-person role, such as an entrepreneur in a start-up, an executive you admire, a parent or other person you respect, or even your best friend.

What Are Your Enterprise's Bad Habits in Relation to Irresistible Forces?

Once you've taken stock of yourself, turn your attention to the habits in evidence throughout your organization. Use your answers to the following questions to determine your enterprise's strengths and weaknesses when it comes to managing irresistible forces:

What irresistible forces are already affecting your enterprise? A good beginning is to compile a list of the irresistible forces that you understand are already impacting your organization. You can learn a lot about your organization's likely future actions by studying how it has acted in the past. Be sure to consider any unique influences of customers, suppliers, distributors, competitors, employees, partners, new technologies, new social trends, demographics, economic factors, financial markets, governmental regulation, and community attitudes.

What has your enterprise done well in creating, anticipating, responding to, and adapting to these forces? It is important to see irresistible forces in a positive light in order to take advantage of their potential to help your organization. For that reason, it's necessary to carefully look for past positive responses. The classic example of a positive response to product tampering, which may occur again, was Johnson & Johnson's immediate recall of all Tylenol products. In making future changes, you want to keep these good habits in place or even build on them to create even more effectiveness. In answering this question, consider the timeliness of the response as well as its appropriateness.

Why did your enterprise do well when affected by these forces? Answering this question will help you get to the causes of your success. These may relate to the skills possessed by various employees, information your organization develops and analyzes, or an ability to focus as a common thread running throughout the organization. Keep asking "why" until you think you have the underlying causes. Johnson & Johnson has since used scenarios of possible future events and values reinforcement to help them be prepared should a product tampering situation recur.

What habits would have helped your enterprise to be more successful in past situations? You might try to rewrite history here to model what would have been an ideal response to the irresistible forces. Then step back to see what habits would have helped your organization to make that ideal response.

What existing habits are in conflict with the habits needed for success? Contrast your current habits with the ideal response habits. Remember when RJR Nabisco was purchased by KKR? RJR's CEO, Ross Johnson, thought the company was too large for anyone other than management to bid on. That belief caused the company to waste resources and stalled progress by fostering a false sense of security. Be careful not to overly model on past situations. The future could be quite different; in fact, you can count on it!

How Can You Replace Existing Bad Habits?

After identifying the existing bad habits, you'll need to work at eliminating them so that they can be replaced with the desired habits. Communication and learning about the bad habits are good ways to begin. Rather than just sharing the conclusions you arrive at, you'll get better results if you take other people in your enterprise through the same thought process of answering the previously listed questions. You'll learn something, too, because you'll often find that the perceptions of others will differ from yours. With more perceptions to work from, you're likely to get better ideas for how to improve.

One way to replace bad habits with communication and learning is to measure performance and share the results. For example, most companies would never acquire oil producing companies if they did the research and discovered that the inflation-adjusted dollar price of petroleum products has constantly declined over the long term. Seagram might never have bought Conoco had they known this fact, and earlier improved the company's acquisition habits while increasing the resources available for acquisitions. One bad habit that needs to be broken is succumbing to the influence of current "hot" fads and factors without studying the long-term context.

Start Becoming a Stallbuster Now

As previously mentioned in the Introduction, the rest of the chapters in this part of the book also contain personal and enterprise examples of stalls, sample solutions (stall erasers), and questions (or stallbusting action guides) to help you think like and become a stallbuster. Be sure to use the questions to relate the lessons of each chapter to your organization. If you haven't already started recording your observations, now is a good time to begin. This book can be a valuable workbook, much like the exercises in a consultant's workshop, but only if you follow through by working on the questions as they arise.

In addition to answering the questions, make a list of your own improvement ideas as they occur to you. Keep the list with you as you read the rest of the book. You'll find that your ideas are apt to change and improve as you read more material and answer the questions at the end of each chapter. Likewise, make notes of how your ideas change. Doing so will encourage you to work more in the area of replacing bad habits because you'll have a written record to show you how much you've learned from when you started reading this book. Finally, identify where your thinking has been stalled so you can see where you need to take new actions. By translating your thoughts into action, the benefits of being a stallbuster will become tangible.

3

"WHERE ARE WE GOING, AND HOW DO WE GET THERE?"

THE DIRECTIONLESS STALL

We're lost. But we're making good time.

—Yogi Berra

A fundamental problem for most organizations encountering irresistible forces stems from confusion within the ranks over what the enterprise's purpose is. This chapter demonstrates the important roles of values, alignment, and understanding of the enterprise's purpose for responding more appropriately to irresistible forces now and in the future.

Encountering an irresistible force (such as a competitor's better way of operating, a new type of technology, or changed customer needs) can be a great benefit to an enterprise. The shock can help everyone realize that the enterprise's purpose needs to be defined or redefined, and then supported by appropriate values and plans. Traditional universities often face this challenge when they have to compete with upstarts like the University of Phoenix or the Open University that provide higher education in more cost-effective ways. In communities served by these new types of universities, the traditional universities are starting to question what their purpose should be. Only good things can happen as a result of such self-examination.

Unfortunately, most organizations are so befuddled by the new pressures that they avoid addressing the question of what the enterprise's purpose should be and become stalled without a clear direction. What does it mean to Harvard, for example, that Bill Gates, the richest person at the end of the old millennium, found it more useful to drop out and pursue his own education than to stay and earn his undergraduate degree? Similarly, Michael Dell is also a college dropout. When some of the most able people in a generation find college to be not very helpful at the dawn of the Knowledge Age, it should be apparent that it's time to reconsider the purposes and ways of providing higher education. For many of these universities, the purposes of providing a thriving faculty environment and serving the needs of students are hopelessly at odds because long-held rules of tenure delay or even prohibit those who are most skilled in many of the new knowledge-led fields from qualifying as instructors.

Enterprises that have a well-founded purpose (beyond simply meeting budgets), like the business team that needed to overcome the weather in order to hold an important meeting, will usually find that an ability to stay focused on that purpose allows them to successfully adapt to the irresistible forces. Having a clear and exciting purpose for the enterprise adds other important benefits, including making it easier to attract and retain outstanding employees. Purposelessness had become so common in work-a-day jobs at the end of the twentieth century that volunteers in nonprofit organizations then often said that they helped out to overcome a sense of meaningless efforts in the paying workplace.

Boxed In: Which Way Are We Going?

In the early days of the cable television industry, technology limitations meant that cable operators could supply their customers with very few channels. Home Box Office (HBO), the largest and most successful pay cable channel at that time, was confronted with the irresistible forces that technology would eventually enable cable operators to offer hundreds of channels and that subscribers wanted lots of variety. Faced with competitors such as Showtime and others who were finding it easier and easier to get into cable households as more cable channels were available with advanced technology, HBO launched a second channel called Cinemax. The new channel served as the less expensive alternative to its HBO service. Home Box Office made it attractive to cable operators to buy their two-channel package, thus reducing the attractiveness of adding HBO's competitors instead.

Home Box Office's parent company, Time Inc., still had a fundamental question to address: Should it primarily build from the Home Box Office base, or should it try to launch dozens of new channels to fill lots of the cable operators' rapidly expanding channel capacity? Initially, the company invested with partners who were starting or supporting new channels, such as the USA Network. The company then pulled back by selling stakes in those channels, enabling the parent company to generate lots of near-term earnings growth from the profitable Home Box Office/Cinemax base with limited risk.

Years later, the parent company realized that each cable channel was an enormously valuable business and more should be added. Turner Broadcasting was acquired for a multibillion dollar price tag to expand the parent company's choices, but, meanwhile, the inexpensive opportunity to launch large numbers of these very valuable channels had been lost.

Why did the parent company make such an expensive flip-flop? The parent company management simply did not decide that the company wanted to be a leader in offering a variety of cable television channels until after the best years to pursue the opportunity were largely gone. A rapid series of changes in top management at the parent company contributed to the confusion as Time merged with Warner Communications to become Time Warner. Each company leader during this time had a different vision and strategy of what the parent company should be trying to accomplish.

Time Inc. had a proud tradition based in the magazine industry, producing prestigious publications such as *Time* and *Fortune*. While cable television offered higher growth, publications offered more prestige. A values conflict ensued. For example, the company invested large sums unsuccessfully to establish a new magazine for cable television listings at the same time that a smaller investment would have undoubtedly succeeded for new cable channels.

Prior to the merger with Warner Communications, the situation was worsened by the risk that Time Inc. might face a hostile takeover bid. New cable channels looked unattractive in this light because the large investments required to expand them would cause lower corporate earnings in the beginning. Lower earnings were commonly perceived as making takeover risk higher at that time. As a result, corporate executives were reluctant to invest in businesses such as new cable channels that could not be profitable for many years. Eventually, a hostile takeover bid did emerge from Paramount following the announcement of a friendly merger of equals with Warner Communications.

The newly merged Time Warner then had a new center and focus: the entertainment industry. Values, vision, clarity, and irresistible force trends were eventually aligned under a new CEO, Gerald Levin. Cable channels were perceived as desirable in such an environment, and Levin had won his spurs in the HBO side of the business so he was comfortable with the opportunities.

The Turner acquisition soon followed. Had Time Inc. merged with Warner sooner, or become an entertainment-focused company earlier, the benefits to be gained from the irresistible forces would have been captured in a much more timely and less expensive way.

Stall Examples

Value Conflicts: Downsizing to Improve Customer Service?

Value conflicts arise frequently in enterprises, leaving those who work in them confused and less effective. A common value conflict arises when a company chooses "head-count reductions" as a key strategy for increased earnings and faster corporate growth.

The message that the employees may infer from this behavior is that the company is going down the tubes; that any improvement in company financial results is going to come from extra work by employees for no more pay; that the remaining employees may lose their own jobs next; that no one is valued by the organization; and that employees should leave if they can find a better offer. Employees who are high performers the organization wants to keep spend their time looking for new jobs, leaving for better ones, or worrying about their futures.

In the meantime, the organization's customers often receive the message that this supplier feels that they, the customers, could be served equally well with fewer people; that many of the key supplier employees they work with now are going to be unavailable to help them in the future, and that the supplier may focus its attention on growing in some other area. Naturally, many customers start looking for new suppliers.

A vicious cycle develops. With less business, the company finds it has too many employees and has to pursue faster earnings growth through more downsizing. And so it goes. If you think this scenario is overblown, look at the history of some companies that downsized themselves virtually out of business. For example, Wang Laboratories was a high-flying company that offered the first word processing equipment through harnessing the potential of modern electronics. The irresistible force Wang faced was that people wanted multipurpose computers (for word and data processing) that sat on desktops and were cheap and flexible. Wang wanted to sell proprietary equipment that was single purpose. The company's sales began to falter when personal computers and competing open software programs for word processing began to appear on the market.

Eventually Wang shifted its focus to become a software company, but only after many thousands had lost their jobs. Constant downsizing to pursue earnings growth for the company created an environment in which the critical software development teams experienced enormous voluntary turnover based on the company's ill-chosen direction. The result was that critical software projects were always way behind schedule. Without that software, the company had little future. Few felt as if they were valued, so the company lost its ability to compete. During the company's critical juncture, Boston-area employers reported getting resumes in the same week from as many as five different former heads of Wang's software development activities.

Wang should have realized sooner the implications of, or reacted more quickly and effectively to, the personal computer. Its growth strategy then could have been a combination of providing personal computers and open-system software for word processing and other applications. In fact, Wang had made some half-hearted attempts as a manufacturer that were unsuccessful in this direction. But the organization's leadership did not believe that success in this rapidly growing marketplace had to be based on using the talents of all its people to aid such a transition. Employees and customers could have been energized by such a changed direction, based on a clear organizational value of serving both customer and employee needs in the best possible way. The value conflict in pursuing earnings improvement through continual downsizing killed that opportunity.

Misaligned and Cast Adrift

How an organization's values translate into the actions needed to adapt to irresistible forces may seem so apparent to its leader that she or he may think other people's views are similarly aligned. However, in reality, no one else may have a clue.

Consider one of the fastest-growing consumer service companies ever. The operation went from zero to over $1 billion in revenues in very little time. It eventually encountered irresistible forces that meant the product line needed to be broadened, and quickly. The CEO was concerned because he was having trouble getting agreement from his key executives about how to implement the next steps in the company's growth. So he brought in an advisor to help him address the situation.

The advisor privately interviewed each member of the management team. They each knew what the irresistible forces were and that adding new products faster was the appropriate response to them. However, none of them agreed on how that product expansion should occur. In addition, each described some other member or members of the team as being opposed to any product proliferation. Not only, then, was there no alignment in the management team about specifically what to do, there was even no alignment about where there was misalignment.

The CEO convened a two-day meeting to address the issues, facilitated by the advisor. The discussions first focused on what the organization's direction should be. With that settled, everyone realized that they all agreed that product proliferation had to accelerate, and the group rapidly began to align itself in a direction to pursue that proliferation. This new direction was different from the initial views of each executive, because it reflected a new and broader purpose. By the end of the two days, the necessary agreement to implement the new direction had developed. In the next six months, the business grew faster than ever before and added more new services than in the previous three years combined. The top executives started enjoying their work more, and even started liking each other (in their ignorance of each other's views, they had initially reacted negatively to each other due to the falsely perceived disagreements concerning what to do about the irresistible force).

Clearly the Way to Go . . . or Is It?

An enterprise can agree about the existence of the irresistible force, have the same values, be aligned, and still make a mess of the opportunity. How? Without clearly understanding all of the dimensions of the irresistible force, a company can undermine its search for the benefits it seeks.

Beatrice Foods in the 1970s provides an example. Financial executives in the company told the authors then that Beatrice had earlier chosen to make growing earnings per share, quarter to quarter, year in and year out, the company's primary goal. It was clear about how to do this, and the company accomplished the goal for well over 30 years—a singular achievement rarely matched by any other business anywhere. Despite this remarkable accomplishment, the company ended up wracked by dissension and felt prey to an attack from a hostile bidder.

The company's purpose in selecting this goal was to obtain a premium stock-price multiple. The company then planned to use its high value stock to acquire other attractive businesses at a more reasonable cost. In the 1950s, the company achieved its hopes with regard to its stock price. Dozens of acquisitions followed. Soon, however, Beatrice Foods found itself unable to find high-profit, high-growth food businesses of sufficient size to expand the company's growth rate. Gradually, all kinds of unrelated businesses were added. This strategy worked well in the early 1960s, the heyday of conglomerates. When investment fashions changed to favor more focused companies, the more diversified the company became, the lower the Beatrice stock-price multiple of earnings became. Still, the nonfood acquisitions continued, paid for in stock.

The rate of drop in the company's stock price multiple matched its growth in earnings per share, so that the stock price itself stayed in the same trading range, year in and year out, from 1977 through 1984. The many senior managers who had sold their companies for stock in Beatrice during those years grew quite unhappy in the face of the ensuing price stagnation. When a hostile takeover bid was received, many company managers supported it. As a result, the company was sold to a group headed by the CEO of a company that Beatrice itself had recently taken over through a hostile takeover bid.

The original irresistible force for Beatrice was the lure and power of a rising stock price and premium stock price multiple to make growing into a large company inexpensive. In focusing on consistent earnings growth, the company had found one factor that could contribute to the stock price performance. Because the company didn't truly understand the irresistible forces that create a premium stock price, the success with earnings growth was offset by the company's indiscriminate and short-sighted use of acquisitions to create that earnings growth. Beatrice executives misunderstood what it took to obtain their stock price results, and worked very hard to achieve a difficult objective . . . but to no avail.

When the stock price stalled, the company should have reexamined its approach to improving stock price. It probably would have done better in growing stock price if the company had provided less earnings per share growth, and stayed a simpler, more focused company that investors could have better understood.

Beatrice Foods chose an inappropriate means (earnings growth from any source) to achieve its ultimate goal of building a large successful company. Instead it should have concentrated directly on all the ways that the irresistible force of the stock market could provide the company with a premium-priced, growing stock price. Misidentifying what needs to be done because of a lack of thorough understanding of the irresistible forces is a common problem among companies that wish to improve.

Stall Erasers
Get More Value from Your Values—
And Walk Your Talk
Habitat for Humanity is one of the fastest-growing large organizations on Earth. This charitable enterprise finds deserving people who can't afford to own decent housing, helps them build such housing at modest cost, and provides no-interest mortgages to finance the purchases. A key element of

Former U.S. president Jimmy Carter works on a Habitat for Humanity project to provide housing for needy families. The organization's strong foundation in religious values has helped provide an irresistible force that has allowed it to operate as one of the fastest growing and most admired organizations in the world. (© Robert Maass/CORBIS)

Habitat's ethic is that the organization is based on Christian principles and sees itself as a Christian ministry. This religious foundation enables Habitat to draw on teachings about "helping thy neighbor" and "loving thy neighbor as thyself." Habitat uses these values as an irresistible force to draw volunteers and resources to the organization. Naturally, the group carefully lives up to its creed. Although the charity operates from explicit Christian principles, people of many faiths support Habitat's work out of respect for the values that Habitat upholds.

To some this enterprise may sound like a fairy tale. Check it out. While conventional builders take weeks and months to complete the simplest structure, Habitat routinely builds housing in hours or just a few days as part of special events. Its members rigorously work to reduce costs, improve quality, and accelerate progress, and are the world standard in much of what they do. They have clear values and a clear mission; it's their commitment to their values and mission that drives their focus on cutting costs and time. That commitment is an irresistible force that Habitat for Humanity harnesses.

Is your enterprise based on values that are this inspiring for you and the rest of your organization?

The Well-Aligned Enterprise Gets Better Mileage

Charles Schwab, the discount broker, has always based its business on providing good service to its customers at the lowest possible cost. It turns out that this operating philosophy is a perfect fit for what customers want and matches a key irresistible force in the brokerage industry. In the early days, the company found that customers who placed an order to buy or sell a security wanted to find out what had happened to their orders. Charles Schwab obliged its customers by placing calls promptly to let them know. To reduce its costs to provide this service, the company became a pioneer in developing computer systems to give its customers more information.

Experience with this dual approach of providing more help at lower cost caused the company to think about other areas where customers would also like more help, at low cost. One innovation was the OneSource service, where customers could buy or sell any of hundreds of mutual funds through Charles Schwab at no cost, and receive the convenience of one account statement for all these transactions. The company blossomed and became a pioneer and the early leader in Internet stock trading as well.

Charles Schwab continues to be a pioneer in offering new services based on computer systems that enhance service while reducing costs for everyone. That's certainly a 2,000 percent solution.

Is your enterprise effectively aligned to serve the irresistible force of customer demand for better services, more services, and lower costs?

Clarity—As Clear as a Bell

Until the court-ordered breakup of AT&T that separated the long distance service from the local Bell operating companies, America's Bell System provided telephone service that was the envy of the world. By contrast, in many other countries the telephone systems became government monopolies that provided less than desirable service at high costs. Even in this new century, telephone calls are difficult to make and receive in parts of many countries.

This tendency for governments to turn telephone businesses into government-owned and operated monopolies was an irresistible force that AT&T had to deal with throughout most of the twentieth century. Early in its life as a company, AT&T realized that its ability to avoid being taken over by a government monopoly depended on having happy customers. Also, as a regulated monopoly, pricing would be dependent on having a lot of assets to serve customers, because pricing was based on a determined level of return on the assets employed by the business. This circumstance meant that the business would also have higher profits and be larger if the company had lots of happy customers. AT&T invested rapidly in new technology, developing redundancies to improve reliable service, and in new equipment. Service was provided on the basis of "the customer is always right," which is especially important when every dissatisfied customer could complain to her or his member of Congress and demand that the monopoly be broken up. The Bell System got the message about what needed to be done to maintain itself relative to the irresistible force of the governmental desire to operate many monopolies for itself, like the postal service. What the company failed to do was to guard against another strong irresistible force: the government's desire to eliminate privately owned monopolies when competition is likely to bring lower prices. It was that failure that led to the break-up of the company after many decades of unparalleled growth and success.

Does your organization understand what must be done to coexist and prosper with *all* of your irresistible forces?

Getting It All Together to Go the Distance

Sometimes the winds of irresistible forces can blow in many and unpredictable directions, and the required actions can be quite diverse. Consider the pricing and demand for commodities like oil. How can you prepare for changing oil prices, even if you have all the values, alignment, clarity, and understanding that you think you need? Royal Dutch/Shell provides an example from the

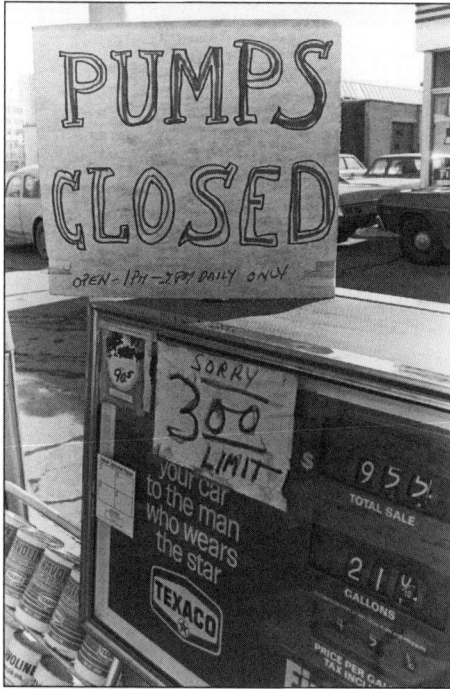

While motorists shivered in their cars waiting for gas during the Arab oil embargo, Royal Dutch/Shell used lessons learned from simulations of such an event to power its profits forward by shifting its sources of petroleum. (© Owen Franken/CORBIS)

period of the Arab oil embargo of being prepared to deal with irresistible forces. Just prior to that time, the company's planning department had been charged with developing a large number of scenarios about what could happen to the petroleum industry in the future. The purpose of this exercise was to provide the groundwork for the company to prepare its options well in advance, and then act quickly and decisively once an irresistible force showed its face and direction.

Shell realized that forecasting these actions might be seen as a waste of time, but the company was fairly sure that the future would lie somewhat in one or more of the directions developed in the scenarios. You guessed it. One of the scenarios called for an Arab oil embargo and an overnight spike in the price of petroleum. When the embargo actually happened, Shell had its plans all laid out in advance, with consistency relative to its values, all the necessary alignment, and required clarity. The company quickly implemented its plans by tapping into new, lower-priced sources of supply not affected by OPEC, making products that would provide the company with a good profit at the newly inflated prices, and focusing on markets where demand would be the least affected. The company saw its earnings rise while its competitors stumbled.

Arie de Geus (author of *The Living Company,* Harvard Business School Press, 1997) points out an interesting characteristic of scenario planning that he learned from his years of experience with this process at Shell. Developing scenarios seems to help people and organizations become more comfortable with how to think about changed circumstances. Thus they are better able to see the new direction and deal with it in a positive way.

Does your organization know about the alternative scenarios that irresistible forces could bring to your environment? Are you ready with plans for those scenarios?

Stallbusting

The preceding discussions show how the lack of a meaningful purpose can cause aimlessness, and provide some examples of how to overcome aimlessness in order to benefit from irresistible forces. Considering the importance of avoiding directionless drifting, how can you and your organization maintain a strong sense of purpose and direction when you are buffeted by volatile organizational conditions?

In the stallbusting section that follows, you can learn how to find powerful, motivating values that will direct your enterprise towards a more empowering and successful future. You can find out how to check for alignment with likely future scenarios driven by irresistible forces. Understanding the importance of values, alignment, and clarity can help you avoid the negative consequences of having a directionless feeling permeate your enterprise.

Use This Check to Retrieve Your Values from the Vestibule

Every enterprise has a core of common values that attracted the people who work there to it and that keeps them there. To avoid succumbing to the directionless stall, you need to make sure everyone in the organization knows what those values are, clearly understands them, and, as a result, knows what to do when irresistible forces arise.

What are your organization's common values? Start looking for the answer to this question by polling everyone in your organization on what his or her values are. The first time you do this, let people simply tell you what the values are that they consider important. If you aren't sure what they mean, ask for more details in the form of an example. Outstanding service organizations like the Disney theme parks and the Ritz-Carlton hotels report a common desire to serve others as an important shared value.

Next, check for commonality by asking everyone to rate or rank the significance of each value that is relatively common. This list will jog some people's memories. The ones that are universally ranked as significant comprise your list.

Is your enterprise operating in alignment with the enterprise's common values? Ask everyone how well she or he thinks the organization is acting relative to its values. Are the values being used for direction, or are they being checked at the door when people arrive at work each morning? Ask for examples of where the alignment between personal values and behavior is both good and bad.

Are You Ready for This?

Irresistible forces are operating all around you. Some could shift in new directions. You and your enterprise need to be prepared for as many situations as possible. Having alternative plans ready to implement at a moment's notice will keep you from foundering and give you a competitive edge. Digital Equipment would have been helped by considering a scenario that called for personal computers replacing minicomputers. Apple Computer would have learned a lot from a scenario in which the company focused primarily on providing software for all computers, rather than just for the ones it manufactured.

What scenarios for "what-if" situations would help your enterprise be better prepared? The key test here is one of significance. If something could have a large impact, good or bad, you need to study it, unless the likelihood is almost totally nil. Microsoft, for example, should consider competition from freeware created by visionary enthusiasts, such as the Linux operating system. Such products are starting to proliferate, the Internet will facilitate them, and the impact on Microsoft would be large.

What actions are required in each scenario? Answering this question involves both deciding whether an action is required and then what that action or direction should be. Shell would have gained no benefit from its Arab oil embargo scenario without having developed some effective ideas for what to do under those circumstances.

Does everyone know what she or he is supposed to do in any given scenario? You should annually check with the people involved to be sure they know their roles in implementing the "what-if" scenarios. This action is particularly important in a rapidly growing company that is adding significantly to its workforce. Some companies have added their own "universities" to share and nurture common values while educating employees in company thinking. The Miller Brewing Company diverts its capacity from making beer to bottling water for communities that temporarily have no drinking water (most often following severe storms and floods). The company has long-standing procedures for identifying when and where bottled water is needed, and for getting the water to those communities in a timely and effective way.

Are We Really on the Yellow Brick Road?

In the Land of Oz, Dorothy always got into trouble as soon as she left the yellow brick road. When dealing with irresistible forces and potential stalls, you need to check constantly that you are on the right path and positioned favorably for achieving success, especially when the road forks.

Are your irresistible forces providing tailwinds, cross winds, or headwinds? Begin by listing all of the irresistible forces that are influencing your organization. (You can probably add to the list now that you started in chapter 2.) Then evaluate how they are affecting your progress. Forces that are helping you are tailwinds. Those that are pushing you off target are cross winds. Those that are holding back your progress are headwinds. You will probably find that the list of irresistible forces and their impacts on you will change over time, so you should update your answers to this question from time to time. A consumer products company that has done this updating finds that its list of irresistible forces changes very rapidly, and the list of which forces are headwinds, cross winds, and tailwinds changes even faster.

How can you turn all of your cross and headwinds into tailwinds? So far in the book, this is the most important question for you to answer. At first, most people think that developing advantages from many of their organization's irresistible forces is impossible. However, with a little prodding, they are always able to find a solution that enables them to do so. For example, a food manufacturer found itself squeezed by retailers' desires to carry fewer choices and to be paid more for carrying those choices, as well as by competitors entering the business. Consequently, the manufacturer's prices were forced down while its spending had to be increased. There seemed to be no way out.

On further reflection, the company realized that if it viewed other companies who were experiencing the same problems as possible allies, the companies could combine in new ways to support each other and become much more effective. Also, relations with retailers could become tailwinds if the food company spent the time to establish a carefully designed, win-win relationship with the retailers. And since the competitive disadvantages were caused by not having enough capital available at a low-enough cost, changing the way the company was financed would quickly improve that situation. With a new understanding of the opportunities, the company quickly benefited by using the irresistible forces to its advantage.

The usefulness of this question was amply demonstrated when a similar food company faltered badly as a result of the same irresistible forces, due to being pulled in so many directions at once as to be directionless and by not considering scenarios. This company sought to serve too many interests in too many ways. Shareholders wanted the company to grow rapidly, become more profitable, use less capital, and be more loyal to suppliers. Customers wanted lower prices and fewer products. It was a very demanding list.

The company finally collapsed from the financial and managerial strain of trying to resolve the irresolvable during a crisis brought on by a totally unexpected shift in irresistible forces. It had focused its growth plans for years on adding new products mostly made with new, less expensive ingredients to meet the demands of its stockholders. Rapid expansion had left the company financially weak, even though it had shown good sales and profit results. Without scenarios, the company failed to realize that its strategy would only work if raw material costs stayed as they were. When raw material costs of the original base ingredient unexpectedly melted down, the company's whole product line became vulnerable to new competitors who emphasized a more "pure" product using more of the higher-quality base ingredient at a very attractive price. To respond successfully, the company would have had to add dozens of new products overnight with a different mix of ingredients. With advance focus and preparation, the company would have had a chance. But the firm had neither the vision, the management skills, the relationship with retailers, nor the financial resources to do this. Almost immediately, shareholders were in revolt as sales and profits plunged, which further distracted the management team. The company tried to do a little of all the things that might help in this situation, and simply saw its situation deteriorate due to its prior inattention to irresistible forces. Too many directions provided a centrifugal force that spun the business apart. A narrow purpose, combined with scenarios, becomes a unifying force—like gravity—in difficult circumstances.

If other enterprises have taken the same path to success that you plan to use to adapt to particular irresistible forces, how have they fared? The answer to this question will help you determine the odds for success with your approach, and how they compare with other approaches. Let someone else's mistakes and successes give you a road map for traveling with the irresistible force winds at your back. This strategy can be especially helpful in newly emerging markets. For example, when consumer products companies begin selling into third-world countries, they usually think in terms of the product sizes used in their home countries. In third-world countries, consumers may not be able to afford to buy so much at one time (as is the case with cigarettes where people often buy them one cigarette at a time, instead of in packs or cartons) or may have a spoilage problem (as is the case with perishables in countries with hot temperatures and limited availability of refrigeration for people). You will learn more about this concept of learning from others in chapter 13.

❖ ❖ ❖

Enterprises can best determine proper goals and directions by carefully considering a variety of factors including the personal and business values of those who work in the organization; the alignment between the company's activities and prospects; and an understanding of the potential implications of irresistible forces for the enterprise's future. Optimal results come when the business direction matches both the irresistible forces and the personal and business values of those who work in the enterprise.

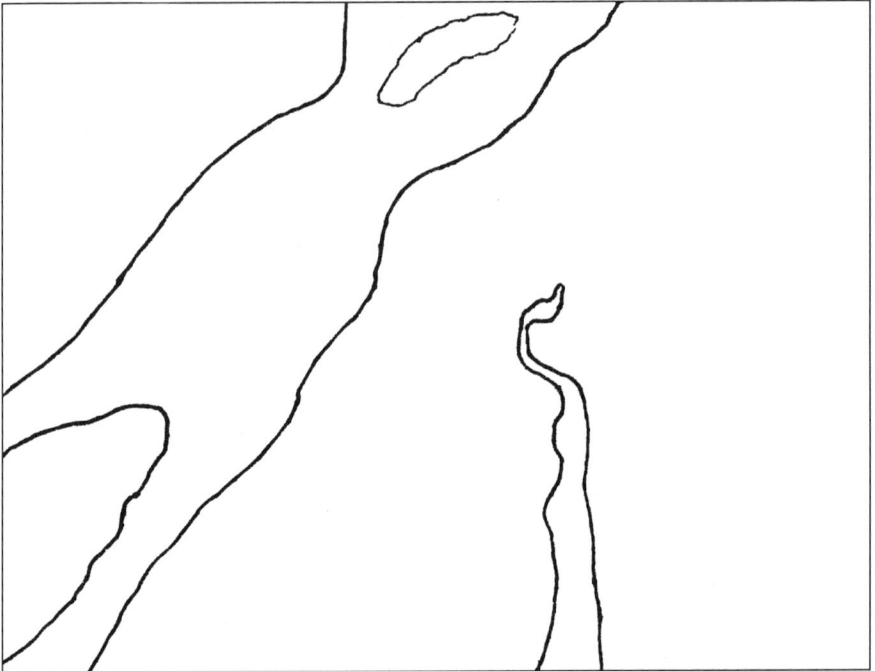

Many actions can leave you with no place to go, like the dead-end crawl way in a cave at the right. Being realistic about your irresistible forces will help you be sure that you are acting in ways that allow you to travel along with the forces, like the passageway through the cave on the left. Wishful thinking can harm you, by making you too eager to pursue opportunities that offer little future potential due to opposing irresistible forces.

4

"BUT THAT'S NOT THE WAY I THOUGHT IT WOULD BE!"

THE WISHFUL THINKING STALL

Neither a wise man nor a brave man lies down on the tracks of history to wait for the train of the future to run him over.

—Anonymous

Assuming that future conditions will be what we want them to be—either for the better or worse—can stall an enterprise unprepared for the irresistible force of an unpredictable future. This chapter can help you recognize the pitfalls of wishful thinking about the future and prepare for both shifts in current irresistible forces and the arrival of new ones through the use of contingency planning.

The CEO of a start-up computer manufacturer in the early 1980s had developed a 20-year picture of how every aspect of the computer industry would evolve. He could entertain any visitor for hours with how his company's plans would enable the firm to quickly exceed many billions of dollars in sales because of its shrewd ideas for capitalizing on the trends he envisioned. Yet the company soon foundered, without ever shipping any computers. What went wrong? The 20-year picture in the CEO's mind bore no relation to what was really happening in the computer industry. The company's plans were perfect for the CEO's forecast, but were terrible for the real situation. Many millions of dollars and years of peoples' lives were wasted because of the CEO's wishful thinking that stalled the company's progress.

No one can know what future conditions will be. You need to avoid extrapolating current trends into the future but, conversely, to also avoid wishfully thinking that this time things will be different. You need to think more about *all* of the significant things that could happen. Such advance thinking will help prepare your organization to act in ways that will take into account these possibilities, such as adopting decision rules that allow plenty of room for uncertainty. In addition, your company will also be much more likely to notice new irresistible forces and have some idea of what to do about them based on this preparation.

Checked Out at the Counter

Data Terminal Systems (DTS) was one of the highest flying technology companies and stocks of the 1970s. The company provided electronic equipment for checking out customers at retail stores such as supermarkets. Established and led by a CEO who knew a great deal about human motivation, the company performed marvelously quarter to quarter based on its finely tuned quarterly management by objectives program: Make your quota, and a substantial bonus would be yours at the end of each quarter.

Like a rocket ship reaching outer space, the company was on a trajectory where its progress kept accelerating due to the bonus program. The company assumed that it had the best technology and the best products, and employees simply had to get out there and sell what the company made. That assumption was true, for a while.

Encouraged by the success of DTS, large numbers of competitors began to build custom equipment designed for this end market. Suddenly, the company's products were not so obviously superior, and competitors were pricing to gain a beachhead. DTS eventually collapsed in the face of this competitive onslaught, and the technology was sold for a song to a larger company.

By wishfully thinking it would continue to be successful based simply on its existing approach to technology products and motivated employees, and by not preparing for the possibility of future tough competition, DTS became stalled and left itself wide open for failure. The company should have been running scared of future competition and have had plans in place to discourage competitors. DTS could have greatly reduced costs and prices through developing more advanced systems that others would have had difficulty duplicating. Or it could have gone into partnership with one of its likely, strong competitors to create a combined effectiveness that no one else could match.

Stall Examples

Wishful Thinking Is Whistled Off the Ice Too Late

Optimism about the future certainly has a positive place in the overall scheme of things, but it frequently fuels wishful thinking. Consider the hockey-stick forecast of the future. Let's say your operation has been doing poorly. In fact, results as measured by revenues and profits have been dropping. You sit down and plan ways to overcome this negative trend. Because the solutions take time and money, you plan for things to get worse in the near term, but you optimistically assume that all your new plans will work, causing the organization's results to turn up at some point in the future. With this viewpoint, a graph of the operation's revenues and profits over time will look like a hockey stick with the past, present, and near-term future going down like the handle of the stick, and the future turning up like its blade as the stick rests on the ice at the point where the handle and the blade meet. After a few years of implementing this plan, you often find that the only part of the hockey stick you can see when you examine the results is a handle still going down.

In the 1980s, a leading business equipment company was faced with declining demand for its most profitable product line. Sales and earnings inched up a little based on service revenues for the previously sold and installed equipment base, but new equipment sales were dropping rapidly. Using a technique called "gap planning," the operation looked for ways to fill the gap between its current direction and what it wanted to accomplish. After rejecting several alternatives, the business executives became excited about creating a new piece of equipment that would greatly reduce the cost for customers. Leading technical consultants from the East were brought in to this Midwestern business, and the consultants confirmed a rosy technology forecast and market for the product.

The company's chief financial officer was unconvinced, so he decided to monitor the situation closely. What he discovered was that compared to the original business plan on which the new product development investment was based, the cost of implementing the project and time to completion increased regularly every six months. At the same time, the estimated future sales and profits from the new equipment kept dropping every six months. He drew a chart showing that if this changing forecast trend continued, the project would be a big money loser. He got nowhere. Everyone else wanted to believe in the product's success, so the project continued. Sure enough, the project was eventually a big loser.

One way to have overcome this problem would have been to authorize the project based on the contingency of meeting interim targets for cost, product performance, on-time completion, profit, and market outlook. Then when those factors weakened, the plug would have been pulled automatically and most of the costs would have been avoided. If the project had been going well, these interim targets would not have harmed the project's ultimate success in any way.

Up, Up, and Away

When a powerful trend has been in place for some time, people lose their ability to imagine that anything different could have occurred. Influenced by the Arab oil embargo and the Iran-Iraq war, the price of oil rose rapidly from a few dollars a barrel to over $30 in just a few years. Pessimists pointed out that nature was making additional oil more slowly than it was being pumped from the ground and consumed, and the newspapers were filled with reports concerning the likelihood of $100-a-barrel oil in the fairly near future.

Many organizations concluded that this high price forecast was a slam-dunk certainty and began taking action to guard against this risk. A highly regarded chemical company, DuPont, purchased Conoco (an oil and gas producer) during this time. DuPont hoped for great things from this purchase. Years later, in 1998, DuPont divested Conoco at a time when oil prices were dropping and had reached the low teens in dollars per barrel. In fact, at the time DuPont sold the oil business (in the largest initial public offering until that time), the price of oil in constant dollars was at its lowest level since the 1930s.

DuPont could instead have used those same funds over the intervening years to develop its position in chemicals or health sciences (a new field of interest that the company pursued at about the same time), or repurchased large numbers of company shares. The opportunity cost (what DuPont could have obtained from the investment in something else minus the benefits of owning Conoco) appears to have been great.

Before deciding on a purchase, DuPont should have studied the price of oil and similar consumable natural resource commodities over time to understand what happens to these prices. It would have observed that these commodities *always* go down in price, as expressed in constant dollars, over time. However, this long-term trend is interrupted by sharp spikes in price from time to time as temporary supply-demand imbalances occur. Following such spikes, customers begin to substitute other goods, conservation efforts increase, producers begin to expand capacity, more resources are found, and technology for extraction improves. The long-term result of these adjustments is to reduce the constant dollar price of the commodity more rapidly than would otherwise have occurred. DuPont should have concluded that the chances of constantly higher oil prices were somewhere between slim and none.

If DuPont wanted to own an oil company, with study it would have realized that it only had to wait a few years and oil companies would be vastly cheaper and readily available. With increased profits per share from any of the alternative investments DuPont could have made in the meantime, the company would have been able to buy four or five companies Conoco's size when oil prices declined. Looking again at the long-term trend for oil prices, DuPont might have concluded that 1998 was a better time to buy than to sell oil companies and avoided its "buy high, sell low" execution of this move into commodities.

You Can Put It in the Newspaper: This Time Will Be Different

Following one of the worst periods ever in the newsprint industry, demand for newsprint and prices began to pick up in the mid-1990s. Manufacturers had avoided building new capacity in North America during the downturn and had actually retired some paper mills. This conservative stance created a supply-demand imbalance in favor of the producers, as an economic expansion in North America increased the amount of advertising in newspapers. Newsprint makers began to sense a bonanza, and prices rose rapidly, despite build-ups of inventories at customers' printing plants and in newsprint mills. Plants began to run at record rates, and newsprint companies began to gleefully plan for what to do with all this newfound wealth. No one could imagine anything less than a boom lasting for at least two years.

Well, the boom was over in not much more than a year. Soon, even more capacity had to be shut down in the industry, as prices dropped to near cash breakeven for many newsprint producers. What happened? Well, the publishers found that they could reduce the number and size of pages in their newspapers a great deal by cutting the amount of news they carried. They could also raise advertising rates very rapidly, and the amount of advertising they carried would drop also. Publishers could protect most of their profits this way, and the result was a large drop in newsprint consumption. The producers kept making paper at record rates, oblivious to the new trends. While some producers tried to restrict supply, others took advantage of the situation to make all the newsprint they could. And just as in every previous occasion when newsprint prices rose to high levels, the newspapers quickly regained the advantage.

What could a prescient newsprint manufacturer have done? The beginning of the boom was a great time to sell facilities that would be unprofitable in the next industry downturn. The manufacturer could then have used the cash received at that time to purchase low-cost mills during the next downturn when debt-laden producers were strapped for cash. This tactic would have improved the company's ability to compete in a low-price, low-demand market in the future.

Many newsprint manufacturers were interested in this strategy, but a belief that "this time would be different" kept them from acting until it was too late. A better approach would have been to sell high-cost mills as soon as their selling price exceeded the price at which low-cost mills could usually be bought in a downturn. That action, of course, would have required assuming that this time might not be different, as it was not.

Stall Erasers
Break the Blade from Your Hockey Stick and Really Score

Rather than assuming that the downward trend will turn up, it is safer for planning to assume that the negative trend will continue. The actions you are taking may fail, or the environment may worsen in ways that you don't yet expect. Think about how the actions you are considering will work out if the downside risks occur. Would you be better off, the same, or worse off? Unless you would be better off or the same, you should probably reconsider your action.

Consider a leading company faced with a decision to lower its costs by purchasing large amounts of transponder time on a communications satellite orbiting in space. If demand for the company's services does not meet the company's projections, there would be a lot of expensive unused time on that transponder. The company decided to look at what would happen if it didn't need any of the transponder time after having purchased it. It turned out that transponder capacity was then in short supply and would be for several years to come based on orders already in hand. A large number of customers would be happy to buy the time at a premium over the company's costs. The company would make money on the investment whether or not it needed all the transponder time.

The business made the investment and did in fact need the transponder time, so the investment was a success. Had the transponder time not been needed, the price of that time rose even faster than the company forecast, so the alternative would have worked well, too. You can be successful more often, too, by using this kind of a 2,000 percent solution. (You can learn more about how to find solutions that always leave you better off, regardless of the irresistible force direction in chapter 15.)

Look Over the Curve of the Horizon

The longer the time perspective you have on any trend involving irresistible forces, the more you can understand about the trend. At a minimum, look back at five complete cycles (from top to bottom and then up again to the next top is one cycle) for prices and demand. In looking at these cycles be sure to understand what happened to cause the cycle to change directions near the tops and bottoms. This analysis will give you clues about the current trend. Then investigate to see what is happening now in terms of those historical trend-changing factors. Consider what else is happening now or could happen in the future that could be new and different in its effect on the trend.

One of the most interesting examples of this kind of thinking occurs in Norman Augustine's book, *Augustine's Laws* (Viking Penguin, 1986, table on page 110). When he wrote the book, Augustine was an aerospace executive at Martin-Marietta Corporation looking at the implications of various long-term trends. He noted that the cost of a fighter-bomber was accelerating so fast that before many more years passed it would take the entire annual economic output of most countries just to purchase a single fighter-bomber. He modestly suggested that this trend would not continue much longer because it could not be afforded. In that observation, he laid the groundwork to predict the end to the cold war arms race between the Soviet Union and the United States. At some point, one side would have to drop out because it could not afford to continue. That is, in fact, what happened. Anyone wanting to predict when the sophisticated fighter-bomber industry's growth would end could have used this same analysis.

Play All the Parts—The Ultimate Role

Referring back to the newsprint example, the fundamental error that the newsprint companies made is that they didn't try to put themselves in the shoes of their customers, the newspapers, in order to anticipate how the newspapers might respond. If they had, they would have realized that newsprint demand would drop faster than they expected. Also, they could have played the role of their competitors to appreciate how much extra supply would be made available. By only considering its own perspective, each newsprint company fundamentally misunderstood the irresistible force of supply and demand during a time of high prices in the newsprint market.

A consumer products company decided to improve the effectiveness of its executives by having them do this sort of role playing. Some young, promising executives in a small division were given this assignment. They enjoyed role playing, and kept asking for more exercises to do. Eventually, they became quite good at it, and located improved ways to run almost every company in their industry better than it currently ran itself. The payoff for their business came in better financial and market share results, because they anticipated competitor actions extremely well through the role playing exercises.

What was totally unexpected, however, was that two of these executives went on to become the CEOs of companies for which they had done the role playing exercises years earlier. Sure enough, the new CEOs immediately began to improve their companies based on the insights gained from their role-playing experiences concerning these same companies. This role-playing skill turned out to be a long-term career 2,000 percent solution for the executives, as well as a near-term benefit to the enterprise that originally hired them.

Go to the Source for Your Fountain of Truth

If you are in an impenetrable jungle and suddenly find that there is molten lava flowing near you, chances are there is a volcano somewhere nearby. You may not be able to see it because of fog or clouds, but you can search it out based on using that inference.

An economist arrived at a company's headquarters in the 1970s and reported on his latest forecasts for consumer income. The numbers showed that those with average and higher incomes would see their incomes grow very rapidly while those with lower incomes would be stagnant. When asked why this might be happening, the economist apologized and said that he had no idea. But he offered to check his numbers and report back. Two years later, he still had not figured it out.

In the meantime, the food and beverage company looked into the phenomenon (thinking there might be a major shift in consumer patterns occurring) and uncovered some possible reasons. The economy was moving into a service focus, driven by highly paid, well-educated specialists. At the same time, global manufacturing competition was prompting unskilled factory jobs to move from North America to lower-wage countries. The company quickly spotted an irresistible force that was likely to continue for decades: the emergence of a mass market for premium-priced and luxury goods to be sold to the new, upscale work force. The company shifted its focus to this phenomenon earlier than others and its "mass class" products prospered. To the best of everyone's knowledge, the economist never did figure out what was going on, even though his forecast was accurate. He may just have thought that his model was faulty, and gave up.

Stallbusting

In this section, you can learn how to avoid wishful thinking about the future by pursuing a clear understanding of the irresistible forces affecting your situation. By being able to grasp the key messages about irresistible forces, you can more effectively utilize those forces to advance your enterprise and your own career.

Bottoms Up

As discussed earlier in this chapter, when planning for the future, you do better when you investigate how you will do if you face setbacks rather than the successes you are seeking out.

What are the worst consequences that can occur if you follow the path you are considering? Let's assume that you are thinking about stock-price improvement. If the action you are considering fails to work, investors may sell, causing the stock price to drop by, say, 45 percent. That drop, in turn, could trigger a hostile takeover bid, which would be very costly to fight.

Is there some way to offset those negative consequences? Perhaps the action could be taken with three partners in a joint venture so that if it failed, it would have no visible impact on the company's profit-and-loss statement. And with the right three partners, failure might be much less likely. You could also find out what other actions investors would like you to take and be prepared to announce one of those if the action under consideration fails. In this circumstance, you would pass the test of being at least as well off or better off if the action fails as long as the expense is not very great. This last vulnerability could be controlled by watching the progress of the action carefully to be sure it is on track before large sums are invested. Perhaps you could arrange to have the partners fund all of the early spending so your risk would be minimal until the later stages. If the program is an expensive partial failure, consider if you could sell it to a partner who will get more benefit from the results than you will. That contingency could eliminate much of the financial downside.

If you cannot offset all the negative consequences, are there other ways to generate additional solutions? By narrowing the risk you cannot cover, you find out where your vulnerabilities are. If these risk exposures are large enough, you can afford to draw on other resources, such as seeking out people whose expertise is greater than yours in that area. In our hypothetical example being developed here, your potential partners are probably a good resource to help design a project that will have limited downside risk. If the potential partners bring substantial knowledge strengths to you, they should also be able to help you find solutions. If not, they may not be the right partners for you.

Check and Recheck

Answering the preceding questions will give you some ideas about how to proceed that should, regardless of the results, at least leave you as well off as you would be by not taking any action at all. But you may have made a mistake in your analysis or forgotten something important, such as opportunity cost. Have others who are independent observers check your thinking.

Who is both competent enough and objective enough to give you an accurate assessment of your thinking? Often the answer will point to someone outside of your business, but usually someone with some knowledge of your general business environment and experience with addressing similar issues. You can find these people by calling experts in the area—authors, executives at other companies, magazine editors, and professors who are active in research or consulting—and asking them who fits the bill. Usually, they can tell you who the right person is or at least put you in touch with "someone who might know." Keep following that string until you find the experts you need.

What market tests of your new direction can be put in place that will give you "real world" feedback on what you are planning? In technology businesses, new products are often provided for free on a limited basis to so-called Beta test sites (customers who are willing to experiment with a product while it is under development) to help the manufacturer work out the bugs and get a sense of how well the product performs before large investments are made in production and marketing. In consumer products, home trials supplemented with focus groups among the users can play a similar role. For stock-price improvement, Demand Measurement Interviews are used to test the waters with shareholders, potential investors, and analysts for actions you might take. Look into similar opportunities for your specific situation.

Find the Cause Before the Result

In looking at irresistible forces, you will often find that their causes have been irreversibly in place for many years. This circumstance is especially true for irresistible forces based on demographic trends. For example, in most of the developed world we can safely assume that there will be enormous growth in demand for products and services associated with aging (due to the graying of the baby boom generation born just after the end of World War II) such as retirement homes, retirement investments, and geriatric health care services. Uncovering the causal events will help you determine the direction and duration of the irreversible forces in play.

What events may have already taken place that will determine the size and duration of this irresistible force? To begin with, you simply want to find events that you suspect could be causes. Test these suspect causes further before making decisions based on them. This testing is most effectively begun in a brainstorming environment in which each person is invited to generate as many ideas as possible, without evaluating the ideas. Then you can decide later which ideas are the more promising ones.

Which of these suspect events is probably a primary cause? You can use statistical tests (if you don't know how, hire someone to do this for you) to see which of the events seem most closely to track the trend. Those that seem to match well should then be tested for their potential connections among people who were not involved in generating these causal ideas.

Have Security Monitors in Place

If the irresistible force has the powerful causes that you think it does, it will follow a reliable pattern in the future. You can test your identification by seeing if the force and its connections to the causes are continuous. A weather station with instruments that show the direction and strength of the wind is the ultimate test of the accuracy of the meteorologist's forecast. So the more you monitor how closely the irresistible force and its impacts match your expectations, the more secure you can be in acting on your assumptions.

You'll probably need help from those with expertise in market research in order to answer the following questions in the best way. If you don't have anyone like that in your organization, hire someone on the outside who has dealt successfully with the same or similar issues of irresistible force.

How can the irresistible force be measured?

How can the frequency of the measurements by increased?

How can the measurements be kept accurate?

How can the cost of the measurements be reduced to modest levels compared to the value of the information to you?

Be Like a Cat on a Hot Tin Roof

That hot-footed cat is ready to jump as soon as its paws get too hot. You should be too because the future is reliably unpredictable in detail. The best ways to be able to move away from a mistake about an irresistible force are to keep your commitments as low as possible for as long as possible and to have contingency plans in place. Your earlier efforts to understand and reduce unnecessary risk will mean that you are less likely to need this nimbleness. Yet, when needed, it can save your enterprise's existence.

How can the costs and risks of pursuing benefits from the irresistible force be kept low, without harming your opportunities? Many people will dive headfirst into the opportunity, but you may be able to ease into the water instead and get the same benefits. This approach allows you to take advantage of important learning that will influence how well you succeed. For example, you may be able to rent rather than buy resources, and you may be able to out-source key activities with a short-notice cancellation clause.

On the one hand, a small-scale beginning may help to keep your costs and chance of near-term loss low. On the other hand, before deciding to start small, consider whether you are in a race with someone else to garner the benefits. For instance, many companies were slow to claim URLs (addresses) on the Internet and then found that someone else already had the addresses they wanted. Large opportunities will almost always eventually require large commitments. Controlling those commitments better before they are necessary will mean you will have more resources when you need to dive in.

What events should happen before it makes sense for you to commit more resources? New programs need to include trigger points, or significant occurrences that indicate whether you should continue with what you're doing or move on to something else. For example, a new product may need to make your potential customer much more efficient before it is considered worth purchasing. Therefore, the efficiencies achieved by customers during tests could be a trigger point to determine whether and when to make the product widely available. Naturally, if something apparently worthwhile but vastly different from what is expected occurs, you can design new trigger points to accommodate your new learning.

What events, should they occur, would indicate a need to steer a new course or reverse direction? These events could relate either to your monitoring the irresistible force to indicate that its power and direction are shifting, or to the effectiveness of your own activities in this area. In the former case, you will want to amend your direction. In the latter case, you will want to revise your plan or how you are executing the existing plan.

❖ ❖ ❖

Enterprises can best avoid the wishful thinking stall by understanding the importance of analyzing irresistible forces so that risk factors can be taken into account and minimized when developing responses. The actions you should seek are those that leave you ahead regardless of the future circumstances you encounter. Be equally suspicious of trends continuing and trends reversing as you make your risk-reduction decisions.

5

"WHAT DO WE DO NOW?"

THE HELPLESSNESS STALL

The only limit [to] our realization of tomorrow will be our doubts of today.

—Franklin Delano Roosevelt

When irresistible forces unexpectedly change a familiar environment into one in which normally appropriate actions no longer work, or may even backfire, executives and workers can find themselves feeling overwhelmed by despair and helpless to respond effectively. By emphasizing adversity as an opportunity to reconsider your thinking and develop a new sense of direction, this chapter points the way to overcoming the helplessness stall and employing irresistible forces to move forward again.

Being buffeted by strong and conflicting irresistible forces can be a bit like being the proverbial little Dutch boy who notices that the dike is leaking. The child can staunch the leak or go for help. Which should be done first? In the story, he stops the leak with his finger and so must wait for someone to come by who can go for help. In reality, many businesses will take neither action, and they then run the risk of drowning as they stand by the widening flow.

That inaction may sound unreasonable, but it isn't an unusual reaction. When the *Titanic* first hit the iceberg, many people decided not to get into the lifeboats because it seemed safer to wait and see what happened than to sit in a small boat in the freezing ocean at night. The "unsinkable" ship then disappeared under the waves less than four hours after the collision. During most of that time, lifeboats were launched with empty seats, because many people felt there was no danger. Many hundreds more lives could have been saved if more of the women and children who were ordered onto the lifeboats had promptly gone into them.

Helplessness is most likely to be experienced in business during extreme booms and busts, and during large market shifts in the mix of demand for products and services. The feeling that people in the organization experience is somewhat comparable to being an airline passenger who, after the pilot becomes incapacitated, is asked with no warning to land the plane despite having no previous flight training. Add to the mix having no working radio to call for help and no instructor on board, and you get the idea. Similarly, when an enterprise and its executives have no direct experience with the circumstances, they justifiably feel that they are likely to falter or fail with new directions. To make matters worse, organizations may reward "staying the course" with subjectively derived bonus payments and punish those who push for change as "boat rockers."

This helpless feeling can also follow the realization that the only actions you can think of violate your values and your past promises. Say, for example, your sales drop in half and are likely to stay there for a year or two, and you have a "no layoff" policy (a rare policy in North America these days, but a good one for attracting and retaining employees). An executive may feel that there is no way out of fixing the business without violating the "no layoff" policy and hurting people who relied on that policy. As a result of these circumstances, progress may stall while the executive wrestles with this dilemma.

In situations involving irresistible forces, delay is often very costly and can even be dangerous. Your organization can quickly recover its sense of being in charge of its destiny by developing better habits related to making more appropriate assumptions. For example, your business will do better if you assume that good choices exist to use the irresistible forces to your advantage. That assumption can help you become more skilled at developing alternatives and create streamlined ways to reach decisions when a crossroads is reached.

Stall Examples
One Big, Unhappy Family
The helplessness stall often follows the wishful thinking stall. Here's an example: Sales and earnings at a large retail chain had been declining for years. The chain's executives were continually forecasting a turnaround that never came (that's the wishful thinking beginning of this painful example). After a decade of steadily sinking performance and continuing layoffs, the company's morale

had reached the bargain-basement level. Optimism had disappeared. Everyone feared additional waves of layoffs or imminently going out of business. The people who worked in the stores were the most depressed because they were overworked, stressed by all of the problems, and in fear for their future livelihoods. A lot of the company's pension plan was tied up in the company's declining stock, so the outlook for retirement looked pretty bleak as well for older employees.

The irresistible force that this company was facing involved a steadily more discerning and busy consumer who wanted better value, better selection, and better service in a beautiful, interesting store environment. This retailer ranked near the bottom in most of these categories, having reduced its effectiveness through cost-cutting to protect budgeted profits. These consumer-perceived reductions had occurred during a time when most of its retail competitors were increasing their effectiveness in these critical ways.

After the company finally improved itself a few years later by moving in a more successful new direction that increased effectiveness, executives were asked why the obvious, needed changes had not been made much earlier. The answer the executives gave was that morale in the stores had reached such low levels that they felt that it was more important to insulate their staff from further pressure by leaving them alone than it was to try further to fix the problems. The executives feared a sudden, final collapse if store employees were asked to do any more than they were already doing.

This perception turned out to be a misreading of the store employees' moods. When needed changes were introduced, employee morale quickly rose and business results soon followed. Morale, in fact, had declined because store employees perceived that the only thing the executives would do in the future was to cut more jobs to reflect lower sales volumes, rather than to address the causes of the sales slide. Helplessness had overwhelmed the organization from the top and the bottom.

Because the executives had no prior experience with turning around low morale among store employees, they felt helpless and waited much too long to make fundamental changes. This circumstance could have been avoided by visiting other retail chains that had previously turned around their negative sales trends in order to understand how employees had perceived efforts to improve. Such an experience would have provided valuable information about how to improve, as well as an earlier understanding of the positive effect on employee morale that efforts to address the fundamental problems would have.

When asked why they had not taken *this* step, the executives admitted that they felt embarrassed to seek help from others. They felt that they should have known the answers already, which added to their feeling of helplessness. The vicious cycle of helplessly spiraling down was quickly ended when a new management team was recruited with experience in turning around similar situations.

Flying Not So High

There may be no stronger source of unhappy surprise than having the customers' and community's perceptions of your products and services suddenly turn from positive to negative with no warning. Perhaps a television program runs an exposé about the safety of your product, testing it in ways that you have never considered or that are actually inappropriate. Or suddenly the government imposes a new standard, and your product has to be phased out in its current form. If you didn't anticipate these risks, your reaction will probably be similar to a bicyclist without a rear-view mirror who is bumped from behind by a speeding truck. You won't know what hit you.

One of the most interesting challenges about these circumstances is that regardless of the merits of the negative reaction you encounter, you have to do something soon or the negative reaction will become even worse. If you don't change your product or service appropriately, you'll be perceived as callous. If you make the adjustment for one country and keep shipping the old product to other countries, you may be viewed as unethical (or even racist in some cases). If the basis of the negative reaction is that your employees may have misbehaved in some way (by bribing someone, for example), you'll be viewed as condoning the behavior if you don't take quick action to suspend the people involved and investigate what has been going on. The irresistible force here is that during the times when you are perceived by society as a positive contributor, you receive the benefit of the doubt from customers and the community in general. As soon as it appears that you may have faltered in your public responsibilities, the presumption seems to shift to doubting everything from your intentions to your ability to your effectiveness.

Many companies have not faced this problem before and don't know how to respond in a crisis. They appear helpless to everyone. You may have observed this condition in the past when an airline has its first big plane crash and many people are hurt or killed. The airline may have always provided great service and good prices, have contributed to the community, and have had a good reputation as a result. But if it appears disorganized and insufficiently caring during a disaster, the airline may be viewed by the public and the families of those involved in the crash as a monster that must somehow have contributed to the accident. Lost revenues can plague the company's path for years as doubts about safety and trustworthiness continue.

A good example of how negativity can be handled can be drawn from the DC-10's safety problems. McDonnell Douglas quickly addressed flaws that had been uncovered and hired one of the astronauts to review the plane's safety and report what he found. That report was featured in the company's television advertising. The company's actions made everyone aware that surveillance by the Federal Aviation Administration and the airlines probably made the DC-10 safer than any other plane that was flying at the time. At first the public avoided DC-10s in droves. But within a year of the advertising campaign, hardly any flyers avoided them. Eventually, the plane was recognized as a safe alternative by the traveling public, following the effective, timely adjustments made by McDonnell Douglas and the airlines.

Stall Erasers
Doubt Your Lack of Choice
Like Captain Kirk on the Starship *Enterprise* in the *Star Trek* television series, movies, and books, you should spurn helplessness and believe that there is always a positive way out of a difficult or unexpected situation. Your job is to find and take that way out. As a cadet at Starfleet Academy, the fictional James Tiberius Kirk was once faced with a problem to solve for which there was no positive outcome included. The purpose of the problem was to see how the cadets handled a setback. Kirk refused to play the game that way, sneaked into the Academy's computer, and reprogrammed the exercise so that there was a positive solution. While the ethics of that approach are doubtful at best, the unrelenting search for a positive solution that lay behind that action is laudable. (It's too bad that Kirk didn't keep going until he found an ethical way out. In other episodes, he did make many difficult decisions that were consistent with his values and those of the Federation, including the Prime Directive of noninterference with other life forms.)

A good example of what can be done to find a positive solution is found in the consequences of many U.S. environmental regulations. The irresistible force here is the common human desire to make all products have less of a negative impact on the environment. These regulations often prohibit companies from disposing of wastes in the way they had previously done, or ban the use of certain inexpensive ingredients because of the wastes they create. When initially faced with such regulations, many companies simply succumb to helplessness. After fighting expensive losing battles with regulators, they reluctantly resign themselves to pursuing more expensive manufacturing processes and earning less money as a result on what is often a higher investment base.

Years later, though, many of these enterprises have reported that some of their workers saw the new regulations as an opportunity to rethink everything the organization did about how the products were produced and distributed to customers. As a result of this rethinking, the cost of the products greatly declined, waste was reduced or recycled into some beneficial form, and the environment was improved as well. Those who worked on these business process improvements saw the experience as one of the most rewarding they ever had.

An irresistible force opportunity for you is to use the adversity you face to stimulate employees to find solutions as a way to overcome initial feelings of helplessness and to stretch themselves to meet the challenge. Employees may take on a challenge of larger proportions than they usually consider tackling in a situation like this because they will find the challenge so personally interesting, exciting, and socially beneficial. You can also use the irresistible force of human curiosity to your advantage by posing "what if" questions concerning what might be done in such situations long before apparently threatening regulations arise. That activity will provide you with many more 2,000 percent solutions.

You'll want to be sure that the people in your organization understand and agree ahead of time on the ethical limitations to finding solutions. You should then encourage solutions consistent with those values. Otherwise, you may find that some want to use the organization's success to justify inappropriate means.

Test the Waters

People who feel helpless often react that way because they can't come up with any acceptable alternatives in their own minds. A good way to circumvent that problem is to find others who have had similar problems and ask them what they would do in your situation. Undoubtedly, you'll get some ideas, and then you can test the more plausible ones on a limited basis to find out which ones actually work.

In *Corporate Creativity* (Berrett-Koehler, 1997), Alan G. Robinson and Sam Stern report that the Japanese national railway company was building a tunnel through one of the many large mountains in that country. Construction was delayed by enormous quantities of water that poured through the rock as the tunneling proceeded. Pumps were set up everywhere, and engineers were engaged to find a way to cheaply draw off all of this unexpected water.

At one of the meetings, a tunnel worker suggested that, instead of helplessly viewing the water as a nuisance, it be bottled and sold to consumers. Why? The worker had tasted the water and found it to be delicious. Encouraged by this discovery, many of the workers had been routinely drinking the water. This ingenious observation led to a way to use the water that generated millions of dollars in profitable revenue annually from the tunnel, while reducing the cost of eliminating excess water.

The irresistible force you can rely on here is the individuality of perception. Finding out more about the problem will usually stimulate someone to see the problem differently, perhaps even as an opportunity. The best way to do this is to experience the problem firsthand, and to try out some alternatives on the spot (like tasting the water in the tunnel).

Stallbusting

In this section we provide questions and directions to stimulate you and your enterprise to overcome your sense of helplessness. This information is designed to make you realize that you are really in a good position to use the changed circumstances to your advantage, so that more progress will occur than would otherwise have been possible.

Burst That Helpless Feeling

You should always view every situation as being one where something positive can be done. You'll be much more effective in adopting that viewpoint if you can first identify what is causing you to feel helpless and then determine how to eliminate that cause.

What assumption or belief causes people in your organization to feel helpless in this circumstance? Those assumptions will usually prove to be at least partially untrue when looked at more closely. For example, many people are concerned about driving on narrow, winding mountain roads because they fear that their car will be thrown over the edge if a tire bursts. As youngsters, many people learned that concern from their parents. However, tires today have been much improved, and you can buy tires that will probably never burst under any condition (some will allow you to drive safely for 50 miles even after you experience a massive puncture). If you have to do a lot of difficult mountain driving, you can eliminate a good deal of your anxiety by learning more about these tires and purchasing the ones that are most appropriate for your type of driving. You can achieve a very low risk level by knowing under what circumstances the tires can burst, so you can then adjust your maintenance of the tires and avoid serious road hazards.

What can be done to eliminate the causes of the feeling of helplessness? One of the best ways to find new alternatives is to involve lots of people with a variety of backgrounds. Chances are, someone already knows of a solution.

Howard Gardner in his important book, *Multiple Intelligences* (Harper-Collins, 1993), points out that each person is uniquely gifted to perform at a high level along some of a variety of types of intelligence. Since the solutions to many problems are often found through the use of intelligence other than those that are primarily reinforced in schools, you should deliberately select people with these diverse capabilities. For example, a problem may not be solvable if everyone only looks out for their own short-term interests (such as who will earn the most money from the first transaction). But someone with great emotional intelligence may see that the problem lies in helping everyone to shift their focus to the best long-term mutual interest (such as how everyone will earn the most money from all of the transactions over time). With strong communications intelligence, another person could perceive a way to explain this perspective so that it can be quickly grasped by the other parties involved.

Confidently Prepare for the Best

Answering the following questions is intended to help you see alternatives where you might otherwise feel helpless in the face of irresistible forces.

How can this setback become the best thing that ever happened to your enterprise? In the case of a faulty product, for example, you have the chance to show that you are prepared for and capable of putting customer needs ahead of your own, and thus win the respect of customers who become more loyal and committed to you. Research on hotels shows that the happiest and most loyal customers are those who experienced a terrible problem that the hotel resolved quickly and happily beyond the customer's expectations. While not a reason to create problems, this experience certainly shows the positive side of seeing customer problems as an opportunity.

Suppose you need to reduce staff and are concerned that this action will hurt morale and customer perceptions. This action can be implemented in a way that raises the quality of your remaining staff by eliminating only those who are the lowest performers and have the least potential. You can also take some of the money you save and provide additional incentives for top performers to stay and do even better in their careers. You can convey your intention to improve the quality of your staff to customers so that they will be aware of the potential benefit to them. Employees normally experience a morale boost when the weakest performers are eliminated because the weak performers usually make a lot of extra work for the high performers.

If you have promised not to do something, such as reduce your performance to customers, your need to consider that reneging on your promise can be an opportunity to explore in more depth the best way to fulfill the intent of your promise. In this case, you can check with customers to learn what their current needs actually are. You can then redesign what you offer so that the bundle of benefits overall is better for the customers. For example, customers may have wanted to receive supplies quickly (causing you to promise fast deliveries) because they usually have to return a lot of the merchandise you provide to them due to your manufacturing faults. If you improve quality, they may be willing to wait longer for deliveries because they won't need to return so much or keep as much inventory. Usually some factor other than the way you have been serving the customer will provide more benefits to both the customer and your enterprise.

How can everyone in your company obtain a benefit from the negative circumstances? Part of the helpless feeling often can be an emotional reaction to having experienced an important loss (in this case, of a positive expectation for the future), not unlike experiencing the death of a parent. Organizations and individuals frequently assume that the loss has only a negative side, but the positive side can often be much greater.

For example, during the early years of leveraged buy outs (LBOs), many management theorists were concerned that the manager-owners doing the buying out would treat employees, customers, communities, and other stakeholders in harsh and negative ways. Managers in the LBOs soon found that making everyone see the LBO experience as a win-win for all was critical to success. LBO executives learned to treat everyone much better than had occurred under the prior ownership, because the debt-laden LBOs had little room for error. Generous profit-sharing programs often meant that everyone who worked for the company was paid much more after the LBO; the businesses grew faster, which improved the chances of receiving a promotion; customers received much better service and products; and innovation increased to provide better services and products sooner. This beneficial pattern occurred in part because incentives were increased, but also because bureaucracy was decreased. In some cases, every employee became a part owner of the enterprise through investing some employee stock ownership program (ESOP) funds. Unless that new employee ownership opportunity was not well balanced with adequate job security, this sharing of risks and rewards often worked well. Virtually bankrupt companies went on to create enormous wealth for everyone involved in owning and managing the enterprise.

How can you create confidence that good ideas will receive attention and action? The best way to do this is to set a good example by asking for ideas, acting on them appropriately and in a timely way, and encouraging others to act on them without waiting for approval when review is slow in coming. Soon you'll have everyone in the organization finding ways to be helpful rather than helpless. Management often takes on too large a burden in crisis situations. Most such circumstances require a variety of actions, each in a different sphere of the organization's activities. Those who are closest to the problem will usually have the clearest sense of the alternatives, but are often intimidated about speaking up for fear they'll offend colleagues or those in power. Researchers report that the joy and fun of finding a good solution that is implemented are the primary rewards needed to stimulate people to find creative solutions to new problems. Be sure that you give people the time and resources to check out their thoughts. You'll be glad that you did. (Be careful, though, about paying and recognizing people for these ideas. Teresa Amabile reported in "How To Kill Creativity" [*Harvard Business Review,* September/October 1998, page 77] that such recognition and pay can reduce creativity except when associated with specific efficiency-improvement programs.)

The 3M company is often cited as an example for successfully encouraging creative solutions. The firm makes it easy for employees to get time and resources to pursue new ideas. Those who succeed are often given the chance to play a key role in the development of the new activity, sometimes with large public recognition, but always with substantial internal recognition and economic incentives as the solution develops.

❖ ❖ ❖

Enterprises can best overcome the helplessness stall by embracing the belief that from adversity always comes greater opportunity, by practicing with crisis "what-if" scenarios before the crises occur, by seeking out diverse viewpoints of crisis situations both from within and outside their organizations, and by fostering an environment that appropriately rewards creative problem-solving.

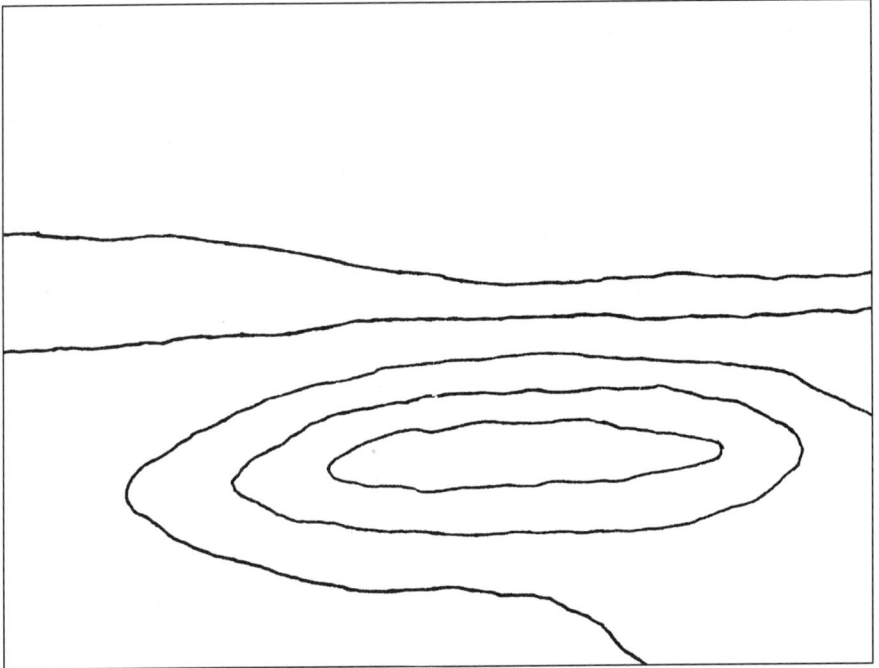

Withdrawing into a defensive position feels comfortable when irresistible forces are making your growth more difficult. Unfortunately, withdrawal may leave you with both fewer options and make you an easier target for competitors.

6

"CIRCLE THE WAGONS!"

THE DEFENSIVENESS STALL

The best defense is a good offense.

—Various

When circumstances turn hostile for their current direction, most organizations will focus on defending themselves from the effects of the changed environment rather than on reaching out to adapt to the new situation. However, this defensive approach creates a diversion from progress and growth. The analysis of defensive postures and how to overcome them presented in this chapter is intended to help you see the advantages of seeking out new paths when the going gets tough, rather than simply hunkering down and hoping for better times and circumstances to arrive.

An enterprise encountering irresistible forces can be likened to a sailing ship. When faced with stormy conditions, the captain can reduce sail, drop the sea anchor, batten down the hatches, and sit below deck hoping to safely ride out the storm. If conditions are fierce enough, this tactic may be the right one. But if you still have the capability to maneuver, your chances are better if you use the irresistible forces to help you get where you want to go; otherwise you may unnecessarily take a merciless pounding.

Consider, for example, that hostile circumstances are affecting others negatively at the same time as they are affecting you. This situation may make these other enterprises willing to become your partners when that option would otherwise not normally be available. The old observation that "politics makes strange bedfellows" can be applied to enterprise combinations as well. It is also possible that hostile circumstances may only be negative if you try offsetting them rather than adapting to the new realities or to your improved perception of existing realities. For example, falling currency values in another country may at first hurt your earnings in selling to the local market using imported goods. However, they may also provide an opportunity to gain market share through reconfiguring your manufacturing to produce locally in that country or by adjusting the prices you pay suppliers.

Keep in mind that your enterprise's strengths can most easily be shifted in a new direction before an irresistible force has done any damage. Psychologically, however, most organizations find it easier to institute change in the face of a very threatening situation, one that may do harm to the people involved. You need to combat delay by alerting everyone early to the future danger to the organization and themselves of taking a solely defensive posture.

Kicking Yourself with Your Jerking Knee

In business, new circumstances are most often first perceived as a threat when budgeted profit or cash flow objectives are not met. Since such potential shortfalls arise almost all the time in enterprises, the organization's first reaction is to look for relatively painless ways to cut costs to overcome the shortfall. This tendency is reinforced by the likelihood that all the senior people in the company receive much of their annual bonus for meeting budgeted results. This so-called incentive creates a common interest in smoothing over the bump in the road so the company can grow profit and cash flow results at the rate it had planned. Enterprises that have public shareholders receive a double incentive to meet this goal because additional compensation is tied up in stock options that will fall in value if shareholders are disappointed in company results. Finally, if the shortfall cannot be overcome, heads will roll in some cases, and that threat is never far from many peoples' minds.

For most companies, this standard operating procedure for dealing with shortfalls often turns into a mad scramble to cut costs with little time for thought about the long-term consequences. For example, for about two decades a well-known packaged goods company had an earnings shortfall early in almost every year in its largest division. The first planned expense to be cut in each year was the money for promotions designed to create more brand loyalty among consumers. Year after year, loyalty to the company's brands in that division dropped, and profits slumped.

But company executives often managed to restore enough profit performance to save some part of their bonus. How? They used defensive strategies.

For instance, they offered special incentives to retailers to purchase products at the end of every year so that retailers often bought four to six months' supply at one time. As a result, the products were often less than perfect when used, and all consumers were trained to look for annual "give-away" price reductions that discouraged them from buying the products year round at full price. Brand loyalty was further harmed as a result.

For this company, reactions to the hostile environment characterized by a decrease of loyal consumers were made worse by the actions taken to protect the budgets. The real solutions (finally taken about twenty years after the irresistible force problem arose) were to improve the quality of the products and to build brand loyalty among the consumers. To facilitate these solutions, the annual "year end load" was eliminated.

Stall Examples
Pardon Me, May I Borrow a Ton of Sand?

Minimizing the importance of any related problems or trying to cover them up are the two most common defensive postures for dealing with irresistible forces. You can always find someone to convince you that there really is no problem even when there is one. And since the bearers of bad news often fear blame or punishment, they prefer to keep quiet about problems. Either way, you end up with your head in the sand and your vulnerable flanks exposed.

Intel learned this lesson to its dismay. A version of its microprocessors contained an error that would in some instances cause calculation mistakes. Outraged customers immediately demanded to have their microprocessors replaced. Intel initially downplayed the problem by assuring customers that they would probably never experience errors unless a certain type of calculation was done with great frequency. Few people were thought to be doing these calculations repeatedly at that time. The company's response only increased the outrage. Customers expected a perfect product for calculations, regardless of their need for that perfection. After a few days, Intel capitulated and announced it would replace all the chips. Along the way, however, the company lost an important opportunity to maintain confidence among its products' users. The irresistible force of having ever more demanding customers and users is something that few enterprises can choose to ignore. Perhaps this is one reason that many personal computer purchasers began to migrate to less expensive microprocessors produced by Intel's competitors in the late 1990s.

Similarly, in the many financial scandals uncovered in the 1990s (such as the ones at Sumitomo and Barings Bank) involving large losses from unauthorized trading in commodities and securities by individuals in major companies, the people involved always succeeded in hiding their errors for years. They invariably used the simple technique of only reporting enough of the trades to show strong profits. These unauthorized "licenses to lose" came about because their superiors in these companies had little incentive to inquire about how the good trading results were being generated. The superiors often depended on a continuation of these false profits in order to get their own bonuses and promotions, as well as hold their jobs. Likewise, the brokers who handled these transactions often knew or had good reason to suspect that the client's internal rules were being broken, but they remained quiet for fear of losing valuable accounts. For a more detailed discussion of covering up as one response to defensiveness, see chapter 9.

I Just Can't Resist, Please Pass Another One

Opportunity is what dreams are made of, and few executives want to dream about anything but success. The opposing irresistible force is the fact that the more opportunities the enterprise takes on, the less likely it is that anything it does will work. The euphoria of going after the new opportunity is often a defensive reaction to the losses of the past.

Some companies have such a large appetite for opportunities that they are drowning in the predictable problems entailed by pursuing many different and difficult directions at the same time. These enterprises are subject to the irresistible force of having their standard processes for accomplishing results break down. Such breakdowns can take many different forms. For rapidly growing companies, the cash to pay for the expansion may be missing. For companies with lots of new businesses under development, there may be a shortage of skilled people to explore these opportunities. For companies that have promised steady economic performance, the wrenching budget-shortfall-driven conflicts already discussed can provide enormous strains.

The psychology of these circumstances is much like that of the Las Vegas gambler with a "proven system" for beating the house. Those who work in casinos report that one of the most common beliefs is that the odds shift in your favor if you have lost a certain number of bets in a row. Losing gamblers will begin to double their bets each time they lose, up to the house limit on these bets, in effect, putting their defensive side forward. If the cards or the wheel run cold (as they do about half the time), the gamblers quickly lose their entire stakes. In the same way, companies that have been failing with new opportunities will usually take larger and larger risks, both in size and difficulty, hoping to make up their losses in one great win. Like the gamblers, seldom do they succeed.

We Just Need to Work on Our Blocking and Tackling

Perhaps one of the most persistent causes of defensiveness is the sense that the enterprise is going in the right direction, but is just not executing that direction well enough. The typical approach: Let's take the most direct route from here to there, and keep it simple. In the nineteenth century, wagon trains headed to California often experienced delays in crossing the Great Plains. Knowing that they must get through the Sierra Nevada mountain passes ahead before winter closed them, many travelers were then tempted to take the shortest route on the map. Those who did often perished or endured other horrible consequences. The reason: The shortest routes on the map had the most difficult terrain to pass through, and so the travelers arrived in more dangerous mountain passes even later than those who took the longer, but ultimately faster, routes.

If you are already experiencing great difficulties, having had that experience should convince you to fundamentally rethink what you are doing. Impetuous actions brought on by impatience will not make things better. For example, in the Gulf War the Iraqis were convinced that the forthcoming battle would entail a massive frontal engagement of ground forces, not unlike those that occurred early in World War I. In such battles, the well-prepared defender often had the advantage. Their experience in the largely inconclusive earlier war with Iran reinforced this thinking. Many lives were lost, but little ground changed hands. Based on that thinking, the Iraqis dug in with little additional thought and confidently waited for the allied forces to be slaughtered.

Actually, the circumstances were quite different than the Iraqis anticipated. The Iraqis were fighting most of the best troops in the world, who also had unmatched fire power and intelligence resources. And when the U.S.-led allies declined the invitation to refight the failed tactics of World War I, the Iraqis were quickly pushed back out of their prepared positions by a combination of punishing aerial bombardments and superior armored assaults. By being relatively immobile, the Iraqis simply made it easier for the allies to deliver their punch. By being less well prepared to fight a retreating battle than a stationary one, the Iraqi defense rapidly grew weaker as it gave ground. If the allied force had pressed its attack through to Baghdad, many observers believed that the result could have been a virtually uncontested slaughter of the Iraqi forces. Fortunately, the Iraqis did retreat because continued hunkering down in those prepared defensive positions would just have cost even more Iraqi lives and equipment. What appeared to be the obvious defensive stance was a most inappropriate strategy for the Iraqis, just as pursuing the obvious will often be for any organization facing irresistible forces.

CEO Speak

Those who attend conferences where CEOs describe their companies report that all such talks reveal only good news and usually deny the existence of bad news. If there is any current shortfall in reported financial results, the listeners are told that this is somehow due to the weather, the number of shopping days involved, or some other factor outside the company's control. The CEOs seem to feel they should be excused by investors for any shortfall unless perfect conditions prevail for their enterprises.

When the CEO or organizational leader takes no personal responsibility for anything and is not candid about organizational performance, a whole culture of defensive doublespeak can develop. Instead of attacking problems, euphonious excuses are sought and articulated. Everyone in the company soon learns to do the same thing. Meetings often degenerate into a vast wallowing in self-pity about all of the bad luck that the group has had. The fact that every effectively performing enterprise had to endure the same "bad luck" fails to dawn on the self-pitiers.

In 1998 AMP, a successful manufacturer of connectors (the small devices that let electricity flow from one apparatus to another or from one part of an apparatus to another), reported poor profit and growth results, which it blamed primarily on weakness in Asian markets. A hostile takeover was launched by Allied Signal, claiming that AMP had do-nothing management. AMP was eventually sold to a friendly bidder, Tyco International. Curiously, one of AMP's key competitors, Molex, did reasonably well during this same period as it quickly adapted by shifting its sales from Asia to North American and European markets. Could AMP have been experiencing the defensiveness stall?

Stall Erasers

When Your House Is on Fire, Call the Fire Department

One of the most dramatic developments of the Gulf War was the Iraqis' burning of Kuwait's oil fields as they withdrew. These oil fires were expected to burn for years and to create one of the worst environmental disasters ever. Fortunately, there are specialists in putting out oil-field fires, but even they had never seen anything of this magnitude. Every expert in the world was flown quickly to Kuwait and put to work. In much less time than anyone expected, all the fires were out. In the same vein, you can overcome defensiveness stalls if you keep in mind that things are not as bad as they seem, if you get the right help. Relying on yourself alone to overcome hostile circumstances is usually a mistake if a capable specialist can help you at reasonable cost compared to the benefits.

Oil-well firefighting companies eliminated the Kuwait fires very rapidly by drawing on their experience in dealing with irresistible forces. The irresistible growth enterprise can learn from their example, as well as the examples of those who routinely deal with irresistible forces. (© Robert van der Hilst/ CORBIS)

Another instance of outside expertise making a difference relates to the familiar Y2K problem. In 1998, a few organizations began to realize that they couldn't fix their computers in time to avoid problems in 2000 and beyond. A few despaired, gave up, and simply sold out. As the end of 1999 approached, however, many highly effective solutions that no one had thought of sooner became available from external specialists. For example, the initial solution entailed totally reprogramming computers in the old programming languages common to the 1950s through the 1980s in order to add the space for two more digits (making 2000 out of 00). There were shortages of programmers who could make these changes, and the "patches" were slow and expensive to make. Then someone finally thought about the issue as a math problem. It was determined that you could leave most of the obsolete programs alone if you inexpensively wrote a short subroutine to simply add the number "50" twice (or 100) for the years beginning in "00" to overcome the computer's presumption that the twentieth century years were involved, and create the year 2000 that way. Yet another enterprise found a way to train programmers to make the standard changes more than ten times faster than the time required by external consultants, at a cost savings of over 95 percent. Both were terrific 2,000 percent solutions for the year 2000 problem. Being open to the possibility of finding help in locating such solutions eliminates the desire to become defensive and inactive when situations go awry.

Take a Deep Breath and Relax

Most circumstances are not nearly as threatening as they first appear. When dealing with the defensive postures that arise in an irresistible-force situation, a good first step is to ask how the changed circumstances could be turned into a benefit. For example, a source of the budget shortfall anxiety discussed earlier in this chapter was the concern that bonuses and stock options would both be decimated. Talking to your investors about the new circumstances may allow you to determine that by taking timely, appropriate action to adapt to the irresistible force, you'll end up with a net benefit over time instead of the feared loss. You'll benefit by operating under the positive influence of an offensive, rather than defensive, outlook. The stock price will soar with the successful changes, and with the higher stock price multiple you'll be able to add the important new resources needed to grow and improve faster in the future. If you do this well enough, the stock option gains may offset your lost bonus for that year.

In the 1980s, Bell & Howell Company moved beyond the defensive reaction of merely explaining why growth in their businesses was slow and decided to speed up the company's growth. It began to shift its mix of businesses to focus its attention into areas where opportunities for profitable growth would be much better. This shift meant selling or shutting down many businesses and spending a great deal of money to acquire and develop others. These adjustments caused a lot of pressure on earnings, and from 1982 through 1987, earnings grew hardly at all. Yet the stock price expanded by several hundred percent, rapidly outpacing the market averages and the stock prices of companies that were providing stellar earnings progress. The reason: Investors saw a company that would prosper greatly in the future because of these changes. They had confidence in the company's management to do the right thing. In interviews done during that time, investors were willing to ascribe value to the company's stock based on positive actions that the company had not yet made or even contemplated simply because they had so much confidence that management would represent the shareholder interests well.

As another example, when the Bell telephone monopoly was broken up by the courts in the 1980s, investors were absolutely convinced that AT&T's stock would be the best one to own. This part of the company was in the fastest growing part of the industry (long distance services and computer prod-

ucts), had the best technology, and would now be free to do more in computers. Investors were told by many security analysts to shun the local Bell operating companies. Yet by the late 1990s, the results of the breakup turned out
to be the opposite of what was expected. Since the traditional way of managing the local Bell operating company offered such limited potential, the Bell
operating companies (Baby Bells) were quick to find ways to expand faster
into new, more attractive business areas such as providing cellular telephone
service and software-based services like call forwarding; acquiring foreign telephone operations in high growth markets; and facilitating the growth of the
customers using the Internet. The deregulation allowed the Baby Bells to move
forward in many more ways, more quickly. Since they felt that competing
solely in the ways they had in the past would not work, the former Bell operating companies overcame the defensiveness stall that could have left them vulnerable. In addition, those who were slower to make the needed changes were
soon acquired by other former Bell operating companies or by long distance
competitors of AT&T. The threat of becoming losers turned the best enterprises into winners.

Don't Get Defensive About Your Mistakes, Profit from Them

Drawing the right lesson from an apparent mistake can produce enormous
benefits. That you didn't achieve the result you wanted doesn't mean that what
you did achieve isn't worth something; it may even be something more important than you started out after. Consider the now-famous story of how Scotch
Guard was discovered at 3M. Company chemists had been working on new
chemical compounds for a variety of purposes. One day, one of these compounds was accidentally dropped onto a sneaker. As the weeks went by, the
worker kept gazing idly at the white spot on her sneaker where no dirt was
clinging. Eventually she mentioned this oddity to a coworker, and ultimately a
profitable new line of research was established that led to Scotch Guard. Post-
it Notes were similarly discovered by accident during research into how to find
very strong adhesives. Every experiment and experience teaches us something,
if we only take time to consider what the lesson is. Learning the lesson should
be our goal instead of minimizing the significance of what happened or trying
to cover it up if it's not the goal we intended.

Peter Drucker exhorts organizations to seek out all of their unexplained
successes and failures, and to determine what really happened. He feels that
this is the best way to make breakthrough improvements. You have just had
an opportunity to learn something, but you have yet to complete the learning. Heeding Drucker's advice, a researcher noticed that a normally effective

model for forecasting the direction of a company's stock price drastically underestimated stock-price growth from time to time. The answer to this apparent anomaly turned out to be that a particularly unusual and desirable mix of investors had been accidentally attracted to these companies, which created a much higher stock-price multiple due to a combination of greatly expanded demand and much reduced supply of stock. A new management process was then developed to allow companies to routinely achieve this result.

In another discovery by the same researcher, an earlier stock-price model had usually failed when external factors affected a whole industry in a significantly positive or negative way. Rather than giving in to frustration and failure, the researcher pressed on. From determining the sources of over- and underestimation came a much improved model-building process that accounted for these factors and that greatly increased forecast accuracy under all circumstances.

Stallbusting

In this section, we present specific ways to overcome defensiveness by turning the unpleasant and the unexpected into learning opportunities followed by effective action. By opening yourself to understanding irresistible forces, your enterprise can achieve greater congruence with the direction of these forces and enjoy much more success.

Be a Weatherman and Find Out Which Way the Wind Is Blowing

In this chapter, we show that companies can be slow to see the cause and effect relationship between a problem and an irresistible force that is creating the problem. In a budget shortfall, for example, people ask: "How can costs be rapidly cut with little harm?" instead of searching for the causes of the shortfall. What's necessary is to change the organization's questions about what to do when problems are perceived. You also need to develop your data-mining to use the valuable information that already exists in your enterprise in order to accelerate organizational learning.

How are irresistible forces causing the unexpected problems and successes that our organization is having? Peter Drucker's question (What is causing unexplained successes and failures?) is a good place to start the search for irresistible forces. The normal mind-set is to assume that more and less positive results are simply a function of management effectiveness. That linkage may be somewhat true, but even if the causes are internal, the likelihood is strong that some fundamental shift in human behavior (such as customers' buying preferences) is involved.

You should pay particular attention to circumstances that repeat themselves, for the odds are high that these are linked to irresistible forces.

How can you determine if irresistible forces are the cause of your unexpected results? You have to become an irresistible force investigator to answer this question. The first thing to check for is whether the variation could simply be a normal fluctuation around the average result. A statistician can quickly help you determine that by seeing how many standard deviations (a measure of the meaningfulness of variations) are involved. If the statistician tells you that the standard deviations involved are significantly high, you are probably on to something.

Talk to everyone who is in a position to observe what might be going on, and ask them to describe any new and different behavior. If you think that the cause may be changes occurring with customers, go talk to customers about what is new in their lives. If you think that the change is with the distributors, do the same thing with them. And so forth.

A toy manufacturer noticed that their company's orders from retailers were off a little. The company ignored this occurrence for a quarter. The next quarter orders were off a little more, but since retail sales in general were up, the toy company thought it was just a matter of time until their toy orders picked up again. In the third quarter having this problem, the toy company decided to look into the situation. It turned out that a competitor's product had become the rage, and the retailers had been offering close-out pricing to move this company's product. The retailers didn't want to reorder any more of the failure, having just spent a fortune to move it off the shelves. Had the toy company understood the source of the problem sooner, it could have produced a "new and improved" version and retained market position in the face of the competitor's popular offering.

How can you detect if your organization is fooling itself? Take the official answer to what is going on and see if all the facts support it. If someone has done a careful study, you should be able to find it. Read the material for yourself. If the study's answer is simply a figment of someone's imagination, you will find a lack of data or poor analysis of whatever data are referenced. That finding should be a sign to dig deeper. You are probably about to learn something.

Find out what is different now than it was before that could be causing the change. For example, if the official explanation is associated with weather, then look at similar periods when weather-based disruptions occurred to see if the effects you experienced are similar. Check to see if companies like yours are having the same experiences at the same time in the same geographic areas. If others are doing better or worse, see if you can find facts that point out why. A retailer might be having more weather-related problems than competitors in Chicago, for example, if the company's stores are on secondary streets that are unplowed during snow storms while its competitors are on main thoroughfares that are always plowed.

Here's another example. A restaurant chain found that its competitors did much better than they in central city minority neighborhoods than in the suburbs. The enterprise's official explanation for this central city weakness had been that the economies were depressed in these areas. Further digging showed that the problem really related to poor service quality. Whenever service improved in a restaurant, sales increased by 20 percent to 40 percent in a few weeks. The chain's minority customers in the central cities had higher and somewhat different standards for service than their suburban counterparts because they were paying a higher price as a percentage of their incomes. After the chain made the needed adjustments, the central city neighborhoods became the organization's best market.

Develop Defensiveness Extinguishers

Leaders can set a good example in overcoming defensiveness. Tell people they'll be appreciated and rewarded for exposing issues that need to be addressed, and behave that way in reality. If you are consistent in your words and deeds, you'll soon have lots of help in finding irresistible force situations that can be addressed. A CEO promoted an executive very rapidly, putting him in charge of ever larger operations. When asked why, the CEO said that the executive was the only division head who reported quickly and honestly whenever his division had a problem, and asked for help.

Do you punish realists? Do you reward honest communicators appropriately? The importance of your answers to these questions can be seen in the following example. A manager wanted to reduce unnecessary injuries in his company. The work was dangerous, and it was much more costly to treat the injuries than it was to avoid them. Despite these facts, costs related to workers' compensation had soared for the company in recent years. That trend in costs was an irresistible force.

Formerly, supervisors tried to hide avoidable injuries from top management, so the manager instituted several new rules that included giving all employees the right to request from top management whatever they needed to improve work safety. Most such requests were automatically granted in a day. Anyone who might interfere with these requests or their fulfillment was warned that he or she would be fired immediately.

Also, when each injury occurred, the injured employee's supervisor had to call the manager within an hour, explain what had happened, and describe how future injuries of this sort would be avoided. A follow-up written report was required in a few days as well. Supervisors hated making these calls and doing these reports, so they became more active in avoiding accidents.

Within a year, workplace injuries essentially disappeared from the company. The benefits exceeded the costs by more than ten to one, and everyone was proud of what had been done. The workers and their families also greatly benefited by having much of their fear of injury eliminated, as well as by the workers actually suffering many fewer injuries.

How have other enterprises encouraged their employees, customers, and suppliers to identify opportunities to take advantage of irresistible forces? This subject is addressed in more detail in chapter 13. For now, it's helpful for you to simply start asking this question. Ask it whenever you meet with people from other organizations, as well as those who visit other enterprises like professors, suppliers, and consultants.

Physician: Heal Thyself

An enterprise can learn a lot about irresistible forces by deciding to look for them, even if they have not yet had an impact on the company. To take this offensive action requires overcoming the defensiveness of feeling that you already know all the answers. The best solution to avoiding defensiveness all together is having a program based on (1) assuming that you don't know what the irresistible forces are, and (2) being open to learning.

Who will be the first to notice new irresistible forces? Many effective enterprises invite outside speakers to brief them about new issues. Futurists, economic forecasters, style monitors, and lifestyle trackers can often offer useful insight. Experts in less well-known fields can be even more helpful.

For example, some consumer trends start in certain neighborhoods in certain cities. Asking about, visiting, and tracking what is going on there can provide years of lead time.

How can we easily track what these scouts will learn? There are two parts to answering this question: finding an easy way to measure and noticing changes is the first; and communicating this information effectively is the second. Such tracking systems often start out well but fall by the wayside when the people in the relevant jobs change. A frequent problem is that the new people have no idea what they are supposed to use the tracking information for. More careful training and documentation are essential to effective monitoring over long periods of time.

What are the implications of what has already happened? Demographics often cast the longest shadow for anticipating current and future conditions. Peter Drucker has pointed out in *Management Challenges for the 21st Century* (HarperCollins, 1999) that births are occurring at a rate below the replacement level of the population in all developed countries. He reports that Italy has the lowest birth rate of any large, developed country. This situation has significant meaning for retirement incomes, taxation, the age of the best customers, what types of products will be consumed in the most quantities in the future, and so forth. How will your enterprise be affected? What other irresistible forces will be created?

Essentially, you need to develop your organization's skill for quickly questioning why things happen, and be relentless in determining what the real causes are. In the same way that Perry Mason often solved the case only at the last minute after an admission by a hostile witness or based on facts dug up by his private detective, you will have to persevere until the causes are clear to you and your organization. The sooner you find them, the more valuable the answers will be.

❖ ❖ ❖

Enterprises can best avoid defensiveness stalls by learning from experience about how to best orient toward irresistible forces. Avoiding self-pity and getting the right help can contribute immensely to a proactive and successful posture.

Independence is a good attribute for an enterprise, as long as you don't take it too far. Being a loner in thinking about irresistible forces can be a lot like burying your head in the sand. With appropriate allies and partners, you can be more vigilant in appreciating irresistible forces. The result will be more appropriate and timely actions.

7

"WE CAN DO IT ALL!"

THE INDEPENDENCE STALL

No man is an island, entire of itself. . . .

—John Donne

This chapter emphasizes the importance of quickly seeking new allies, adding different resources, and being open to new ideas to adapt to irresistible forces. Reliance on old standbys and taking few chances may actually present greater risk during a time of crisis than trying your luck with the appropriate new people and perspectives.

Being able to rely on trusted employees whose track record is well known is one way that enterprises and their leaders develop the confidence to address the changing face of their operating environment. However, when irresistible forces move in totally new ways, this approach will usually be the wrong one. For example, if Latin American countries suddenly develop a powerful trading block with a single currency (an idea under discussion), your enterprise would need to draw on resources from the enterprises and individuals in those countries to make the most of your new opportunities. Putting only your best North American or European people and allies to work on the problem would go only so far to improve communications with Latin American companies and customers, and would thus limit your success.

Companies should assume that substantial shifts in the values of foreign currencies and related economic changes and crises will be constant irresistible forces in the years ahead. You need to diagnose the threats and opportunities that arise from such shifts to determine which skills and resources are needed in a particular circumstance.

The Internet has provided a good example of this problem of inappropriate self-reliance. Some major companies made an early decision to be on the Internet. Levi Strauss launched its Web site in 1994. After spending a reported eight million dollars, the firm decided to stop selling its clothes on the Internet in 1999. What happened? First, it took the company four years to decide to sell its clothes online because it couldn't decide how to avoid alienating its bricks-and-mortar retail customers. Then the company made many missteps, such as dropping all of its advertising for e-commerce and failing to think through a returns policy utilizing its retail customers and its own outlets. Having effective allies and resources at the start would have helped Levi Strauss think through and implement its online retailing. (See "Denim Disaster" in *Forbes,* November 29, 1999, page 181.)

Stall Examples

Don't Bother Me with Your Help— Can't You See I'm Busy?

Irresistible forces have a way of arriving at what appear to be inopportune times, often when those who normally deal with new issues are already occupied with other pressing matters or when budgets for new initiatives are already committed. As a result, an appropriate response is usually delayed. Having the same people deal with every important issue causes lost momentum just as closing off several lanes of traffic for construction creates a bottleneck and a snail-trail of cars and trucks during "rush" hour.

In the early 1980s, one of the fastest growing and most successful high technology companies in the United States experienced just such a bottleneck. The company served an important segment of the personal computer industry and enjoyed the leading market share position. Suddenly, a large number of new technology trends combined at the same time to require a change in the company's existing technology. The company correctly perceived that its current products would be made totally obsolete by new methods of manufacture from any one of several different directions. Fortunately, the company had a tremendous research department that responded very well on all fronts. Within a year, terrific technical progress was made in all the areas of concern. The company was relieved and pleased.

Yet the company was soon devastated by other irresistible forces related to rapid growth and had to be sold at a fraction of its former value to a larger company. Why? Although the company conquered the irresistible forces brought by the new technology, that effort took up so much of the research group's attention that enormous blunders were made in manufacturing due to insufficient support from the researchers.

The company always had the irresistible force of rapid growth to deal with. In its industry, this growth meant doubling the company's manufacturing capacity every 18 months in order to hold market share. As a result, new facilities constantly needed to be planned, new equipment ordered and installed, and new employees trained and supervised.

To prepare for this growth, the company had always relied on two people: the head of manufacturing and the technical supervisor of one part of the manufacturing process. The head of manufacturing developed serious personal problems and had to be replaced with little warning. Just before leaving, he erratically and for no apparent reason canceled all orders for new manufacturing equipment for the next year without telling anyone. Since the equipment normally took a year to be delivered, it was a year before this information came to anyone's attention. The head of the technical process was then asked to do the impossible and fill the wide capacity gap. Feeling that he was under too much pressure and seeing little personal benefit from solving the problem, the technical supervisor left to join a competitor. As soon as he left, the technical process he supervised crashed and no one could resurrect it. The company then had to rely on costly outside suppliers who themselves had limited excess capacity to share for this emergency, causing both company sales and profits to evaporate. That crisis marked the end of the company's success.

For many years the technical supervisor and the research department had been assigned to document this particular technical process so that it could be properly maintained without the technical person's special knowledge, experience, and skill. Because of the time pressures on everyone involved to deal with the various irresistible forces, the documentation never took place. The most important part of the manufacturing process and the technical skills to support it were foreign to the rest of those who manufactured the product. Without the ability to perform these crucial steps, the company lost all of its cost advantage at a time when it was capacity constrained. What a dual blow!

Years earlier advisors had recommended that the company diversify its sources of this technical process so that just such a collapse in production capability would not be catastrophic. The irresistible forces had also conspired to keep key personnel too busy to work on that alternative, as well, until it was too late.

The lesson here is that key people, no matter how capable or appropriate for the specific job, must always be left with enough time and resources to deal with *all* of the essential tasks related to irresistible forces. This attention to irresistible forces must be a top priority, superseding the importance of any other given task. Otherwise, the irresistible force you ignore may be the one that gets you.

"We're Number One"

One of the primary causes of the independence stall is a sense of confidence that as a successful enterprise "our people" are better than anyone else's people. That feeling relates to a common psychological problem. Most people see themselves as superior to the vast mass of humanity in almost every area of activity, but measuring actual performance usually reveals average accomplishment.

In an organizational setting, individual weaknesses often become magnified and the feeling of superiority stronger. A financial advisor was asked to investigate whether a company should emphasize dividends, acquisitions, or share repurchases as the primary way to grow stock price. The company had been doing plenty of each. It became curious about the issue after security analysts kept publishing reports showing that if the money spent in the past on acquisitions had gone for share repurchases, the company's earnings-per-share would have been much higher.

The results of the investigation clearly showed that share repurchase had been the way to go in the past, but that this activity would be beneficial in the future only if earnings-per-share *before* the share repurchases were going to grow above a certain annual rate. Otherwise, faster dividend growth would be the right approach. Management couldn't imagine that its earnings-per-share would not expand rapidly (since it had done so for decades), so massive share repurchases were undertaken. Within a year, earnings-per-share dropped by a wide margin because of irresistible forces the company had been paying too little attention to. The company eventually surmounted these irresistible forces after several hard years, but other ones shifted that once again hurt earnings.

Had the company waited to do the share repurchases until these troubled times, it could have bought back twice as many shares with the same amount of money. Its stall had been an unwillingness to have anyone question its future business success. The same financial advisor had pointed out several warning signals about these future problems that the company had ignored. A favorite reaction by this company's senior management was to assert that "No one can understand our company from the outside—we're too unique." So the lesson is you not only have to be willing to talk to others, you have to be willing to pay attention and act on what you hear as well.

The financial advisor reports that many hundreds of companies have made similar claims in the past. If that's the case, then these companies may well have problems because of an inability to work with allies and outside resources. If it is not the case, then these firms have a severe case of the independence stall. Neither circumstance is desirable.

Stall Erasers
Looking Sharp, and Finding the Right Answer
When sales falter in a region, the sales force may want to maintain its independence from interference and contain the problem by creating a solution using only its own people, perhaps by putting more salespeople into the field. This approach seems logical when no one knows the cause of the problem for sure, but proves to be flawed when more information is available. For example, when Russia's economic woes led to a default on government debt in 1998, many distributors of foreign products in Russia were unable to pay for inventories of imported goods as the ruble plunged in value versus foreign currencies. So sales by many companies exporting to Russia ground quickly to a halt. Some exporters tried to solve the problem by going into Russia and selling directly to the retailers themselves, then handing the orders to the Russian distributors. Since the distributors had too little money to buy the goods, they still couldn't order much.

The Gillette sales force quickly perceived that more help was needed in Russia, and added financial people to its team. Their solution involved amending Gillette's credit policies to undertake the currency risk for three days after the order was received (during which time the product could be received and shipped to the distributors' customers). This policy enabled many distributors to borrow the needed foreign currency working capital to support a "cash and carry" policy with the distributors' customers, who were ready and willing to pay cash to get the supplies. Soon Gillette's sales in Russia began to recover. The Russian situation called for financial thinking and changed credit policies, not more sales people as many other companies perceived (see "Gillette Won't Meet Profit-Growth Goal While Emerging Markets Face Turmoil," *The Wall Street Journal*, September 30, 1998, page A3). The companies who understood the situation avoided unnecessary costs by focusing on solving the credit issue. They didn't attempt to do everything for everyone, including directly selling to the distributors' customers on the distributors' behalf.

When Being a Copycat Helps
North American companies often pride themselves on their ability to innovate and create exciting new products and services with great benefits for all.

However, these same innovations often have an Achilles heel, such as a design that adds unnecessary costs for providing or maintaining the product or service. The engineering department that does such a wonderful job of providing these exciting innovations may not have any responsibility for manufacturing the product or providing the service, and may miss these issues totally. Patents can make the problem worse by providing rich profits that suggest little need to improve during the period when competitors are excluded. In contrast, cost reductions and improvements in effectiveness pursued during the protected period can greatly expand the market and help to discourage competitors when the patent does expire.

Let's examine what happened to Xerox when the protection period offered by its patents ran out. Xerox produced the first plain paper copier, which was an enormous improvement over the existing wet copiers. When its copier patents began to expire in the 1980s, Xerox was astonished to find that Japanese competitors were selling small plain paper copiers in the United States at prices that were below its own costs for making similar machines. How could this be? The authors interviewed some former Xerox officials to find the answer. According to them, Xerox executives from the United States flew to Japan to visit Fuji Xerox, the company's joint venture with a Japanese company, and learned that its own joint venture could also afford to profitably sell small Xerox copiers at prices well below U.S. manufacturing costs. As the executives discovered, the designs in Japan had far fewer parts, so fewer suppliers were required and the machines were less expensive to assemble and needed less maintenance.

Quickly heeding these lessons, Xerox launched a successful improvement of its copier quality and costs led by designs that emphasized equally innovation, low manufacturing costs, reliability, and ease of servicing. Without the Fuji Xerox experience, it might have taken Xerox many more years to learn how to most effectively design its innovative products in order to create the most success for the organization.

When a company has the field to itself during the period of patent protection, adding partners who can provide friendly competition through alternative ways of thinking can be an excellent way to prepare for the inevitable day when unrestrained competitors will arrive. Otherwise, needed innovations will be rejected summarily as not being consistent with the best thinking of the company's top innovators. Those who rely only on the perspective of one design team in one location will find themselves increasingly vulnerable to all kinds of irresistible forces: changing customer needs, currency shifts, competitive pressure to be more effective, and new ways of providing the goods and services to customers.

Allies Are Us

Organizations provide many reasons why they prefer to rely on their own people. These concerns include:

- The frequent rate of failure among joint ventures
- The difficulty of getting a high priority for resources needed from allies
- The time spent working with allies
- The effort it takes to attract allies, often unsuccessfully
- Disagreements with allies over future directions
- Allies' slowness to respond
- Inexperience in obtaining benefits this way

These are all, in fact, legitimate concerns that must be dealt with successfully before allies can be usefully added as a critically effective, on-going resource for adapting to irresistible forces. The important perceptual change is to realize that whichever enterprise has the largest number of the most effective allies will win. Time to attract and develop allies must be a high priority for the operation, even before irresistible forces arrive and shift. Becoming effective in this area is a required core competency for the present and the future.

In some industries, this approach can even be extended to turning competitors into unwilling allies. Consider Microsoft, the company that sells more software than anyone else in the world. During the antitrust suit against Microsoft that began in the United States in 1998, a great deal of attention was focused on the company and its historical practices. A wide split occurred in public opinion during this time. If you read the newspaper accounts about how people reacted to the case being brought, most people were pro or con based on their view of the company's history. On the one hand, younger people credited Microsoft with every innovation that has occurred in software—from word processing, to spread sheets, to communications through the Internet. These younger people saw the suit as threatening all technical progress in computer software and the Internet. On the other hand, older people pointed out that Microsoft's innovations were almost always based on the work of others, which the company either purchased inexpensively (such as the basis for DOS), or emulated quickly (the Windows version of the interface that Xerox and Apple had earlier developed). Older people often favored the suit against Microsoft as a way to expand competition by providing more incentive to innovate in the absence of the Microsoft giant.

Prior to 1998, Microsoft sought to maintain relations with all of the companies in the industry so that its interests would be served, even when those relations were not always friendly in the early stages. The catch phrase for this effort at Microsoft could have been: "How can everyone help us?" This help came in the following forms:

- An expanded universe of innovative software that could work with Windows, making it ever more attractive to use Windows

- A broad base of smaller companies that could provide prototypes of new software "look and feel" features that Microsoft could improve on and incorporate into its own competing products

- Feedback on its own new products from large numbers of top software developers before they were launched so that the new Microsoft products would work better and be more appealing

- New bundles of software features that were not present in any single competitor's programs, presenting important convenience advantages for customers

- Advanced information on which competitors could establish large new markets before committing resources to develop similar products

Microsoft's approach of drawing on both contacts with allies and carefully monitoring competitors to enhance its own effectiveness in product development worked very well. Relying solely on its own innovations and resources, the company would have been far less successful.

Your industry may not allow you to co-opt competitors and allies in the same way. A more traditional approach to creating allies was used for decades by Corning. Having chosen a strategy of concentrating on glass and glass-based technologies, the company found itself with skills that it could not fully exploit by itself in many end-use applications and other geographical markets. So the company joined with dozens of partners around the world to develop technologies, products, and markets. The result was that Corning grew to be many times the size it would have been otherwise.

Stallbusting

In this section, we cover how to break out of overly relying on internal resources and solutions, and how to get and keep allies to help you become more effective in adapting to irresistible forces. By reaching out to others, you expand and diversify resources available to you and your organization.

Date Matchmakers

Chances are that perfect allies for you are also out there looking for allies and have not considered you. The main reason that your two organizations are not currently allies is that you have no current business relationship.

How can you make contact with potential allies? Individuals and organizations are springing up who specialize in helping you find allies. A CFO joined an organization of other CFOs who were not competitors of his company. At a meeting for prospective members, another CFO (herself not yet a member of the CFO organization) for a small customer worked with the first CFO on a planning exercise for adapting to irresistible forces. As a result of this experience, the customer CFO suggested that both CFOs could do better if they met and worked together on joint projects in the future. Within months, sales to the customer company increased substantially, based on the projects initiated by the two CFOs. From this experience, the first CFO's company developed a policy of having each senior executive work regularly with her or his counterparts in customer and supplier companies to establish closer and more effective relationships.

Cross-industry groups of all kinds can provide similar sorts of exposures and experiences. Experts who often come into contact with people from other enterprises and cultures can also play this role for you, by helping you consider who would be the best allies. Unfortunately, many companies construe this advice as encouraging them to work primarily with their investment bankers for this purpose. That approach can bear fruit, but investment bankers are often more highly compensated for developing acquisitions than for crafting informal business alliances. They may follow their pocketbooks as a result.

Keep in mind, too, that having helped someone when it was not expected will often generate a life-long friend. Young people are often surprised to learn that they will bump into the same people again and again for the rest of their lives. After all, it's a big world and it's natural to assume that you will only be meeting new people. Having been surprised by that observation, they fail to realize that their interactions with these same people will have a large bearing on their future success.

A public speaker some years ago made a promise to himself that he would be sure that everyone who heard him speak would enjoy a better life as a result. He decided he would teach each person in the audience how to set personal and career objectives, and offer to discuss these objectives with anyone who cared to follow up at any time in the future. Every time the speaker met someone who had once attended one of these talks, the hearer would begin by telling the speaker what a big difference the objective-setting training had provided. The rest of the meeting then would tend to focus on how the grateful hearer could now help the speaker. Over time, dozens of the most successful people in the speaker's field came to credit part of their success to the speaker, and the speaker added allies faster than he had the opportunity to call on them for assistance. You can do the same. Magnified and reflected goodwill toward you fills a reservoir of untapped desire by successful, effective allies to help you.

How can you become good at finding allies? If you haven't been seeking allies much, you may be wondering how you can possibly become good at it. You'll find it helpful to start looking at groups with which you already have well-established relations. These organizations include your existing partners, customers, distributors, suppliers, and employees. Each can be turned into an ally in many ways that you may not be pursuing today. For example:

- Ask your partners for suggestions about how you can help each other.

- Ask your customers how you can help them and their customers be more successful.

- Ask your distributors how you and they can make each other more effective.

- Ask your suppliers what else they can do for you that you have not asked them to do before, and to describe the benefits.

- Ask all employees how you and they can be more successful by helping each other in their present role as employees. Also ask if they would like to set up their own businesses and become external suppliers to the company, and how they could be more effective in that role than as employees. For some, this question will be remarkably liberating and valuable, while others will be confused. For the confused, suggest that they visit independent businesses in their field that were set up by people who used to be employees of their customers.

- Ask those to whom you outsource what else you can do together to be more effective. This group may also include your outside accountants, attorneys and other advisors.

- Ask each of these groups who else they think you should know and work with, and ask them to make the introductions.

Of particular interest to you should be experts and operations that have more experience with the irresistible forces that are important to you and your enterprise. Such people and operations should both have knowledge to share and be in a position to make relevant introductions based on a good understanding of how an alliance could be beneficial to both parties.

How can you let others know that you are a good ally? Having a reputation as a good ally will bring more alliances your way. A wonderful way to add to this reputation is to help your ally get recognition for the results that have come from your alliance. Chances are that the ally will acknowledge your help along the way, and your reputation as someone to work with will grow also.

Be Schooled in Charm

Business alliances are usually based on long-standing relationships between one or more people in both companies who work behind the scenes to maneuver their organizations into taking the right action. These cross-relationships are often closer than those the same people have with others in their own enterprises.

How can you keep allies? Such long-term relationships are best when based on mutual respect, interests, fondness for each other, and shared objectives. These people will realize that the relationship needs to become more like a family relationship than a business friendship. Over the years, many successful allies report sharing vacations, family visits, anniversaries, and other important occasions. This commitment may seem strange to you until you find the right ally, but keep it in mind for when you do, and give it a try.

Those who already are good allies will be in the best position to attract and work effectively with even more allies. Your perspective on keeping allies should include people in other parts of your current enterprise as well as external enterprises and groups.

Let's Get Specific

A good way to narrow your search for allies is to consider the combinations of allies who could be most effective in working with the irresistible forces facing your enterprise.

Who are the allies that will make you and your enterprise most effective in working with the irresistible forces? To answer this question, you need to start with a perspective on the whole range of activities that your company does and should be doing. Then, considering that broader perspective, overlay your understanding of where irresistible forces will make a difference. The intersection of the two perspectives should be the top priority for where allies are needed.

For example, if you have innovative designs but even more innovative competitors, what skills are needed to overcome the irresistible force of ever more innovative competition? If you are a manufacturer, the answer to this question will probably include new ways of producing the goods, new ways of providing error-free performance for customers, more customer-friendly ways to work with your company, and faster availability of future innovations. Some of the best practices for what you do reside in other parts of your own company. Internal allies in manufacturing innovation, market research, service innovation, and new product design will be helpful at a minimum.

But don't stop there. Now look for external allies who can further extend your effectiveness in these areas. Such external allies could include people in organizations that monitor best practices in manufacturing and customer preferences in your industry, custom designers of systems to improve service, and those who study how to streamline innovation processes.

How can you attract these potential allies? You'll have to get to know them or know them better before you can answer this question. The key point of creating an alliance is for potential allies to see you and your enterprise as an ally with whom they cannot be without. This point may sound paradoxical, but you have to have something that you can do for potential allies that will either make them much more effective or save them a lot of time.

The ideal ally, then, is one for whom you can provide this assistance with very little effort on your part. A good way to start is to ask your potential allies what issues they are facing that you may be a good resource for. A corporate planner once held a conference of operating executives and found that business planning was taking up too much time. The corporate planner then worked with the executives to design a new process that both produced better plans and actions, and reduced the time involved. The changes were possible because of the desire of all involved to spend more time on the important challenges posed by the irresistible forces of changing consumer responses to the company's products. The executives earned much higher bonuses as a result and were eager to work with the corporate planner in the future when he posed areas of possible mutual interest.

How can you make your ally and you both more effective? To have the time and resources to work with you, you will need to help your ally. The sooner you provide this help, the better. For example, if your ally's energies are consumed by a problem of declining profitability caused by a changing irresistible force, you could independently search out solutions that you are better equipped to locate before being asked. If the market research department works for you, you could commission a small study to find out what responses will work best in the ally's market place and share those ideas with your ally.

You might also have the market research people do a best practice study to find out how others have best adapted to what you uncover.

Send Internal Myopia on Vacation

If you are a leader in your enterprise (whether formally or informally), you have an opportunity to ask questions that can expose the weaknesses of internally dominated thinking. The best questions are those that expose the lack of external testing of your organization's thinking. Those in your company to whom you pose such questions will soon realize that you'll inevitably ask about external testing, and will soon learn to do such testing in advance to avoid the potential embarrassment of being unprepared when you inquire. Of course, the best way to begin this change is to warn everyone that you will be doing this questioning about research and to explain why you are doing it. Use stories of successes and failures that people themselves have experienced to help bring home the message.

How can you use personal examples to help others learn the benefits of having allies and a broader perspective? A great way to begin is to isolate some area that is troublesome to everyone about an irresistible force. Let's say that your company is beset by rapidly dropping prices for your products or services. Perhaps the solution is to accelerate cost reductions fast enough to surpass competitors and the rate of price decreases. You might take an area where you are responsible for costs and use internal and external allies to create a vastly lower-cost solution. You should later share this experience as a case history for everyone of how you used allies to achieve the solution. Then, you could follow the case history with some private thoughts for each person about how they could apply the same approach in their own cost areas.

Once everyone is good at using this approach for costs, you can pick a new example in another irresistible force area and repeat the experience.

How can you involve the rest of your enterprise in activities that will teach them to seek out and become good allies? Personal example is once again a good path. Cross-industry research organizations are one of the fastest-growing ways that executives are creating more involvement among their colleagues in seeking out and becoming good allies. You can ask those you are already allies with about such organizations, and get involved in them yourself. Through contacts in those organizations, you can get ideas about other organizations from which people in your company would benefit in terms of new perspectives and allies. Share your successes and insights with your colleagues and help them get started down the same path.

Ultimately, they'll learn best by having hands-on experience in developing their own relationships and seeing the benefits flourish as a result. While they are just beginning to learn how to cultivate allies, you should coach them by asking questions about what each is doing to be sure they are locating the areas of mutual advantage concerning irresistible forces. IBM does well at establishing alliances in their successful outsourcing relationships where they operate the information technology (IT) function for customers. Without IBM understanding what its customer partners want (both in and out of the IT function) from the outset, there can be no basis for a successful alliance. Without coaching your colleagues may develop new relationships, but never learn how to use the alliances for greater company growth and success.

How can you permanently abolish internal myopia? Challenge your enterprise to implement close to the ideal best practice for adapting to important irresistible forces (see chapters 15 and 16). Setting the goal of finding the best way that anyone can ever adapt to an irresistible force as a normal objective for your organization requires a broad perspective on alternative ways of operating, what the future best practice will be (see chapter 13), and emerging capabilities in other enterprises. By encouraging this perspective, you'll permanently smash the lenses that only permit seeing choices from the internal viewpoint and add the benefits of having strong tailwinds to aid your progress toward breakthrough gains.

❖ ❖ ❖

Virtually all companies suffer from the independence stall. Enterprises can best avoid the independence stall by rejecting views that have not been thoroughly tested externally and by embracing the benefits of alliances as a top priority.

8

"HOW CAN WE MISS?"

THE OVEROPTIMISM STALL

The man who is a pessimist before 48 knows too much;
if he is an optimist after it, he knows too little.

—Mark Twain

When a company feels confident about the steps it is taking,
overoptimism can stall an enterprise by keeping it from flexibly
addressing issues as they arise. When irresistible forces shift,
the company's overoptimistic actions will lead to achieving
much less than full potential, or possibly even disaster. This
chapter provides you with a guide to avoiding the pitfalls of an
inflexible approach.

Simply choosing a new direction for your operation is not enough to ensure
success with irresistible forces, particularly if the new direction is a result of
overly optimistic thinking about what you can expect to accomplish. You may
simply set off in a direction that is even less advantageous than the one that you
have been pursuing. But creating a new direction for a business is stimulating
for most people. Having conceived of a more successful future, organizations
can become addicted to the excitement that comes from a sense of certainty
that they will succeed. Similarly, faced with contrary evidence that circumstances have changed in ways that are harmful to the new business direction,
too many executives will ignore it due to the sense of certainty they developed
when the plans were originally made.

Overoptimism has many sources, but the impact is the same: A misplaced sense of confidence about the company's ability to succeed causes the organization to inflexibly commit its resources to one path—a wrong one. When IBM first began to falter in the late 1980s, one reason for its inflexibility about changing its practices undoubtedly related to the remarkable success it had enjoyed over several decades.

In other instances, overoptimism is based on believing that you have done a better job of preparing for the future than your enterprise has done before. This mistake is often made by people new to planning exercises and new to the top executive roles that include responsibility for strategy. In addition, the people in the organization can simply be more optimistic than current or future conditions warrant because they are unwilling to face up to the bleakness of their prospects (this is frequently a problem in low-profit industries like paper manufacturing). They have to believe in a better future to avoid despair.

Another cause of overoptimism is that your company's information is faulty. Your organization will be much more successful in assessing your alternatives if you take the time to be sure that the information you are relying on is timely and accurate. Without such checking, you can become subject to the problems of many entrepreneurial organizations, namely, "fire, ready, aim."

Stall Examples
Walking on Air
A visitor came to meet with executives at a leading video-game cartridge manufacturer in the early 1980s. Within weeks of that meeting, the company would declare bankruptcy. Within months, most of the workforce would be gone. Within a few years, few would remember the company at all. Yet, at the time of his visit, he had never seen such a happy, excited, and optimistic group of people.

While the visitor waited in the reception area, one of the world's most popular athletes came bounding through the doorway. This man was a celebrity endorser for the company's products. Before going to his meeting, the athlete signed autographs for anyone who wanted them and pranced around the room describing how awesome the company was and how great its products were. At one point, the receptionist came out and did a little dance with the athlete.

As the visitor was escorted down the hallways by one of the company's senior executives, he found that he had to adopt a semijogging pace because the executive also was bounding along like the athlete had been. Clearly, the man was walking on air.

During the meeting, no executive would concede that anything bad could ever happen to the company. With a big smile, the senior people would always reply, "We can handle that!" to any observation about difficult industry conditions. The executives happily pointed to several new buildings that were under construction to handle the anticipated growth in the company's future volume. "Nothing can stop us now" was another phrase frequently heard during the meeting.

The visitor cautiously sniffed for signs of illegal substances, but smelled none. The executives were simply high (at that moment at least) on their optimism.

Ironically, all of the problems that would soon crush the company were well known and had been reported quite frequently in the business press. The company's executives simply couldn't see any connection to themselves in reports of excess retail inventories of video-game cartridges, teenage boredom with the latest games, and parental rebellion over how teenagers were spending their spare time and money. While these might be problems for other companies, these executives felt that those concerns didn't apply to them.

Subsequent events showed that the company had been actually more vulnerable than most to these problems, triggered by the irresistible force of male teenagers demanding much better quality and variety of games than anyone could deliver at the time. (In fact, another decade would pass before sufficient improvements were made for video-game cartridges to again capture the attention of teenage boys in a major way.)

It's Straight Up . . . in Smoke, That Is

Put the average company into a high-growth situation (for its industry) for the first time, and you'll soon see overoptimism sprouting everywhere. In the aftermath of the Arab oil embargo and the subsequent rise in the cost of energy, Americans began using all sorts of new ways to reduce their energy use and costs. One idea for home heating was to cut wood to burn in wood stoves and fireplaces. Soon, every wooded neighborhood was abuzz with the sound of busy chain saws. Prior to the oil shortage, chain saws had been avoided like the plague by suburbanites who didn't want to be confused with the woodcutters and gardeners they hired. Now, you couldn't walk like a man unless you could buzz through tree trunks and limbs with the best of them.

McCulloch was the leading chain saw manufacturer at the time. Black & Decker, the home-power-tool giant, quickly purchased McCulloch at a hefty price to be able to benefit from the seemingly limitless potential of chain saws. Soon, Black & Decker was optimistically describing itself as a company about to be transformed by its chain saw business. Capacity could not be expanded fast enough. And business did, indeed, take off . . . for a while.

Within a few years, though, everyone who thought they wanted or needed a chain saw had one. Many people who took to the backyard woods found that cutting down trees and making smaller pieces out of the logs with a small chain saw was hard, dangerous work repaying little for the time and effort. The person using the chain saw also had to cope with a tremendous racket, obnoxious fumes from the gas engine, and an irritating need to keep sharpening the small chain saw blade. And many of these nouveau woodspeople didn't know that wood has to be dried and aged before it will burn properly. So they often endured smoky, smoldering fires that left the whole house smelling terrible and provided little heat.

Wood is a poor way to heat most houses. The fireplace sucks the heat from the house up through the chimney, leaving the rest of the house colder. A wood stove is great if you're at exactly the right distance from it, but too hot or too cold otherwise. And it's a real drag to have to constantly haul wood to feed the fires and clean out the ashes.

Pretty soon, suburbanites found that they liked warm clothes better than wood fires as a way to save money. Used chain saws began to be sold at garage sales for a few dollars. Moreover, even those who loved cutting wood with their chain saws usually had no use for more than one. Black & Decker basked in the glow of its then remarkable record of growing earnings from quarter to quarter at 15 percent per year. It began to believe the chain saw market would perform like its core power-tool market. However, some important differences were overlooked. Power tools are inexpensive, and if you add a new feature, many householders will buy a new one to get the benefit of the feature. Chain saws are much more expensive, and few people were willing to replace them. That's where the irresistible forces took hold

Entranced by the rising sales numbers, chain saw competitors proliferated and the market was jammed with products. Then chain saw sales dived. Black & Decker reversed course and dumped its chain saw business. A lot of money went up in smoke in the process. Overoptimism was costly in this case because the irresistible forces driving chain saw sales were not understood by Black & Decker before it entered the business.

Can't You Count?

Accounting systems are designed to accurately report how a company did financially as a whole, using generally accepted accounting principles to make comparisons easier from company to company. Such systems are often totally misleading when it comes to accurately describing which areas of the company are providing the positive financial results. One restaurant chain learned this lesson to its chagrin when it sought to improve its earnings. The company received money from operating its own restaurants, from selling supplies to itself and to its franchisees, and from franchising and licensing fees when others owned and operated the restaurants.

The accounting records accurately showed how much revenue each area generated. Company-owned and -operated restaurants were the biggest source of revenue, followed by supplies, followed by franchise fees. The company had a lot of overhead in operating the various parts of its business, both in the home office and in the field in order to supervise its own restaurants, franchisees, and supply operations. After looking at all of this overhead, the company could clearly see that it needed to generate considerably more operating income to support it. Because the overhead was not allocated by activity area across the company, it seemed optimistically clear to everyone that the company-owned and -operated restaurants needed to be expanded the most because they already provided the bulk of the operating income to offset this overhead. The company was also convinced that it did a much better job of running restaurants than its franchisees did. Almost any company restaurant was newer, bigger, and had better equipment than the franchisees, which reinforced this impression.

Yet a curious thing had been happening. Although the company had been rapidly expanding company-owned and -operated restaurants, its overall earnings were declining. This occurrence failed to make an impression on management when looking at the accounting results, so the company kept redoubling its efforts to expand these company-owned and -operated restaurants even faster. Results grew worse.

At this point, the company asked outside advisors to help improve its profit growth. Working with internal cost accountants, the advisors found that almost all of the company's overhead costs actually were variable costs needed to operate the company-owned and -operated restaurants. In fact, when the costs were properly applied to the activities they actually supported, the only place the company made money was on the royalty fees from the restaurants that were operated by franchisees, the area that initially appeared to have the lowest profit potential.

The accounting system had so misrepresented profitability in the company-owned restaurants that management had not only greatly overexpanded in this area, it had also permitted itself to spend money in unwise ways. The company eventually learned that it had never once made money in company-owned restaurants. The franchisees were usually much more effective restaurant operators than the company was. To further compound the error, the company was constantly trying to persuade franchised restaurant operators to take on the innovations that were, in fact, losing lots of money in the company-owned restaurants. The franchisees fought back aggressively, souring relationships between them and the franchisor.

In retrospect, it was clear if you thought about it that all the company's earnings must have been derived from franchisee income and licenses. There were very few costs associated with those activities, so almost all of the franchising and licensing operating income was actually profit before tax. This operating income amount from franchising was always much more than the company's combined pretax income. The rest of the activities *had* to be operating at a loss.

Why had executives continued to believe that they were great restaurant operators? When asked, they replied that they had hired only the best people, had carefully trained them, and had done a great job of supervising them. By comparison, the franchisees were characterized as less well educated, less talented, and did a poorer job of supervision. These executives had missed the irresistible force that someone running his or her own business will do a better job in most cases than someone who is hired to run the same business. In a restaurant, an owner-manager will often attract 10 percent to 40 percent more volume than an average hired manager by doing whatever it takes to please the customers, which makes them want to return. The marginal profits on that incremental volume will be 60 percent to 80 percent of the increased revenues. The professionally managed restaurants will be lucky to overcome that disadvantage with better people and training. The smaller, less expensive franchised restaurants also cost less to operate, providing a further edge.

Based on more complete accounting and an improved understanding of its economics, the restaurant company overcame its unfounded optimism. It went on to become much more successful by allocating its resources according to the most effective actual use, rather than based on where its greatest revenues and most talented people seemed to be. Highly effective people don't always overcome irresistible forces. The 2,000 percent solution is always to use irresistible forces as tailwinds pushing you forward to key accomplishments.

Stall Erasers
Temper Your Optimism with First-Hand Information
As currency volatility increased in the late 1990s, Molex (an electrical component manufacturer) had reason to be concerned. It produced more than 40 percent of its annual income from selling products in the very countries that were experiencing the most difficulty with their currencies. In many cases, the

company also manufactured products in those same countries. The company also knew that it faced an irresistible force: Almost all profit growth in its industry comes from new products, and these are expensive and time-consuming to design and produce. Reduced demand for existing products would mean a drastic drop in profits.

But Molex was a company proud of its "can-do" heritage of growing faster and with better financial ratios than the bulk of its worldwide competitors. It immediately reacted to the currency plunges by taking all of its best people and putting them into the troubled countries for as long as it took to understand the irresistible forces affecting the local economies. By not just optimistically relying on its past successes and making a commitment to finding out what the company was facing, Molex's actions made the difference between additional success and failure.

Here are some of the things it found, and what it did to adjust. First, in some countries, the local currency was devalued by more than 50 percent. This circumstance meant that imported materials now cost double or more what they had before. Molex moved quickly to raise prices for customers in the local markets where the currencies had dropped to reflect those changes. Second, the local economies were thrown into severe recessions by the devaluations, which meant that local customers would not be buying very many products. Molex quickly fanned out its salespeople to locate new customers in other countries (such as in Europe and North America) who would want to buy imported goods built in Asia at much lower prices than Molex had formerly charged. Third, Molex kept its commitment to expanding new product development, and focused more on the needs of its newest customers who were least affected by currency and economic changes.

A year later Molex had experienced only a single quarter of modestly lower earnings since the currency volatility started, revenues and market share climbed every quarter, and financial ratios actually improved. Other companies in the industry had severely reduced profits that continued for a much longer time.

Give Your Optimism Regular Reality Check-Ups

Many people admire the success that Wal-Mart enjoyed in the retailing industry at the end of the twentieth century. For many years the company grew its number of stores, the sales per store, and the efficiency of its operations at an impressive rate to become the world's largest retailer. Throughout the time that founder Sam Walton was CEO, much attention was focused on the aggressive goals that he would encourage the company to meet. Walton was famous for not only setting the goals, but also for recognizing his people when they met the goals. In fact, as his payoff on a bet that the goals would not be met during one year, he dressed up in a grass skirt and danced the hula for the amusement of everyone.

What many people don't know is that Wal-Mart also operated one of the most useful corporate air forces in the world. Each Monday, almost every executive left the headquarters in Arkansas to begin visiting stores around the world. The visits continued at a hectic pace (using the private planes to allow more visits to occur) through Friday, when the planes filled with executives returned from the field. Then, the whole executive group met on Friday night or Saturday morning to report what had been learned that week and to devise solutions to be implemented when they returned to the field on Monday.

Wal-Mart people were justifiably optimistic about the future of their company, and one reason for their optimism is that they were never more than a week away from addressing any irresistible force that they found affecting their operations. As a result, their on-site experiences allowed them to discount any overoptimism that arose.

Don't Be Bedeviled by Smugness

In a U.S. genetic engineering company that develops pharmaceutical products, the company's founders and scientists disdained the views and processes of the federal government's Food and Drug Administration (FDA). The company knew (correctly) that the regulators at FDA were much less capable and knowledgeable than they should have been in genetic engineering. Whenever the FDA raised an issue, the company's officials would sneer as it explained to the FDA people that they were wrong. As you can imagine, the FDA examiners were soon concerned that the company was out of control because of the unfriendly attitude.

And the FDA was right. The company had bypassed some important procedures in its pharmaceutical trials. While correctly believing that it knew a lot about genetic engineering, the company's superior knowledge didn't extend into making safe and healthful pharmaceuticals. In that respect, the company was clearly deficient. When the FDA finally found out, it gave the board a choice: Go out of business or replace all of your senior executives and scientists with people we can work with. Naturally the board complied, but it took the company more than five years to recover from the prior management's refusal to acknowledge that the FDA was one of their company's irresistible forces. The company's initial overoptimism about overcoming the FDA's views cost it hundreds of millions of dollars in lost revenues and profits, and life-saving developments were unnecessarily delayed.

Disagreements Mean Healthier Profits

Overoptimism is bred by homogenous thinking. One way to overcome that one-sighted tendency is to task at least one thoughtful person to consider what the organization should do if future conditions change, and challenge the prevailing view. As an example of the problem, one fast-growing U.S. health maintenance organization explained that all of its senior executives were focused on getting new customers. When many types of customers (such as those on Medicare) became unprofitable due to changing health-care reimbursement practices by governments and employers, the company was slow to shift away from the unprofitable accounts.

Another company in the same industry had many fewer problems because one member of the top team viewed his job as balancing the optimism of his colleagues. So even if this man was not pessimistic about something, he would play the role of devil's advocate for that position to stimulate more balanced thinking. Early on, the "independent" thinker pushed for not taking on accounts that could become low-margin if reimbursement practices changed. As cost containment pressures assaulted the company, it was little affected because it had avoided taking on those potentially profit-threatening customers in the first place. Alfred Sloan often played that same independent thinker role at General Motors during that organization's successful climb over Ford in the first half of the twentieth century.

You can obviously improve on this solution by being sure that all of your teams are created with as much experience and psychological diversity as possible. Many organizations encourage teams to undertake simple psychological tests and to share the results with one another on the team, so that each person will be aware of as many of the biases as possible that the others may or do have.

Stallbusting

This section demonstrates the importance of analyzing and monitoring irresistible forces to prevent overoptimism from stalling your progress. Skill in this area will provide your enterprise with a competitive edge because overoptimism is difficult for many companies to overcome.

Keep Both Eyes Open for Irresistible Force Risks

As you have read, some companies ignore or underestimate important irresistible forces, optimistically viewing them as gentle breezes rather than raging hurricanes that can tear the organization apart. To overcome this sort of misunderstanding and overoptimism you need to constantly focus on identifying what the most important irresistible forces are.

What are the irresistible forces that had, are having, and could have strong positive and negative impacts on your organization? To a person sitting calmly in an underground shelter, the raging tornado overhead doesn't seem too threatening. Many organizations have succeeded in such sheltered environments because they have yet to be subject to the full fury of the irresistible forces. But they often fail to make the connection until they leave the shelter. For example, many chemical companies initially reported in 1997 that the overseas economic problems had no impact on their operations. Two years later, many of these same companies were showing very weak profits as demand and prices for chemicals slumped in many markets with devalued currencies. These slumps in turn caused worldwide prices to be lower because of oversupplies of products and excess capacity. If those companies hadn't been overoptimistic about their positions in the worldwide economy, they could have been more successful in dealing with the irresistible forces.

What is the best way to monitor these forces and spot new ones in the future? Monitoring is a tricky function. If your technical analyst understands what's going on but no one else does, you won't be much better off than if you were completely unaware of what's happening. The best ways to monitor are ones that everyone participates in and understands. You can learn more about this subject in chapters 11 and 12.

Keep an Optimism Thermometer Where It Will Do the Most Good

Organizations have patterns of optimism and pessimism that can be used as indicators in helping to understand what is going on. Corporate controllers have known this for years, and some will secretly keep records of the accuracy and inaccuracy of the forecasts they receive from different people in the enterprise. New company-wide forecasts are then adjusted to reflect these historic patterns by business area. Done over time, you'll find that the levels of optimism wax and wane.

Where can overoptimism lead to big mistakes? Based on learning about which irresistible forces are the ones that matter for you, you should next analyze where those forces come to bear on your organization's decisions. That's where it is critical to watch out for overoptimism stalls. If an irresistible force affects demand for your products, then anything you do to develop new products, adapt existing ones, produce or deliver these products, and make money while you do so will be at risk. This is particularly a problem when a company enters a new market.

Here's an example. In the 1960s, Heublein, the vodka giant, overoptimistically decided that its liquor marketing expertise could cross over into the beer industry. Hamm's was purchased as a vehicle for innovative new products. But it proved to be a big disaster because beer is subject to irresistible forces not applicable to vodka. It was later divested in the 1970s at a loss. Heublein could have grown Hamm's sales with the new products (including an early version of low-calorie beer), but Heublein lost money on the increased volume because its costs were high due to small-scale facilities and low market share. Costs in brewing versus competitors vary primarily with the size of the breweries, distance to the customers, and ability to spread advertising costs over larger brand volumes.

The challenge that organizations face is that many of these product opportunities require planning against a moving target in the future, a moving target whose location will shift with the irresistible force.

How can the harm from overoptimistic-based mistakes be limited or reduced? One good way is to seek more flexibility in how you deal with irresistible forces. (See chapters 13–16 for more discussion of flexibility.) You want to be more flexible so that what you have been doing can be quickly adapted to better fit the irresistible forces affecting product or service demand. For example, you might always plan to have 40 percent of your new products manufactured by others who are effective and much larger than you are, so that you can quickly reduce or expand capacity if your forecasts turn out to be wrong. Also, if you're in a fashion business, you might always have some work going on in alternative fashion areas should the direction you're following be received coolly.

How can you create an advantageous mix of optimism and pessimism in order to bring out important perspectives about irresistible forces? Perhaps the best way to achieve this mix is to ensure that key teams in the organization always reflect a diversity of thought about irresistible forces. Any time that you find a quick and easy consensus forming, you should be skeptical that you are on the right track, unless the irresistible force is following precisely a path that you have had experience with before and there is little chance of an unexpected diversion.

Looking for this pro-and-con mix in your suitably balanced team by no means requires you to reduce the presence of optimists. Research shows that optimists accomplish more than realists or pessimists because they attempt more and are more confident that they'll succeed. However, you don't want optimism to run amok and instigate action when none should occur. You don't want to simply have happy volunteers for *The Charge of the Light Brigade.*

How can you use optimism within your organization and keep it from evolving into overoptimism? For some companies, a good solution is to use the sense of optimism in the following areas: to keep morale high, to ensure enthusiastic implementation, and to enhance the organization's energy level. Then shift the focus of that optimism into a new and more beneficial direction: Replace certainty about the current direction with certainty that changed directions will be required, and that your enterprise will aggressively seek out ways to benefit from shifts in irresistible forces. At the same time, an appropriate dose of humility about implementing these new directions will be helpful. This change in focus can turn the risk of overoptimism into a way to enhance the organization's ability to deal with shifting irresistible forces. A good way to keep this focus is to have the financial group prepare brief reviews of past performance to highlight where overoptimism has been a problem, and to draw lessons from what went wrong.

❖ ❖ ❖

Enterprises can best avoid overoptimism stalls by recognizing the dangers of incorrectly assumed, misplaced, or misinformed confidence about the current direction and by working on continually and accurately analyzing the past, present, and future effects of irresistible forces and how to turn them to advantage.

9

"THROW ME A TOWEL"

THE COVER-UP STALL

Only the mediocre are always at their best.

—Jean Giradoux

Enterprises often unwittingly encourage their people to be seen
by others only as successful. When problems arise, then, this
desire can encourage downplaying the seriousness of the problems or even to covering them up. In this chapter you can learn
about the dangerous consequences of such inappropriate
actions and how to avoid and deal with cover-ups before they
cause serious or even fatal damage.

"To err is human, to forgive, divine" is a maxim that the irresistible force
enterprise could rewrite as: "To err is human, to find out about the error
quickly and forgive as much as possible is in our best interest." Frequently, the
path to progress in new areas involves a move forward, a setback, another
move, another setback, and so forth until major progress results from the combined benefits of learning from the mistakes and more favorable conditions.
Like the robot minirover on Mars making its way through a boulder-strewn
field, progress is inevitable but it's not smooth. Robots aren't troubled by the
setbacks, but people often are.

When irresistible forces cause major setbacks for a company, many people
will want to characterize the problems as being limited in scope and duration.
They will often try to hide the problem from others both inside and outside
the business in hopes of redeeming the situation before anyone finds out about

it. They frequently will then proceed to take outsized risks in a vain effort to get back to where they started. Often, the actions that got them into trouble originally were at odds with the irresistible forces, and these actions can continue to misfire.

This tendency is harmful to companies in two ways: First, the enterprise is delayed in perceiving and responding appropriately to the problem; and, second, the business is exposed to additional harm through the inappropriate actions taken during the cover-up period.

In most organizations, the ethic of the school playground or prison yard prevails: No squealers! An irresistible growth enterprise actually needs a different sense of community: "Errors only hurt us if they are ignored or covered up. Cover-ups threaten us all, because they harm us and can even undermine our continued existence."

Clearly, cover-ups must be avoided. To achieve this goal, the environment within an enterprise must be such that individuals feel comfortable reporting problems. In addition, companies need to take a tough stance toward those who engage in cover-ups and be extremely vigilant in rooting them out. It is essential that these principles be well accepted by everyone as part of the irresistible growth enterprise's values.

Stall Examples

I'm Just Doing This in the Best Interests of Everyone Involved

Adverse new circumstances are almost universally viewed as being fleeting by those with the authority and opportunity to do something about adapting to the irresistible forces involved. A revealing example of this psychology at work occurred in the U.S. savings and loan industry during the 1980s.

At that time, the country was wracked by a high rate of inflation. Under presidents Carter and Reagan, the Federal Reserve sought to bring that inflation quickly under control by raising interest rates, which soared and stayed high. For savings and loan institutions (S&Ls), this situation was a disaster. These S&Ls had almost all of their depositors' assets tied up in long-term home mortgages at interest rates well below the then-prevailing rates paid to depositors. To keep the depositors' money, the S&Ls had to continue to offer interest rates well above what they could earn with the money from existing loans. Shareholders' capital rapidly evaporated amid the mounting losses.

Such circumstances had occasionally occurred in the past, and the U.S. government had always stepped in to rescue the savings institutions. That experience lulled the S&L executives into a fatal lassitude about their circumstances during the Reagan years. At a time when they could have raised more equity capital, sold the mortgages for a loss, and closed down unprofitable operations, the executives procrastinated, hoping for better times.

Finally, these executives began to realize that no government bailout was on the horizon. Unwilling to face the music for their procrastination, they desperately looked for new places to put depositors' funds that offered enormously high rates of returns. Some began investing alongside borrowers in new commercial ventures, such as residential shopping centers and resort developments. Others bought barrelfuls of high-yield bonds (later dubbed "junk" bonds). Still others began to speculate by buying second mortgages that had poor collateral. The problem with all of these investments was that they, too, would fail if interest rates stayed high (or went higher), because the high interest rates would harm the underlying activities being financed.

This problem was compounded later by the federal government stepping in and requiring that all of these assets be liquidated at "fire-sale" prices whenever an S&L got too near to running out of equity capital. Although many of these bets would have paid off handsomely if held over a decade or more until a time when interest rates were much lower, the government liquidations tended to cause still greater losses in the short term. Each liquidation then made the holdings of the remaining solvent institutions less valuable, threatening them with liquidation as well. This circumstance put the S&L executives in a situation like the gambler who puts all of her money on one hand of poker only holding a pair of eights. Unless she wins in the short run, she's out of business. And many of these institutions did just that—went out of business.

Many of these executives considered themselves to be pillars of the community and felt that they were doing the right thing at every step of the way. Visions of the movie *It's A Wonderful Life* may even have been on their minds. As you can imagine, some executives were less than candid with their boards and regulators about what they were doing. Their desperate actions (in making very risky loans and investments) in the end caused the losses to multiply enormously. Taxpayers were forced to make good on their deposit guarantees for these institutions to the tune of many tens of billions of dollars.

Everybody's Doing It

Banks are not immune from problems with their loans similar to those experienced by the S&Ls. A changed economic environment can mean that asset values drop, cash flows dry up, and the bank is holding a note from a borrower who cannot pay and whose collateral isn't worth very much. Some analysts say that this sort of situation was a major cause of the poor economic performance in Japan during the 1990s, as banks there scrambled to hide the extent of the losses that they had already taken in economic terms, but had not yet charged to their balance sheets.

Banks that have looked into how to recover on such troubled loans noticed something very interesting, however. The loan officer who originally authorized the loan tended to be very sympathetic to the borrower, often taking the step of lending even more money. If the adverse irresistible force turned around very quickly, this approach worked out all right in some circumstances. However, if the adverse irresistible force of a poor economy or weak demand in an industry continued for many years, this policy caused a disaster, as some argue happened in Japan. In fact, the banking examiners and those who supervise them in Japan are often those who formerly worked as loan officers, and had lost their previous jobs when the loans they had made were not repaid. Naturally, such examiners are likely to be sympathetic to the banks and bank officers they examine.

In this kind of clubby environment, executives and loan officers draw a lot of comfort from knowing that everyone else both in and out of their lending organization is taking the same approach to not being very active in calling bad loans. In the process, billions can disappear, with the rate of disappearance compounded by more bad loans being granted to the same people. In the case of Japan, the government rules abet this cover-up problem by making it easy for banks to argue that these are good loans. That position, too, sends a message that the institution should not seek to aggressively protect its depositors. As a result, an insolvent institution may keep losing and wasting money long after its own capital has disappeared.

Feeling Lucky?

Financial institutions and companies now place huge bets on the future economic environment of everything from currency values, to commodity prices, to interest rates, to common stock indices. Because the sums involved are often enormous and the potential profits regal, those who make decisions about these bets are often rewarded with a piece of the gain when they succeed. Even in the worst times, these decision-making jobs tend to pay extraordinarily well, so they are well worth hanging on to.

Meanwhile, the rapid shifts in values for currencies, commodities, and financial markets can often leave the enterprises that are trading in these markets exposed to enormous losses. This exposure results from the vast amounts of borrowed money involved, which means that a company doing such trading can lose far more money than it initially put up as its own equity capital. Taken to extremes, such losses can cripple or destroy otherwise healthy businesses.

In recent years, we have seen a number of these debacles. One of the most interesting to consider for our purposes is the trading (apparently unauthorized) that has been ascribed to a single person, Nicholas Leeson, on behalf of Barings Bank, for many years one of Britain's oldest and most well regarded financial institutions. Having taken large losses, the trader decided to try to recoup by making even larger trades (reportedly beyond his authorization). He was somehow able to operate without being detected by the firm's management, with the result that the subsequent losses grew larger. By the time the losses from the trader's unwise decisions were uncovered, the bank had no equity left and had to be dissolved. Had the trader followed his firm's rules better or had the firm stopped him before the losses became too large, the bank would still be functioning today and providing an economic contribution to its many customers and employees.

Show Your Slip, or You'll Slip Up

Psychologists who do surveys concerning personal fears tell us that the most common fears are of public speaking and public embarrassment. Most people will go to great lengths to avoid either circumstance. This is an important point to consider because it helps to explain why so many people take enormous risks for their companies and themselves to avoid an alternative that is far less threatening in reality than the path they are taking.

To fully understand this psychology, however, we must also consider the research that shows how most people perceive risk aversion. This work is well documented in the decision-making literature.* Briefly, what this research shows is that people prefer to avoid a loss over seeking an even larger gain. This characteristic means that no matter how good the ultimate consequences may be of being candid about the impact of the irresistible force, people will act to avoid the negative near-term consequences of public embarrassment.

Both the Nixon cover-up of the Watergate burglary and the Clinton cover-up of the relationship with Monica Lewinsky (referred to by some as "Monica-gate") appeared to be influenced by this psychology. In the case of Nixon, an early admission of error and an apology would probably have avoided the Watergate hearings and his subsequent resignation. Nixon felt

---

*See, for example, *Smart Choices* by John S. Hammond, Ralph L. Keeney, and Howard Raiffa, Harvard Business School Press, 1999.

pressed to resign from office because of the public reaction to the cover-up, not because of the burglary itself. Similarly, subsequent events suggest that the American public would have accepted an early acknowledgment of the Lewinsky relationship and sincere apology by Clinton. The impeachment hearings could have undoubtedly been avoided, since the special prosecutor, Kenneth Starr, based his referral to the House of Representatives on the alleged cover-up.

Now, anyone can understand why these two men didn't want to confess their errors and be subject to public embarrassment. In retrospect, however, it seems clear that sharing their faults early would have been the better course for them and the country.

Hicks Waldron, former CEO of Avon Products and Heublein, was once asked what he valued most about one of his executives. Waldron's answer was revealing, "The man always calls me to tell me about his problems as soon as they arise or he finds out about them. That way, I have no surprises, and I can work with him to resolve the problems before they get worse." Many CEOs share this philosophy.

Yet many people in companies feel that they have to be perfect in their jobs, which means not making errors. That is an unreasonable self-expectation. Where does this feeling come from? In addition to fear of public embarrassment, most people also overestimate their talents. This universally high self-esteem is helpful for encouraging people to try things, but can get in the way of their being effective when misaligned with irresistible forces.

Stall Erasers

Listen Up! Treat Your Irresistible Force Messengers Well

On a 1998 visit to the Cabinet War Rooms from which Winston Churchill and the British War Cabinet functioned during World War II bombing raids, the authors read an interesting letter on display from Churchill's wife to her husband. Written during the early days of the war, this letter tells of having been approached by an officer working for Churchill who recounted to her that Churchill was being very unpleasant to anyone who tried to bring up difficulties. The officer reported that everyone had given up trying to reason with Churchill and just went along with his ideas (even when they were very wrong). Churchill's wife wisely reminded Churchill that people used to like to work with and for him, and that he needed people to tell him what he needed to hear. She counseled him to kindly seek out other views.

As a devoted husband, Churchill was willing to accept this unpleasant message from his much-adored wife. Audio tapes available then to visitors at the War Cabinet Rooms recounting the experiences of those who later worked with Churchill indicated that he subsequently pulled back a little from pugnaciously pursuing his own ideas, and no longer pushed people to tell him what he wanted to hear and to do exactly what he demanded. He gave enough room for people to push back, and many disasters were averted. For example, Churchill soon after had a plan to take most of the Royal Navy into an action near the Continental coast, without air cover, while the Luftwaffe was still strong. The admirals properly pointed out that this was folly in the face of the Luftwaffe and U-boats that the fleet would encounter (substantial irresistible forces if defenses were lacking), and Churchill listened . . . even though he made his disagreement clear. For the rest of the war, Churchill received the news he needed to hear as a result. He never thereafter ordered his military advisors to go against their best judgment, although he would firmly test their thinking every step of the way. He spent every spare minute contacting those around the world in the best position to know what the circumstances were, so that he could accurately assess the odds the British people were facing.

Churchill's early war behavior isn't unique; most organizations have the same problem. Leaders are inclined to tell people to "get the results" that the leaders want. Knowing that they are between the proverbial rock and a hard place, people tend to stop sharing the causes of the problems they encounter to avoid being told to get the results anyway. The smart ones start sending out their resumes, knowing that they may be selected as scapegoats when the leader's desired results fail to occur.

Still Water Breeds Mosquitoes, Not Progress

You have probably seen a stagnant pond. The lack of movement on the pond's surface makes a perfect breeding ground for mosquitoes, and makes it easy for unattractive debris to cover the surface as well. Put a little movement into that pond's water, and you'll have many fewer mosquitoes and a much more attractive pond.

New CEOs coming into stagnant companies understand this lesson very well. They also know that their own movement won't stir the waters nearly as much as the movement of all the people in the firm.

A corporate officer in a newly invigorated company, led by a new CEO brought in from outside the organization, shared this experience. The company had had almost no revenue and earnings growth for many years and was doing little about it. It had been the industry leader just five years earlier, and now was half the size of the rapidly growing current leader.

The first day on the job, the new CEO called a meeting of all the corporate officers and asked each of them to outline what needed to be done to get the company moving again. He indicated that he wanted the answers within five days. Then he waited. In the next few hours, the executive recounting this story wrote and turned in her report to the CEO. The CEO later told her that no one else produced a report until five days later, and some people even missed that deadline.

The CEO excoriated everyone except her for taking the company's needs so casually. News reports indicated that almost every one of the executives who waited five or more days to report left the company within a few weeks. The replacements were told that their futures depended both on results and on sharing rapidly what they were running into. The company soon began to make progress again. Making mistakes and reporting them were okay, as long as the risks were understood and shared in advance.

Irresistible growth enterprises should seek effectiveness, rather than personal perfection for its own sake. Most companies will make much more progress by doing a lot more and having some of it not work out, than doing almost nothing at all and making few mistakes.

Stallbusting

In this section, you can learn how to shift attention to using irresistible forces proactively to avoid the need for cover-ups in your organization; how to reduce the number of cover-ups that your organization suffers from; and how to shorten the duration of cover-ups that do occur. By addressing these issues directly, you can create a more effective organization that enjoys high morale as well.

Can We Talk?

Most organizations act as though errors will never be made and give those in the organization no guidance as to what to do about errors when they are. That attitude fosters a cover-up mentality. An excellent way to improve your organization is to have a clear understanding of what should be done about avoiding and dealing with errors.

What errors do you want to encourage in your organization? Your reaction to this question may be that you never want to encourage errors, but that stance will retard your progress. Particularly in areas such as developing improved ways to do things, you and your organization will and should make lots of errors. Otherwise, you'll never produce anything that is much better than what you are doing already. Also, inexpensive errors can be a good way to train people to be more successful in avoiding expensive errors. A good example of that opportunity is to give hands-on experience in simulated environments (in the way that many highly technical jobs are taught today) where the cost of mistakes is nothing more than sirens going off on a computer screen and a little time spent to do the simulation.

What errors do you want people to report immediately to others? A well-trained group will already know how to resolve most errors, and the people who find the errors should simply resolve them immediately. But errors that happen repeatedly should also be reported and evaluated. Knowing that a certain error happens often can help focus attention on finding a way to overcome the root causes of the error, rather than having to repeatedly deal with the consequences. Also, recurring errors can be a clue that an existing irresistible force is taking a new direction or a new irresistible force is at work, either of which may require a totally different kind of action.

How can you motivate people in your operations to report errors, including their own? The best way to encourage people to report errors is to make the cost to the individual of alerting the organization about a problem relatively small or nonexistent. You might even consider rewarding such communications under some circumstances, such as when personal safety or the firm's existence is in peril. You need to be sure that the people who report their own and others' errors are, at the very least, praised for doing so. Otherwise, the fear of embarrassment or being thought of as a "stool pigeon" will inhibit reporting. To make this approach to errors more effective than just having a reporting system, you will also need to encourage people to recommend what actions should be taken to deal with the causes and consequences of the errors. Recognition and rewards should be even higher for those who excel in this area as well.

An important step in this direction is to have the leaders throughout the organization set a good example. Many CEOs never take responsibility for anything in their operations. Leaders should seek out opportunities to describe errors they have made, what they did about them, what benefits accrued from telling others about the errors, and why they are glad that they have acknowledged and addressed the causes of the errors. This behavior provides the irresistible growth enterprise with a powerfully necessary learning opportunity if you are to elicit the same behavior from everyone else.

Encourage each person to measure her or his own performance in order to locate more opportunities to avoid errors and correct repeated ones. Pratt & Whitney, the aircraft engine giant, uses the following approach at its plant in West Haven, Connecticut. Publicly visible boards in each manufacturing area track daily productivity by shift. Any time goals are missed, the team immediately discusses the causes and adjusts. Most good quality management programs do something similar. Training in how to do such measuring will make it a lot easier for people. If you have a total quality management program, this training can be combined with the background that people need to work as members of quality teams.

Often, the most serious cover-ups are revealed by whistle-blowers. If it happens that you need to fire a whistle-blower for reasons unrelated to the revelation, be sure that there is no alternative and that everyone understands the reasons why. Be sure the person had been rewarded appropriately for the service done by the whistle-blowing, if appropriate. Otherwise, you won't be hearing any internal whistles in the future.

How can you make honesty about errors part of your enterprise's core values? First, you need to have a process whereby your organization identifies and promotes your core values. Second, you need to reinforce those values through repetition, new forms of communication, training, and personal examples. Third, you should screen when hiring to identify people who have shown already that they include candor and honesty among their personal values.

Showing people that honesty is the best policy is highly effective. A Mitchell and Company survey of institutional money managers in 1999 reported that the most harmful thing executives can do to hurt their company's share price is to hide problems from investors and their fellow employees.

No Cover-Ups Allowed

You can't afford to have anyone think that they can get away with a cover-up, either by keeping things quiet or by avoiding negative consequences. Having reporting methods in place to raise red flags about the potential for covering up and being unequivocal in dealing with anyone who violates company policy concerning covering up are your best weapons in this regard.

How can you improve your ability to detect cover-ups? Your internal and external auditors and other technical experts can be very helpful to you in setting up measurement and monitoring methods to expose inconsistencies that suggest that someone may be covering up something. Have them work on the areas where you have the most safety, reputation, and financial exposure. Before putting these measurements in place, seek the advice of those who work throughout the company about how this can be done in a way to show a basic trust that people will avoid covering up. Consider the analogy that almost everyone gets a smallpox vaccination, and as a result no one in the firm has to worry about getting smallpox at work, even though no one thinks that anyone now has or is likely to get the disease.

Carefully keep an eye on those who resist your new measures. They may have something to hide or may want to hide something in the future, or their values may not match those that you are encouraging. In any of these cases, they may be a source of future problems in this area of cover-ups.

In addition, establish a system for identifying problems based on contacts with customers calling to order from you, ask questions, or complain about deficiencies as a way to keep problems out in the open so that they can't be easily hidden. Certainly, the more visible the performance of each part of the organization is, the less likely it is that a cover-up can occur.

How can you continually exhibit your enterprise's intolerance toward cover-ups? Making an example of those who violate your organization's policies in this area is critical. The higher the level of the person who is the example, the bigger the impression you'll make. You'll have to be careful to be fair. If everyone is covering up and continues to do so, you can't just fire one person and expect to make the point. In such a situation, you may want to have an amnesty policy for old cover-ups, and a new date after which everyone will be expected to be forthcoming.

Of critical importance is to give the sense that *no one* is immune from this policy, and that there is always someone willing to listen to problems. For example, in one division a junior executive watched with chagrin as his boss weaved drunkenly into the office every morning, and later weaved out to visit a local bar every afternoon after a brief nap on the couch. Everyone in that part of the company knew that the boss was an alcoholic and was making lots of expensive errors. The junior executive had tried to talk to the boss about the behavior, and was brushed off.

After much soul searching, the junior executive shared his concerns with the company's CEO, a man of well-known honor. The CEO warned the junior executive that he should not make such accusations unless he was sure. The junior executive stood his ground and was soon vindicated in the subsequent investigation. The CEO insisted that the junior executive receive a promotion and a new boss, because the CEO wanted to send the message that the junior executive had done the right thing and in the right way. The junior executive went on to enjoy a distinguished career that was always noteworthy for its ethical probity. Soon, other nonperforming alcoholics in the organization were being turned in by their subordinates as well, and the company sponsored counseling for those troubled executives to help them back to sober reality. Business performance improved.

❖ ❖ ❖

Enterprises can best avoid cover-up stalls by fostering a culture that accepts the fact that errors will be made and that they can be benefited from, but only if they are exposed sooner rather than later, and by enforcing an across-the-board policy of appropriate punishment for covering up.

10

"LET'S TAKE A CHANCE!"
THE UNDERESTIMATION STALL

The future isn't what it used to be.

—Variously ascribed

Knowing about the existence of irresistible forces, getting organized to deal with them, and seeking advantages from them are
not enough to achieve breakthrough gains and irresistible
growth. You need to understand the degree, frequency, and
volatility of these forces and decide which your business should
pursue—and to what extent. This chapter emphasizes the importance of accurately evaluating irresistible forces and your enterprise's capability for dealing with them. With that information in
hand, you can realistically choose which Irresistible forces to
pursue and which to avoid to your best advantage.

Underestimation is a stall unique to those who are adept at identifying and
seeking out advantages from irresistible forces. Before learning the irresistible
force management process (described in Part Two) that the irresistible growth
enterprise should use, you need to be aware of this potentially most dangerous
of all stalls.

Irresistible forces are not only powerful, they are usually also volatile.
This combination of power and volatility make for a very difficult management environment, even for those who pay a great deal of attention to taking full advantage of irresistible forces. Keep in mind that no matter how
good your navigation skills are, some boats are simply too insubstantial to

Hurricanes are a good example of the kind of irresistible force that can be too strong. In this picture you see the severe damage done to trees that were not flexible enough to withstand the winds. (© Raymond Gehman/CORBIS)

weather the most severe of storms. Pursuing irresistible forces that you think you can handle, but actually cannot, will often be your organization's worst possible choice because you are unwittingly courting disaster. Those who focus on irresistible forces that are less powerful *and* less volatile will have a large advantage in achieving the full benefits of being an irresistible growth enterprise.

American International Group (AIG) is one of the world's most successful insurers as measured by growth and profitability. Much of its new revenues have come from outside the United States, over a span of many decades. At a time when many saw worldwide insurance markets as limited in size and too risky, AIG realized that the potential volatility could be managed—as long as excess competition did not occur in the markets it entered.

In the United States, there are major profit cycles in property-casualty insurance that run from underwriters taking on excess risk at too-low prices at the bottom to selling with firmer prices for taking on much less risk at the top. Having a large number of tough competitors forces insurers to take on the challenge of competing in a market where prices are often too low. AIG found that in many non-U.S. markets in the past, the government regulators were quite concerned that insurers stay solvent. To encourage this result, the regulators severely restricted the number of licenses issued. Thus, excluding the inherent volatility of the local market, the competitive sources of profit cycles were much weaker than in the U.S. As a result, AIG benefited from two irresistible forces that could help it—limited competition and more rapid growth in the local economies it selected. A less careful organization could have looked at the same situation after World War II, and chosen instead to go after the fastest growing countries, without considering the likelihood of growing competition. All things being equal, the fastest growth countries would probably have the fastest rate of new competitive entrants and experience the widest swings in local economic growth. This combination could be lethal to an insurer's solvency if the forces coincided in too many countries at the same time. AIG didn't have to worry about that problem. If local regulation turned against such controlled competition, the company had plenty of warning and enough time to reduce its position. It could merely sail ahead in the relatively calmer seas of favorable regulation, enjoying the tailwinds of both forces.

In choosing irresistible forces as environmental partners, many companies err by underestimating what *could* happen. A frequent cause of this misevaluation is a too heavy reliance on *historical* patterns of fluctuation, rather than on analysis of the *potential* for future fluctuation in degree and frequency. Your choice of irresistible forces to pursue and avoid for your advantage will play an enormous role in your future success. You need to carefully match your resources to the challenges you will face. This is your most important strategic activity as an irresistible growth enterprise. In this chapter, you can read about classes of irresistible forces that can be the most dangerous and can learn ways to overcome this tendency to underestimate the potential of irresistible forces.

Stall Examples

The Shortest Route Is Not *Always the Quickest Route to the Top*

If your organization wants to get to the top of the heap, beware of a greased pole as your sole means of conveyance. From a distance, a greased pole may look like a regular pole. You need to check your assumptions about how reliable the route to the top is before you commit to climbing the pole as your only approach. Otherwise, a lot of time and resources can be lost. In the same way, many irresistible forces can look like a sure thing from a distance, but closer inspection can reveal impediments that will delay or deny your progress.

Because of interest rate volatility, financing a business primarily with debt can be like trying to reach the top of a greased pole without a crane. Property developers usually borrow almost all the money they use to create their developments. But many property developers fail to recognize the potential explosive volatility from the combination of higher interest rates and excessive debt. Many count on selling what they have developed soon after it is complete to reduce their financial risk back to normal levels. Otherwise, they will inevitably lose lots of money at some point if the development is unsuccessful. Interest costs alone will quickly turn a development that is making some money into a loser, if the developer can't refinance with equity or meet the interest payments.

Gauging interest rate trends is serious business for a developer because the lenders normally expect them to personally guarantee the loans for the development. This requirement means that having a failed large development often causes a personal and business bankruptcy for the developer. Bankruptcies are unpleasant, to say the least, and make it much harder to do the next development. Succumbing to bankruptcy is a little like getting near the top of a tall greased pole and then falling to the hard ground with no cushion or net.

What makes a situation like this even more challenging is that the best time for starting such developments is usually near when the business environment looks the worst. That's when there is little immediate need for new developments, interest rates are high, money for borrowing is scarce, and the outlook for the development business is bleak. As soon as interest rates start to decline, all of those circumstances start to improve as well. The longer and more that interest rates improve, the better the environment gets for beginning a new development. However, at some point, that advantageous environment becomes risky for making money from new developments after interest rates start to rise again. This future rise will eventually hurt the business prospects for the development and make it hard to sell or refinance the project with equity to replace the construction debt.

Many developers fail to consider the underlying potential volatility of a seemingly good environment, and often act as though the favorable tide in interest rates will not reverse itself. This belief is especially risky because those who try to forecast interest rates generally agree that it cannot be done for very long with very much accuracy. Consequently, developments that take more than a few weeks to complete and sell to someone else at a good price are always potentially running their developers very close to bankruptcy, unless they finance the development without borrowed money. If you take away the debt, the potential for obtaining a gain is greatly improved because then developers have more time to weather adverse circumstances.

Would You Like a Hula Hoop?
Can I Pay You to Take It?

The cyclic nature of trends is also evident in fads involving consumer and industrial goods and services. Usually engaged in by people who want to stand out from the crowd, fads are then reported by the popular press and quickly picked up by those who want to be "in with the 'in' crowd." For example, in the 1970s encounter groups were touted as a way to improve business communications. Executives had to sit in circles on the floor while holding hands with their peers, and then explore embarrassing personal experiences and attitudes with the group. Some people were so humiliated by the experience that they quit their jobs rather than continue with this "public therapy in the workplace" process. The fad soon ended, as a result.

Increasing popularity eventually turns the fad into the new conformity, and those who don't want to be conformists lose interest and move on to the next novelty. Eventually only the most rigorous of conformists are left with the original fad, which by then is no longer a fad, so sales quickly drop at that point.

Few enterprises can benefit from fads because their sources and timing vary so much. Take extra care when you think you may be relying extensively on faddish irresistible forces. Consider a property developer who rented her buildings to a company that was producing the latest fad toy item. When the fad passed, she soon had a bankrupt tenant and a difficult situation on her hands. Neither she nor the tenant had foreseen that the toy was going to be a fad item. She had inadvertently added fad risk to the normal risk of interest rates and excess debt.

When the Rules Change in the Middle of the Game

Many irresistible forces cause an unexpected impact because of a change in the rules of how businesses are allowed to operate. Since external rules are usually something over which you have limited influence, the rules themselves can be irresistible forces. The irresistible forces unleashed by the rules or by changing the rules can be especially volatile because the rules may constantly change. Governments, trade groups, accounting standards organizations, and testing companies are just a few of the rule-setting bodies in our society that can create or block the opportunity to make breakthrough gains.

The rule changes usually occur because someone has properly pointed out that the existing rules are causing or not preventing some result that is less than completely desirable. For example, accountants may have a rule that permits people to take income before it really should be credited. This activity can potentially harm investors who misperceive how well the organizations are doing and thus pay too much for the business results being reported.

An example occurred involving residential property developers around 1970. Prior to that time accounting rules allowed the developers to take the entire profit from the sale of undeveloped land whenever the purchaser made the deal, even if the mortgagor was the developer. In reality, most of these purchasers eventually just walked away from their mortgages, and the profits from a completed sale at full price were never earned. Then the accounting standards were changed to prohibit taking the profits until the developer-held mortgages were paid. Stocks of some of this sort of residential property developer plunged by over 90 percent in a short period of time, devastating their shareholders and the prospects for these companies to raise equity to continue and expand their operations. Yet the only change that occurred was to the accounting rules. The economic performance of the units was going to be the same until the next time the developer needed equity capital. Changing the rules essentially wiped out a whole sector of the industry for undeveloped residential land.

Many organizations that depend on one particular set of rules for their rapid success are inclined to forget this dependence and thus are blindsided when the rules change. Don't be one of them.

But I Was Counting on You!

It's not just the overt rules that can get you. You also have to beware of the assumed rules that may have governed organizational practices in an industry for many years. In the software business, it has been common practice to provide advance notice of new standards and software to all those who need it. In the antitrust lawsuit brought by the U.S. Justice Department against Microsoft in 1998 was an allegation that Microsoft had not followed that practice in connection with Netscape and one of the new versions of Windows. The allegation was that Microsoft was trying to use the information as a bargaining chip to get large advantages from Netscape. Whatever the truth of the matter, Netscape, seemingly quite surprised that Microsoft hadn't followed the "rule," clearly felt that it had suffered significant economic harm because it experienced delayed access to the new Microsoft standard.

I Didn't Think the Other End of the Board Would Hit Me in the Face When I Stepped on It

Irresistible forces can also have not-so-obvious connections to other causes, including other irresistible forces, that can make their future direction and volatility hard to assess. Not seeing these connections and underestimating the volatility can produce negative consequences with surprising speed and leave companies totally devastated.

The first practical portable personal computer was built by Osborne. Although very large and heavy by today's standards, it met with immediate acceptance, and the company's sales boomed. Knowing that demand for an improved portable computer would increase, Osborne developed a second-generation product that was to be more powerful, lighter, and easier to use. Investors and customers were extraordinarily excited about this prospect. However, Osborne had miscalculated and made an error from which it could not recover. After announcing the new product, it was delayed beyond the company's expectations. In anticipation of the new model, orders all but disappeared for the existing model, and the company didn't have the financial resources to stay in business until the new model was ready. Osborne perished because it wasn't really prepared to deal with the demand stimulated by the irresistible force of desire for better and less expensive portable computing.

Always consider the potential unintended consequences of your actions as well as the positive relationships you have to irresistible forces. (We explore this subject in depth in Part Two, especially in chapters 12, 13, and 14.)

Stall Erasers
Interesting Developments
Having adapted to using irresistible forces to aid your progress, you must also prepare yourself for the likelihood that the same irresistible forces will shift in new and unpredictable ways and degrees at unforeseen times. One way to be prepared is simply to operate as though much greater and more frequent volatility will occur.

Returning to the property development example discussed earlier in this chapter, some developers use a variable risk management strategy to grow their businesses. As interest rates drop, they use less and less debt leverage. At some point, they stop developing, even though the near-term environment for starting new developments looks very good. At such times, they begin to take parcels of land they have assembled and gotten through zoning commissions and sell the parcels to other developers who will pay top dollar in their rush to expand. Thus, by the time the interest rate cycle turns toward higher rates, those developers are sitting on large amounts of cash and no debt. To keep their operations busy, such developers often have a management company that rents and maintains properties for owners.

Then as interest rates rise and business conditions worsen, they gradually look for places to begin assembling low-cost parcels of land from distressed sellers (often other developers). This strategy allows the savvy developers to buy low and sell high while keeping their risk much lower during all phases of the interest rate cycle. Handled conservatively enough, this strategy can use the volatility as well as the level of interest rates to allow the developer to always make lots of money and always have appropriately limited risk. The large residential builders in the United States often use this strategy very successfully.

The wise developer further hedges the interest rate and business cycle risk by developing properties on a smaller scale that allows the developer to survive an occasional stumble, while focusing on projects with the least risk of not being able to be sold quickly. Others will reduce the sale risk by creating partially-captive operations financed by partners who will buy most of the properties as soon as they are complete. Some developers have used publicly traded real estate investment trusts (REITs) in this way. Done properly, these programs can become 2,000 percent solutions.

Get into the Right Doll House

Enterprises often need to develop new products or services to tie their futures most firmly and effectively to the irresistible forces of their choice. Where several irresistible forces are available, wise organizations will pick those that have the greatest likelihood of stability and continuation, as well as good growth trends. Demographics can provide just such an optimal irresistible force.

For example, consider the demographic trend of the low birth rate in developed countries since 1970 (and even in some developing countries, such as China where having only one child is a governmental policy), which means that the number of one-child households is increasing. Parents tend to spoil the only child, which means that expenditures for each child's toys and games will probably grow. Those who provide better quality, more expensive choices (such as American Girl dolls) will probably prosper at the expense of those who produce mass-market products that succeeded in the multiple-child family (like Mattel's Barbie dolls). No wonder Mattel acquired the company that makes American Girl dolls in the late 1990s. Because demographic trends are widely reported, you'll have several years of notice if the number of multiple-child families starts to increase in developed countries. All you need to do is monitor the trend and be prepared to act when you notice a change. Unless you are in the diaper business (or some other industry that serves newborns and their parents), the inevitable delay between births and the impact on your products or services will give you the time to make highly optimized adjustments.

Make It Snappy!

Rapidly evolving customer needs and new technologies have meant that many products, services, and methods of producing goods and services have become obsolete. When obsolescence looms, businesses are most commonly faced with a difficult choice: Destroy what they have on hand by using a new skunk works operation, or acquire nimble competitors and hope to adjust. How nice it would be to create more choices for the most volatile circumstances!

In the late 1990s a new organizational model was developed that is well suited for operating with the most volatile irresistible forces: Establish a business that needs little capital and is very flexible in providing goods and services. Amazon.com (the Internet retailer) was an early example of this kind of business. The company grew from nothing to a major factor in the retail book marketplace because it required little investment (other than funding start-up losses) to operate its business. Its success gave the company an equity market capitalization (in early 2000) that was larger than the rest of the retail book publishing and retailing industry combined. Going forward, the company had the potential to grow faster in book retailing for a time because it didn't have to build retail stores, could carry less inventory than a store-based chain needed to, and was supported by equity investors more interested in long-term growth than near-term profits.

In the manufacturing sector, making products to order is another enterprise alternative that also provides capital management advantages. In these circumstances, the company making a product may only order the components it needs after actually receiving the order for its product and having been paid by the customer. In such a business involving lean manufacturing, the producer may have negative working capital (like a supermarket) rather than 60 to 90 days of outstanding receivables and another 60 to 90 days of inventory. A key advantage of this approach is that the company does not have to worry as much about having a lot of obsolete product should the irresistible forces shift against it. However, it does have to be sure that its designs are closely tracking the evolving customer preferences. By selling directly to even small customers in many cases, these suppliers will also be able to reduce their risk of missing important shifts in market trends driven by irresistible forces. Dell Computer was an important innovator of this approach in the computer industry.

Stallbusting

In this part of the chapter we provide questions for you to ask yourself and your enterprise's colleagues in order to better comprehend the potential volatility in irresistible forces affecting you. While no business can be immune from the potentially negative impact of irresistible forces, you can be better prepared to deal with the impact than are other companies that are like yours. Thus you'll have a compelling competitive advantage that will often turn out to be decisive in your marketplace.

Insulate Your Enterprise from the Cold Headwinds of Changed Irresistible Forces

Examples in this chapter show how some businesses wrongly consider irresistible forces to be more stable than they are. The irresistible growth enterprise should assume, instead, that irresistible forces will always change, sometimes more suddenly and unexpectedly than ever before. The company that operates from this assumption will be well positioned to use the volatility brought about by irresistible forces such as globalization, interlinked economies, shifting financial markets, and changing consumption patterns to be even more successful.

How can you use future volatility in irresistible forces to allow your enterprise to have less risk and grow more rapidly than when irresistible forces are stable? In answering this question, you are wise to consider directions that will be rewarding both if the irresistible forces are more volatile and if they are not. Scenario planning for both options will often allow irresistible growth enterprises to locate superior strategies, ways of operating, and safety measures that are good for the enterprise, regardless of what happens next. That is the sort of solution you should seek out.

The phrasing of this question is designed to focus your attention on the unthinkable, which will help you to identify new choices that you have not yet considered. One such possible solution could be to target improving ways to serve both the needs of customers whose requirements will be most stable as well as those whose requirements will vary greatly if circumstances change. You can then smoothly shift the amount of attention paid to each market based on what actually happens. To achieve this positioning might mean having both "booming economy products" and "recessionary products" under development at the same time. This approach can even help you prosper in mixed markets where some customers are experiencing good times while others are not.

How can you streamline your operations to make them more flexible for more rapid and effective adaptation to changes in irresistible forces and to new irresistible forces? As presented in the Stall Erasers section, you can start your thinking with some of the ideas already discussed including rapid provision of custom products and services; getting goods from suppliers on a just-in-time basis; getting paid in advance by customers; and using electronic commerce. (Chapters 13 through 16 can be used to further stimulate your thinking in this area.) You should be sure to consider large changes, far beyond what anyone else has done before. You already live in an age in which the large, inflexible organization is an endangered species. In the next few years, more and more of them will become extinct.

According to Joan Magretta in "The Power of Virtual Integration" (*Harvard Business Review* March-April 1998, pages 77–84), which is an interview with Michael Dell, Dell Computer has used an innovation in enterprise design that has served it well in this regard. As the company grows, it subdivides its customers into narrower and narrower categories and subcategories, and reassigns management quite frequently so each executive and manager can focus on the needs of one ever-narrower sliver of the customer universe. Dell said, "If you just lump diverse customers together, you can be sure that some of them will come last on some manager's list, and he may never get around to solving their problems."

Dell expanded on this point in his address to the Comerica Economic Forum in Dallas on September 10, 1998: "We've been pretty aggressive in our company about surrounding ourselves with the best talent we can find and structuring our business for success, even to the point of dividing up peoples' jobs. This has now become part of our company culture. . . . Six months later, because of growth, their job is the same size it was before, and they say, 'Please cut my job in half, I've got too much!'" Rather than constantly stretching people beyond what they can handle, this policy of dividing jobs in half with growth keeps people operating at their optimum effectiveness. Also, it makes it much easier to attract and retain outstanding new people by offering them many opportunities for personal growth and promotion, with less risk of excess hours and burnout than in traditional organizations.

Conservative Financing Is the Right Foundation

Borrowing money enhances risk, and voluntarily taking on greater risk that is avoidable will normally be a bad idea when dealing with irresistible forces. If you succeed in capturing the potential momentum of the irresistible force, you'll never be able to retire the debt; you'll simply be refinancing and increasing it. That position leaves you exposed to credit crunches, interest rate volatility, and times of capital shortages. In case you think that's something you needn't worry about, consider the circumstances of September 1998 when the savings rate of U.S. consumers turned negative for the first time since the Great Depression of the 1930s. If consumers in the largest economy in the world can't save much money from their incomes during an economic expansion, where will the funds come from for borrowing in the future as worldwide growth increases? This point certainly suggests that we could be entering an era of scarce and increasingly expensive debt. In the aftermath of Russia's default on its bonds in August 1998, many low-rated borrowers found themselves temporarily unable to get money anywhere. Some high-risk consumer lenders went out of business because no one would buy their debt at reasonable prices. The same thing happened during the clean-up of the S & L debacle described earlier. That circumstance may occur more frequently in the future.

Also, inflation all but disappeared in the United States during the 1990s except in the form of home and securities' prices. Since a change in the investing mood could quickly burst inflated stock prices, the careful organization would naturally see the early years of the twenty-first century as a good time to have little debt *and* lots of cash immediately available. If prices continue to deflate in many markets from commodities to high technology, cash holdings will expand in purchasing power. Debt will be ruinous unless interest rates also turn negative (as actually did occur with Japanese government debt during 1998).

How can you change the way you finance your operations so that you'll be less affected by adverse shifts in the availability and cost of capital for enterprises like yours? Besides having low costs, little debt, lots of cash, and being prepared to fund unexpected needs, you should develop helpful new sources of capital that will be captive to you. For example, if your suppliers gain more profits from what they supply you than you do in using their goods, you may be able to arrange to pay them more slowly than your customers pay you so that you have no net investment in these supplies.

Of critical significance is managing the organization's cost of equity. An enterprise's capital management will be a key skill throughout the twenty-first century as new forms of economic growth replace the old ones based on traditional manufacturing and established forms of service. This aspect is extremely important for publicly held companies because of the power that public stock gives to acquire assets at a bargain price, motivate and attract employees, encourage customers, and reduce costs.*

---

*For more details on the benefits of managing the cost of equity, see "Become a Master of Capital Management" by Donald W. Mitchell (*Directors & Boards,* Summer 1998, pages 41–45).

How can you expand your organization with less capital and more flexible investments? Companies that require less capital will be able to grow faster than those that need more will. For example, eBay quickly established a large and profitable position in Internet auctions by bringing together millions of potential buyers and sellers, while not needing to take an ownership position in the goods being auctioned or providing a physical location for inspection and sale of the goods. Those Internet sites retailing only their own products usually are not nearly as profitable nor able to grow as fast as eBay and those following similar models.

Travel the Road Less Threatened

You can overcome the effects of the underestimation stall by identifying and using the irresistible forces that are less threatening to your enterprise. For example, carefully analyzing your target customers and considering the way you serve them will enable you to sidestep certain irresistible forces in favor of others.

Which irresistible forces that you face now could you avoid if you changed your business model? Note that this question is not designed to assume that you want to avoid these irresistible forces. It is designed to sensitize you to the risks that your current business model provides so that you can later decide which forces you want to be subject to and which ones you do not. Creativity researchers have discovered that you'll do a better job of identifying alternative directions if you withhold your judgment concerning the alternatives until after you've identified all the possible choices you can. You'll find it most helpful if you begin by looking at extremes. For example, if you now do business only on the Internet, what would be your changed exposure to irresistible forces if you never did business on the Internet? You can do the same for considering different target customers and ways to provide them with goods and services. You get the idea.

Which of the irresistible forces you can avoid contain risks worth eliminating? Many companies believe that their stock-price multiples are held down by business volatility. But a few routinely sell stock near peaks in their multiples and buy back near multiple lows, thus reducing cost of capital while expanding its availability. These companies usually boast a stock-price growth advantage compared to competitors. They turned a potential risk into a competitive advantage.

However, if your enterprise would have a hard time coping with fad business conditions (and an irresistible force will make part of what your company does subject to fad trends in the future), working under those conditions might be something to consider avoiding. Conversely, if everything you do is about to become subject to fads, you may have no choice but to develop the skill to prosper in that type of environment. A little controlled experience with fads might strengthen your enterprise in that case, as happened with the companies who found added wealth in their stock-price multiple volatility.

Which irresistible forces give you the best combination of competitive insulation, manageable risk, and opportunities for breakthrough gains? Your answer to this question will be improved by involving as many people as possible from different types of work and psychological perspectives in your company. For example, if you have only financial people work on answering the question, they may eliminate irresistible forces that marketing and operations people see as desirable. One person's daunting irresistible force is another person's tiny hurdle.

❖ ❖ ❖

Enterprises can best avoid the underestimation stall by thoroughly understanding the need to choose their battles, that is, to pursue the use of only those irresistible forces appropriately matched to their organization's capabilities and resources.

❖ ❖ ❖

In Part Two you can test all of the ideas and conclusions you've come up with so far by learning about a management process for leading your enterprise into the best positions to be able to take advantage of irresistible forces. Don't be surprised if you change your mind about some things. Your practice in answering the questions posed in Part One, however, will be beneficial in preparing you for the powerful perspectives you will develop in Part Two as you move beyond being stalled into the positive habits of the irresistible growth enterprise.

Practice Effectiveness Scale

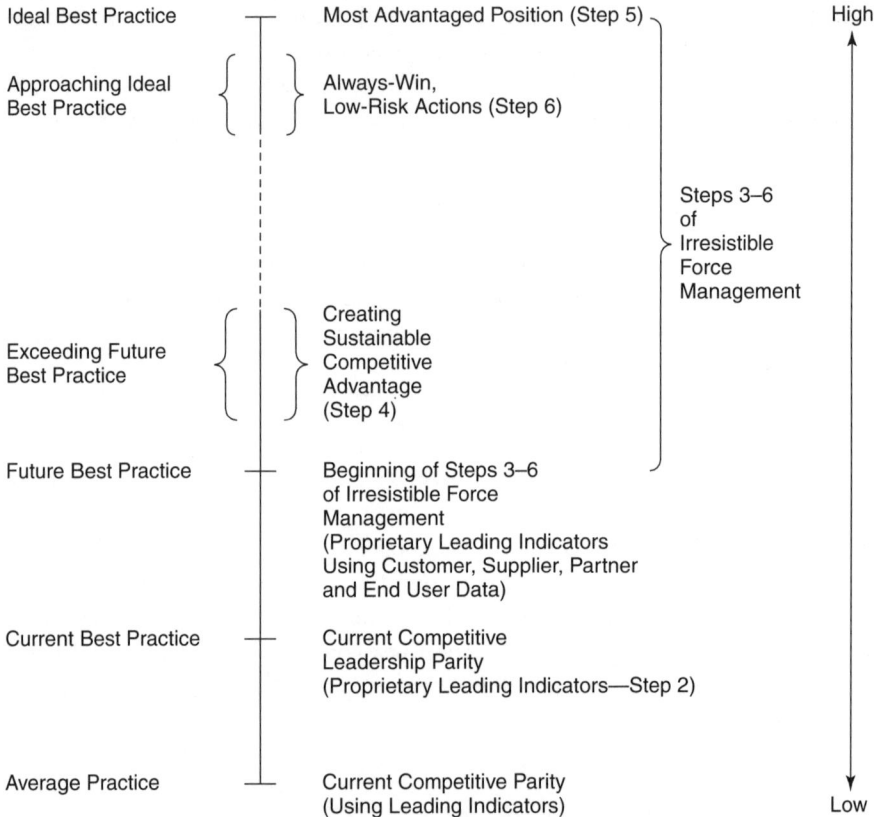

Ideal Best Practice	Most Advantaged Position (Step 5)	High
Approaching Ideal Best Practice	Always-Win, Low-Risk Actions (Step 6)	
		Steps 3–6 of Irresistible Force Management
Exceeding Future Best Practice	Creating Sustainable Competitive Advantage (Step 4)	
Future Best Practice	Beginning of Steps 3–6 of Irresistible Force Management (Proprietary Leading Indicators Using Customer, Supplier, Partner and End User Data)	
Current Best Practice	Current Competitive Leadership Parity (Proprietary Leading Indicators—Step 2)	
Average Practice	Current Competitive Parity (Using Leading Indicators)	Low

Part Two includes a number of terms and business concepts that may be new to you. Referring back to this exhibit should help you keep them in perspective. The focus of Part Two is improving on the best of what enterprises do to create, locate, identify, anticipate, and adapt to irresistible forces.

PART TWO

IRRESISTIBLE FORCE MANAGEMENT

An optimist is someone who thinks the future is uncertain.

—Unknown

To become an irresistible growth enterprise, it isn't enough to simply stop fighting irresistible forces. You must capture the benefit of those forces by being constantly aligned with them. To create the ideal alignment, the bad habits, or stalls, explored in Part One need not only to be eliminated, but also to be replaced with a new set of better habits. In this part we present an eight-step process for acquiring these habits. It is a process that should be continuously repeated. Each time you use the process, you will develop and reinforce these new habits for capturing momentum from irresistible forces, the source for achieving breakthrough gains.

The following steps can help you to identify what the irresistible forces are, track their direction and strength, locate the best ways to adapt to them, in some cases create new ones, and make continuous changes in your company's directions in order to become an irresistible growth enterprise:

- Step One is to recognize how measurements can help your company identify and understand more about irresistible forces (chapter 11).

- Step Two is to use your own leading indicators to anticipate shifts in irresistible forces (chapter 12).

- Step Three is how to identify the future best practices for locating, anticipating, and adapting to changes (multidimensional management) in irresistible forces (chapter 13).

- Step Four is to find ways to extend your vision to identify best practices beyond anyone else in the future (chapter 14).

- Step Five is to identify the ideal best practices for the multidimensional management of irresistible forces (chapter 15).

- Step Six is to determine how to operate close to the ideal best practices for locating, anticipating, and adapting to your irresistible forces (chapter 16).

- Step Seven is to learn how to enhance your people's abilities to achieve the benefits of irresistible force management for your enterprise (chapter 17).

- Step Eight is to repeat steps one through seven for improved effectiveness in using the irresistible force management process (chapter 18).

We believe that this irresistible force management process is the key competency that will distinguish the most successful enterprises in the twenty-first century because it will help you create the flexibility needed to achieve the most benefit from ever-more volatile irresistible forces.

This book's fundamental point is that no matter how successful you and your operation have been, you are performing well below your potential. If your company is typical, you're getting full benefit from irresistible forces (such as demographics, customer preferences, and business conditions) only a small percentage of the time. Most of the rest of the time you're struggling to fight off the negative effects of irresistible forces acting as headwinds, rather than changing your orientation to use the forces as tailwinds in your favor. And it is rigidity that keeps you struggling, for inflexibility is the primary reason for the frequent, large gap between an enterprise's potential and achievement. Here are the most significant reasons why:

At best, rigidity keeps you firmly focused on your organization's goals while denying you the majority of the most effective tactics to achieve those goals. If your company isn't increasingly relying on irresistible forces to accomplish goals, you are going to fall geometrically behind companies that do because the power and variability of these irresistible forces are rapidly increasing. Rigidity keeps you from seeing and acting on your company's best opportunities. When you reach your goal by one of the longest routes possible, you'll have wasted lots of time and resources that could have been used to get there much sooner with less effort.

At worst, rigidity can put your existence into doubt, like an oak tree suddenly facing a hurricane. Companies that have done little to adapt to irresistible forces can quickly disappear from sight. Retailing provides this kind of example on a regular basis, as customer needs and preferences and supplier economics shift in ways that make an existing retailing business model obsolete. When was the last time you remember going into a Woolworth's or an S.S. Kresge store?

To have the most advantageous strategic position, you must act first to better align your enterprise with the most important shifting irresistible forces. This position allows your company to capture more benefits sooner, use fewer resources to get those benefits, and avoid costly problems. Each time you execute this superior adaptation, you'll create substantial advantages over the other organizations that either miss the shift in irresistible forces or that belatedly follow you in adapting to those shifts. Making irresistible force management a strategic platform for your enterprise will reward you with irresistible growth.

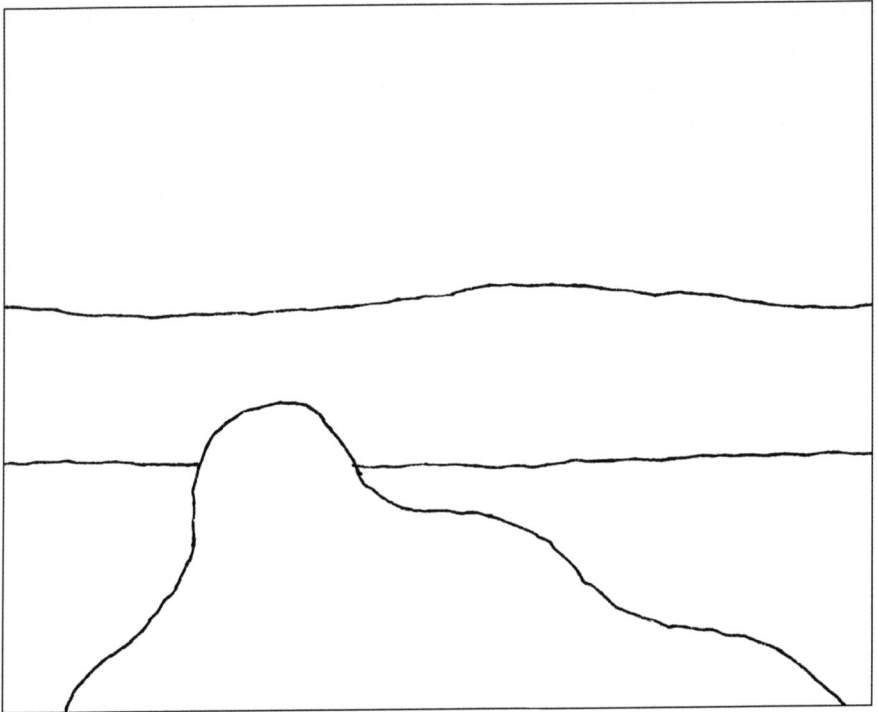

Using measurements to identify and understand more about irresistible forces will expand your horizons for perceiving opportunities for your irresistible growth enterprise.

11

KEEP THE TAPE MEASURE HANDY

STEP ONE: RECOGNIZE HOW MEASUREMENTS CAN HELP YOUR COMPANY IDENTIFY AND UNDERSTAND MORE ABOUT IRRESISTIBLE FORCES

Experience teaches you to recognize a mistake when you've made it again.

—Unknown

Many irresistible forces go totally unnoticed by the organizations they affect. This chapter shows you the value of continuously measuring all important aspects of an enterprise's environment in order to detect, quantify, and track those forces. When it comes to irresistible force management, only constant assessment of the factors that can determine your success or failure will keep you current and on track.

Lights, Camera, Action!
Recognizing the Importance of Measurements

In the movie *The Truman Show,* Jim Carrey stars as a character who lives his whole life from birth on a television set that he believes is the real world. By carefully observing that certain circumstances occur in too-predictable patterns, he eventually realizes that he is on camera. If it hadn't been for noticing the strange occurrences around him, the young man would have missed the most irresistible force in his life, the will of the director. Using his newly found knowledge, he decides to leave the set and join the rest of the world.

So it is with irresistible forces in your world. Success in dealing with them must begin with perceiving them. Since human beings normally pay little conscious attention to 98 percent of what's going on around them, it's not surprising that executives miss important shifts in irresistible forces. Measurements are powerful tools for drawing attention to significant changes. By assuming that virtually anything can change and placing measures on your enterprise's environment to monitor that assumption, a business can much improve its potential for grasping shifts in irresistible forces.

From this point onward, please think of any reference to "forces" as meaning "irresistible forces." In that way, we can make the remainder of the book's content a faster read for you.

Set Sail: Let the Wind Blowing from Any Direction Speed Your Journey

Enterprises that detect the arrival and departure of irresistible forces can more easily adapt to using those forces to their advantage. For sailors, the wind is a key irresistible force. Because the winds are often light in Newport, Rhode Island, anyone who had the right sails in place and positioned properly when the breezes shifted gained a large advantage during the America's Cup trials there. Historically, canny captains scanned the clouds and the waves for any clue about what the wind was going to do. However, in one of the last America's Cup events in Newport, the approach to anticipating the wind was taken to the ultimate. A team set up a weather station adjacent to the course to measure and forecast the shifts in the breeze. That information could be conveyed to the captain five to six minutes before the shifts occurred. One year the information proved decisive. For the next America's Cup trial in Newport a few years later, every competitor used a weather station.

Let's Shop until the Trend Drops

Businesses are finding that real-time feedback can be extremely valuable to their success. Consider mail-order shopping. Let's say you bought something from a catalog a few years ago and nothing similar since. When the catalog seller thinks it may be time for you to replace this item, you may be prompted to do so the next time you call to place an order. If you then say you're interested in buying the same item again, the catalog representative can refer to your computer record and describe what you bought before, ask how it suited you, and tell you about current items that might be acceptable replacements.

If you make any casual comments while placing your order, such as your color preference or the size of your family, those bits of information can be logged into the computer record. Then other related purchasing suggestions could be made. You may be asked if any of your family members has a special occasion coming up for which you'll need a gift. More probing questions will elicit what that person likes and what kind of gifts you like to give. If you then do buy a gift, chances are you would be reminded to buy that person an appropriate gift at the same time next year for that same special occasion.

If an overview of customer interactions shows the mail-order company that a new trend is developing, such as changes in customer tastes, the firm can quickly shift its purchasing to emphasize those items that will be in more demand by consumers and reduce the acquisition of items that will be in less demand. By identifying which items are looked at as well as which are actually purchased, orders placed over the Internet can give even more information to the mail-order provider.

Clearly, measurements can help you anticipate conditions so you can correctly outfit and position your enterprise to get the most benefit from those circumstances.

Identifying Irresistible Forces by Taking the Measure of Your Environment

When you visit your primary care physician, someone takes a number of vital measurements including your height, weight, temperature, and blood pressure. From this information as well as the results of any testing that was done prior to your visit, your physician draws a baseline for comparing your current state of health with your past, how you compare to others in your peer group, and what would be desirable for you in the future.

Similarly, a business needs to sample its history, current situation, and desired future along a number of dimensions. These perspectives include understanding what is happening with customers, employees, suppliers, those who help distribute the products or services, partners, investors, regulators and the communities in which you operate. Just as a fever can alert a physician that an infection may be present, shifts in trends affecting these stakeholders can likewise alert your business to the presence of important irresistible forces.

Take Me to Your Users

The best uses for many products are often revealed only after the products have been tried out in different ways by customers. For example, consumers discovered that Arm & Hammer baking soda makes a good deodorizer in the refrigerator. Church & Dwight capitalized on this application through advertising and greatly improved sales of its product. Many intended uses also turn out to be unimportant. Consider that relatively few sports utility vehicle owners regularly drive their SUVs on unpaved surfaces. Optimizing that feature, then, would probably add costs while not improving sales very much. The successful and unsuccessful experiences of those who use your products or services constitute forces that you ignore at your peril.

In many businesses that sell through a distribution channel, no one has direct contact with those who actually use the products. Observing what customers do with a product can be a real eye-opener. Jell-O's marketing and test kitchen personnel spent some time in kitchens watching parents and their children making Jell-O. Many parents mixed up highly concentrated Jell-O and then used cookie cutters to create shapes their children could play with as well as eat. This observation led to the famous Jell-O Jiggler program that improved Jell-O sales.

The first semimoist dog food, Gaines Burgers, was produced in the shape of hamburger patties. The competition quickly noted that users typically broke up the patties into bite-sized pieces, especially for smaller dogs. The competition then launched a semimoist dog food that resembled uncooked ground beef and was packed loosely so that the dog owner could simply open the pack and pour out the contents. No more messy handling! Users switched in droves to the more convenient form of the product, which, incidentally, was also less expensive to produce than the patties were.

Let's move on to the car lot. Buying a car has always been like a wrestling match. The buyer is pitted against the salesperson who, naturally, wants to sell at the highest possible price. The buyer often fails to negotiate on price, or does so poorly. But an irresistible force is building up. Rather than feel like helpless victims in a macho bargaining process, many people simply want to pick out a car and be sure that they get a fair price. Voila! Saturn comes along and offers that opportunity to all, and soon Saturn dealers are outselling Chevrolet dealers in similar locations by more than five to one (despite having a limited model range).

Car buying services have sprung up on-line. You indicate what kind of car you want to buy, and dealers who have or can get that car for you in your area bid for your business. With no negotiating involved, you simply pick the lowest bid. Use of these automated services has exploded. Now that's a 2,000 percent solution for car buyers and the Internet intermediary!

They are responding to the same irresistible force that is helping the Saturn dealers: the purchaser's desire for no-stress car buying at a fair price. This irresistible force in the car business has probably been around for quite awhile, but no one noticed the opportunity it held until recently. Talking to customers just after they bought their cars and thinking about what they said would have turned up this opportunity long before now.

Go to the consumers and distributors directly and pay attention to what they have to tell you as a start to recognizing the irresistible forces in your industry.

Supply and Demand

Suppliers are an often-ignored source of information about irresistible forces. Your firm's suppliers know a lot about what you're doing wrong, but may seldom tell you. Why? Because usually no one in your organization wants to listen. Supplies are commonly bought against detailed specifications through purchasing agents. Such purchasing agents usually don't have the knowledge or the authority to change the specifications to something more appropriate. Their job simply is to get the specified product, at the right time, and at the lowest price from reliable suppliers. And those who designed the product that requires the supplier's component are normally as happy as the proverbial clam, confident in their belief that the product's design couldn't possibly be improved. From the designers' point of view, for a supplier to suggest a change is tantamount to criticism or even an attack on their competence.

Why do suppliers often have a superior view of what you need? Whatever else is going on, the suppliers usually know more about the alternatives than you do. For one thing, they may be supplying several companies in the industry, and know that the component purchased by your competition works a lot better and is cheaper. For another, suppliers know a lot about the trade-offs in cost and performance that go into one specification versus another. The supplier may be in a better position to judge trade-offs than you since your purchasing agent wants the lowest possible component price. The supplier may sometimes be able to give you a more expensive component that will work better and allow you to use less expensive other components or have lower assembly costs for other parts of your product. As a result, the cost of the entire product is greatly reduced.

You can turn the situation around and encourage information sharing with your suppliers by offering incentives, often called "gain sharing." Let suppliers know that if they'll share improvement ideas with you, you'll reward them with a share of the benefit you receive as well as make their position as your supplier more secure. You'll probably also have to encourage your own people to listen by having them share the profits resulting from the cost savings.

Nobody Does It Better

Recognize that your competitors' actions, both effective and ineffective, can be one of your biggest sources of irresistible force information and help give you the insight to develop a competitive edge. Take Kentucky Fried Chicken (KFC) and Church's Fried Chicken. In the 1970s, KFC's largest competitor was comparatively quite small, and so would have been easy to ignore. But Church's had several interesting characteristics: The company had a higher profit margin (profits divided by sales), charged lower prices, enjoyed higher sales per restaurant, and provided customers with larger portions than did KFC. Many of KFC's successful profit improvement programs in the 1970s had their beginnings in the competitive benchmarking studies of Church's that revealed the sources of those advantages.

Having a methodical competitor that always operates the same way makes it easier to analyze its actions and take advantage of what it demonstrates about existing irresistible forces. Procter & Gamble (P&G) once had a highly predictable pattern. P&G's competitors from different categories occasionally exchanged notes on what had worked to derail P&G's marketing programs. More and more companies learned that you could tell when P&G was about to enter a geographically limited test market with a new product. If the market test didn't pay off according to P&G's plan, its brand managers would retire for more study (for up to two years) before making another move. If the competitor hit that test market with everything it had, there was a good chance to deter P&G for a while. The relatively high cost of defending the test market was much less than the cost of defending against a wide-scale marketing expansion, so it was well worth taking the chance. Eventually P&G changed the way it test-markets products to avoid this vulnerability.

Until Death Do Us Part

Partners are also an important source of information about the identity and direction of irresistible forces. A partner may do more business than your company does in another part of the world where the forces come into play sooner. For instance, the best way to see the future of outsourced overseas software development at the start of the twenty-first century is to visit India, where this activity has become a major industry supplying companies around the world.

Global operations increasingly involve multiple partnerships to accomplish specific purposes. The forces that make such partnerships necessary are the rapid development of an interlinked world economy, the formation of rival alliances using partnership forms of competition, and the need for skills or resources that exceed the capabilities of any one organization. Even Coca-Cola, the global soft-drink powerhouse, is heavily dependent on its partnerships with local bottlers, in which the Atlanta giant often has significant investments. Partners also provide useful perspectives into the complexities of operating globally by exposing you to how local irresistible forces differ. The partners reflect and respond to the local cultures and values within the framework of a worldwide organization.

Working with partners also exposes your business to more irresistible forces, such as the needs for a common purpose, coordination, and effective communication. A partnership-driven enterprise is much harder to make work than any other form of organization because any one partner can scuttle the foundations of success. If a partner loses interest, or priorities change in his or her business, the partnership may soon dissolve due to a lack of commitment or change of direction. Operating a partnership is more like running an organization primarily staffed with volunteers, like Habitat for Humanity, than an ordinary business. You have to keep maintaining everyone's attention and support in order to succeed. Some say that the partnership organizational form is itself an irresistible force that every enterprise needs to master in order to prosper.

Taxachusetts

Governments have the ability to set and change the rules by which your company operates. Consequently, most managers do monitor for shifts in these mandates. You will need to be judicious, though, in preparing to react to changes that the news media might suggest are forthcoming. Government action doesn't always match up with such reports.

For example, in the 1970s it was widely expected that Senator Edward Kennedy of Massachusetts (the nickname, "Taxachusetts," stems from the unusually high tax burdens imposed on the Commonwealth's citizenry) would be able to push through national legislation establishing government-run national health care. Of course, such legislation hasn't been passed yet; but the likelihood of its occurrence back then was considered by many to be so strong that dozens of major companies dropped out of the health insurance industry at the time. The decline in competition due to the threat of the legislation became an irresistible force in favor of those who remained in the business. The winners in circumstances like this will be the enterprises that measure the impact of possible, as well as actual, changes in laws and regulations. Those who recognize that the subjective perceptions of future occurrences can strongly influence the holders of those perceptions can certainly gain a competitive edge.

Deregulation at the national level in the United States has provided a similar fair wind for those who were nimble in aligning themselves to take advantage of new opportunities. Deregulation of broadcasting allowed broadcasting companies to become much larger and more profitable, and opened up improved ways of serving customers, as has been shown by clear channel communications. Deregulation in the airline industry has made it easier for new companies to start up and, in the telephone industry, has made possible the success of newer long-distance carriers like WorldCom.

The privatization trend in Europe has been a similarly important irresistible force. As long as many firms were state-owned enterprises, political considerations (such as maintaining employment and keeping prices low) dominated decision making. When the public took on ownership directly through purchasing shares, these organizations began to act more freely like traditional for-profit enterprises.

Good Neighbors

Every business has some level of contact with the communities in which it operates or where its employees live. In some cases the enterprise has a large impact on its local communities through the spending that the firm and its employees do locally, through volunteer activities to support local well-being, and sometimes through its own impact on the cleanliness of air and water near factories.

Community relations can be a powerful force for or against an enterprise. For example, in California's many congested cities there is often a tendency to legislate and set regulations that make growing a local business slow and costly. As a result, many of California's fastest growing businesses do much of their expansion outside the state, even when they plan to remain in the United States.

Interestingly, a less prohibitive stance concerning environmental regulation is gaining popularity in the United States. Citing local relevance neighbors affected by discharges of pollutants often favor solutions that are more flexible than those pushed by government legislators and regulators. This irresistible force has changed the way that pollution problems are solved. Typically, all affected parties now meet to share information and to find a solution with which everyone is comfortable. Where enterprises have developed trust with their neighbors, the resulting savings in avoiding federal regulation can be worth tens of millions of dollars while creating happier neighbors. Chemical companies have been particularly successful with this approach.

Neighbors can play a role in other ways. If the local community attracts and retains outstanding people, your enterprise's ability to employ a skilled labor force is enhanced. You'll be able to choose from people who already live in the community and to attract others interested in moving to that community. Some residential communities are considered so desirable that people will work for less money just to be able to live there. This attractiveness can be an irresistible force in your favor.

Researchers like Rosabeth Moss Kanter (in *World Class*, Simon and Schuster, 1995) have pointed out that the most successful companies and suppliers in an industry congregate in geographic clusters. The more similar companies that move into such clusters, and the more competition there is, the more successful the companies will be. A 2,000 percent solution for you is to determine if you are making the most out of having your enterprise operate in the most competitive and effective geographic clusters.

Stallbusting

Measurements can be used to assess virtually anything in your environment to get information about irresistible forces. Once you recognize the importance of measurements, you can begin to take specific actions to avert stalls and initiate new thinking habits for irresistible force management. This section can help you learn what areas you should have measurements in, how to start measuring, and what to do with what you learn. You can then build on this experience in chapter 12 to create even more focused and beneficial measurements.

Compile an Irresistible Force Inventory

Irresistible forces are easily dismissed or ignored, so you need to make a conscious effort to focus on and track them. Your starting point should be an irresistible force inventory. Irresistible forces are like the wind, constantly shifting in direction and intensity. The inventory can also help you by providing a baseline against which you can measure the force and its changes in the future.

What irresistible forces are affecting your company and its stakeholders now? Answer this question by making a list. Using a computer will make it easy for you to add notes to your list in the future. Consider the question from the point of view of those who use your products or services, your customers, distributors, partners, employees, suppliers, competitors, governments, and the communities in which you serve and operate. Add another dimension by reflecting about those times when your enterprise was unusually successful or had disappointments. Were there irresistible forces at play on those occasions? What were they?

What do you know about these irresistible forces? You should pay special attention to identifying what you believe are the causes of these irresistible forces. If your customers and those who use your product or service want more convenience and quality, inquire further to ask about the underlying motivation. Maybe deadline pressures require that your products and services do more for them in less time. Again, what is driving these pressures? Always look beyond immediate causes to determine if there are other forces that you can turn to your advantage.

It will also be helpful for you to note when the irresistible force began, how strong the force is now, whether the force seems to be getting stronger or weaker, and how the irresistible force is affecting your company. If you have ideas about how the irresistible force may affect your enterprise differently in the future, make note of those thoughts, too.

Use Measurements to Check Your Perceptions of Irresistible Forces

It's very likely, as you begin the unaccustomed process of analyzing the irresistible forces in your inventory, that your initial conclusions now will be inaccurate or out-of-date. Measurements can help refine your understanding of the forces affecting your enterprise, as well as their relative importance.

How can you measure or assess the nature, strength, direction, and impact of each irresistible force? You must find the important clues about these forces so begin by considering more measurements than you may actually need. These measurements should include as many dimensions as possible. For example, how does each irresistible force affect users, customers, distributors, partners, employees, suppliers, competitors, government, and communities? How is the influence different for your various products and services? Are you affected more or less than competitors are?

You'll need to use both external and internal measurements to get a complete perspective. For example, government data may give you a handle on what is happening to a certain category of customer (such as those defined by a Standard Industrial Classification [SIC] code) that is of interest to you. Industry data may be helpful for perspectives on competitors, customers, and users. Your own market research may be very valuable for adding business- and product-specific perspectives concerning competitors, customers, and users as well. Be sure to also gather data on users of competitors' products for comparison.

You may be surprised by how many valuable measurements are available. Most businesses capture very few measurements about their irresistible forces. Even those that are captured may be stashed inaccessibly in different parts of the organization so that they may have never been seen together. Make sure that effective communication and evaluation of the measurements and their meanings are part of your measurement program.

How do the irresistible forces actually differ from your own and your company's initial perceptions of these forces? If you are like most people, you'll find that many of your perceptions about irresistible forces are off-target to some degree or another. In addition to analyzing how perceptions differ from the actuality, it's important to understand why those misperceptions have occurred. Were your perceptions once accurate, but circumstances have since changed? Are your perceptions based on interaction with your largest customers, who are not typical of everyone who uses your products and services? By answering these kinds of questions, you'll learn a lot about the strengths and weaknesses you and your business have in developing information about your enterprise's environment.

Pick One Irresistible Force to Study in More Detail

Continue your exploration of how measurements can help you address and use irresistible forces to your advantage. Focus now either on the force that is having the biggest impact on your organization or on the one that you are most interested in better understanding.

How many measurements can you find for the targeted irresistible force? The purpose of making this detailed examination is to give you and your colleagues experience in seeing how measurements can extend your ability to understand and use irresistible forces. If you do this investigation well, you should find more than triple the number of measurements you have uncovered so far. For example, if your customers have customers, find measurements concerning them. You can do the same for suppliers, partners, and competitors.

Using the expanded list of measurements, how many more irresistible forces can you find? Powerful and inexplicable trends usually have other forces behind them. Without looking for the causes of the irresistible force you've identified, you could miss these other important forces.

If you find this detailed study to be valuable, pick another irresistible force and repeat the process. Keep repeating the process until you no longer uncover any important benefits worth your time and effort.

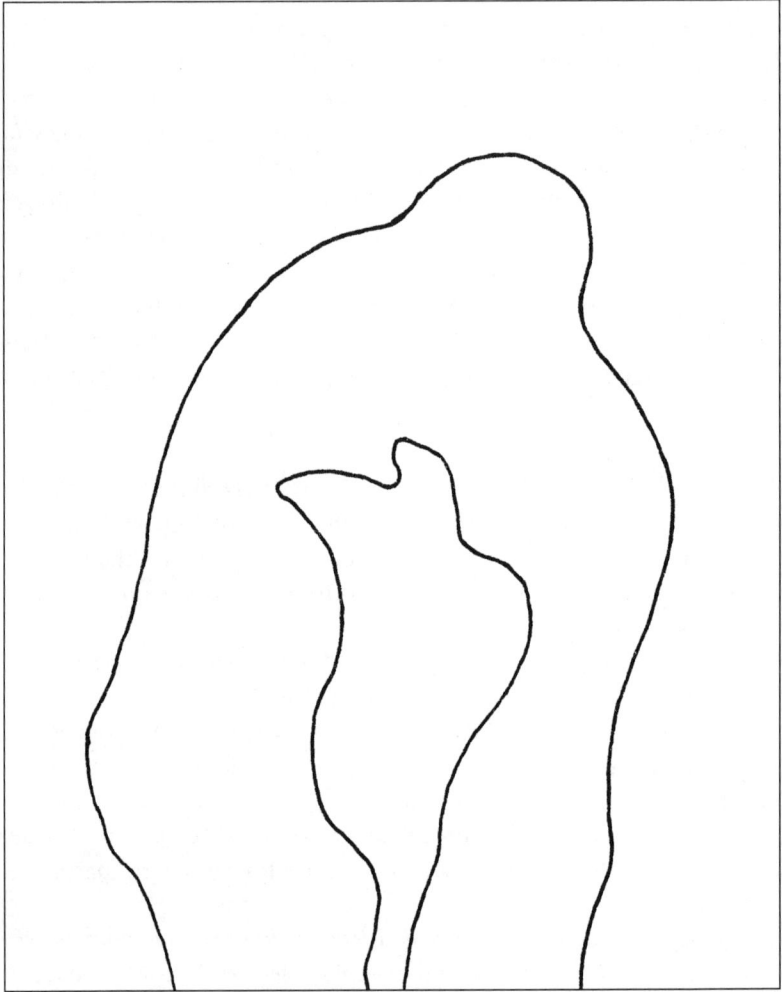

The future shape of irresistible forces can often be seen by looking more closely for clues inside current trends.

12

USE MEASUREMENTS TO PREPARE FOR ALTERING THE PATTERN TO FIT YOU

STEP TWO: USE YOUR OWN LEADING INDICATORS TO ANTICIPATE SHIFTS IN IRRESISTIBLE FORCES

If the window of opportunity appears,
don't pull down the shade.

—Tom Peters

Measuring irresistible forces after they have been operating for some time is not as valuable as anticipating the beginning of, or changes in the direction of, such forces. In the realm of economics, much attention is placed on "leading indicators" that are used to predict the future direction of the economy. In this chapter you can learn how to find the leading indicators of the irresistible forces that affect your enterprise, and determine which measurements are best for anticipating important changes or rapidly identifying that such important changes have already occurred.

Understanding the Importance of Tracking Trends

Managers can easily become confused by not knowing what to do with their initial measurements of the company's internal and external environments (as developed from the directions in chapter 11). Some measurements will prove to be good for anticipating, some for describing what is happening now, and others for providing insight into the past. To be most effective, your organization needs to identify and pay close attention to those that allow you to anticipate and to measure what is already happening in order to prepare for and adapt to irresistible forces.

How Low Can You Go?

From one year to the next, the length of women's skirts usually changes in response to the wearers' desire for novelty. Once established, the trend in length generally continues unabated in the same direction towards shorter or longer until an extreme is reached. When hemlines reach the ground, it's safe to assume they won't get any longer. At that point it's also safe to assume that only slightly shorter skirts won't hold much appeal. So you can predict that when skirts reach maximum length, fashion will move in a totally new direction due to the irresistible force of the desire for novelty. You have just found a leading indicator of an irresistible force change.

If for example you sell fabric to dress manufacturers, being aware of the leading indicators of fashion trends—wanting novelty among them—is critical to your survival. If you aren't prepared for the new designs, you could get stuck with unpopular fabric that you'd have to dispose of at a loss.

Rigged to Win

Imagine for a moment that you rent drilling rigs and crews to petroleum companies exploring for oil and gas. You would like to rent your rigs out for the longest period of time at the highest possible price. To achieve this goal, you have to decide how many rigs to build or buy, staff, and operate. If you have idle rigs, you have to decide if you should take a long-term contract at the current rental price or hold out for an even longer-term contract or a higher price.

Exploration rig demand is heavily influenced by the level and direction of oil prices. The best environment for you is a combination of high and rising oil prices. The oil companies will project a rosy future, and will pay very high prices to get to the oil sooner. The worst environment is having both low and dropping oil prices because oil companies will forecast a great drop in profitability and cash, and drilling will shrink dramatically.

An accelerating trend in oil prices turns out to be a better indicator of your future business level than is the absolute level of or trend in oil price. If you are a rig operator, you watch that oil price trend every day. When you see it start to slow or change direction, you may have to shift your strategy in a heartbeat.

Checking the Barometer

Weather forecasters find that changes in the barometer are valuable leading indicators of weather conditions. The following examples provide ideas for finding the irresistible force barometers that your organization should use and how to interpret them.

The Chicken or the Egg?

Let's take our oil rig example a little further. If you want to do more than watch the oil price trend as the barometer of your future business, you can try to identify the barometer for changes in oil prices themselves. The benefit of this latter approach is that you'll have more warning than anyone else in your industry, because it is generally believed that oil prices cannot be forecast. Fortunately, you don't need to forecast the actual prices, only their direction, which is a much easier task. The advance warning on the oil price direction will allow you to hold out for higher prices for your oil rigs and crews when you anticipate higher demand, and rent out quickly at current prices when prices for renting your rigs are about to fall.

How might you obtain this advance warning? For your needs, you don't have to be exact in forecasting the trend. You just have to do better than the results you would get by guessing blindly. Even relatively modest insights can provide large benefits over time. With that reassurance in mind, begin by breaking down the problem into constituent pieces. Start with the supply side. Experience with the Arab oil embargo in the 1970s should remind us all that the supply of oil has a big impact on the price level. Generally, OPEC's aim is to limit output to keep oil prices high. Non-OPEC countries and some less cooperative OPEC nations may not always share these goals. These countries may expand supply to offset economic crises in order to raise cash quickly. You can begin your analysis, then, by monitoring supply, quota agreements, and paying attention to the countries that may pump extra oil.

Next, you should look at demand for oil. Demand is driven by the level and direction of economic activity. You'll want to establish some connection between the leading economic indicators for the world's economies and future demand for oil.

You should consider other factors that can complicate the picture. For instance, how much oil is already in storage and in transit through pipelines and tankers? An unusually large or small inventory can accelerate the timing of a changed price direction. Investigate whether there is sufficient refinery capacity to handle the available oil. Some types of crude oil require special refineries for processing. Refineries require periodic upgrading and maintenance, and spot shortages can occur when those activities take place. Accidents can also reduce supply. Consider, too, that a lot of oil goes into home heating. Mild or harsh winter weather will have a big impact on demand. You'll have to check your El Niño and La Niña charts for clues. Governments can change the way they tax gasoline, encouraging or discouraging consumption. Further, vehicle styles can impact fuel efficiency and consumption. SUVs burn a lot of gasoline compared to compact cars.

The next step is to evaluate the usefulness of all of this information and these potential indicators by seeing how well these data series predicted the direction of oil prices in the past. Pay particular attention to clues from past environments that most resemble the current conditions. From these data and observations, you can begin to develop rules about what combinations of circumstances have an above-average likelihood of predicting oil prices rising or falling. Multivariate correlations can help (if you are not sure what these are or how to develop them, find a statistics or math major to help you).

As you begin to apply these rules to make your decisions, you should keep track of how well they work in practice. If they work significantly better or worse than you expected in helping you anticipate oil price trends, you should study further to understand why. A streak of better or worse prediction will often help you isolate additional factors to consider. What you learn will often help you to identify better decision rules for the future.

When the Shift Sticks

Knowing *when* the shift's cause will be triggered is critical to your success because you need time to prepare. The more important the information is, the longer it will take you to adjust. Having a lot of advance warning is especially important if the required response will be to develop new products or services, or to redirect your organization in some fundamental way. You should also be aware that some irresistible force changes occur slowly, while others are almost instantaneous.

Let's look at some different examples of time lags that have proven to be confusing to managers. Consider the collapse in many Asian economies beginning in 1997. Many people point to the currency crisis in Thailand as the beginning of the problem. That event, in turn, was made more likely by a much earlier devaluation in the Chinese currency. If you keep looking backward, you find that the primary cause for this chain of events is attributable to earlier overspeculation in Asian economies. Mountains of loans were made to fund all kinds of dubious investments, such as high-priced office buildings in saturated markets, unneeded infrastructure projects, and excess local manufacturing capacity that could not compete with imports. This misdirected investment activity had been going on for more than a decade before the crisis. Anyone who watched capital flows into and out of these countries and how new capital was used could have accurately identified the potential for a crisis years before it occurred.

When word of the collapsing Asian economies reached the United States, almost all public companies quickly responded to investor questions about how the event would affect their businesses. The answers usually were framed in terms of how much exporting to Asia the company did. Unless the amount was more than 5 percent of total company sales, most executives and financial analysts felt that there would be no material impact on the company. However, a few analysts held the view that a more important factor than exports to Asia would be increased competition from Asian companies. This conclusion was based on noting that these companies would now be selling their products at hard currency prices 30 percent to 50 percent lower than before to reflect the devaluation of many Asian currencies. While these pundits certainly had a point, they were off on their timing.

When currencies and economies collapse, the financial system usually collapses too. During the crisis, then, Asian companies had difficulties with liquidity and financing. Because of the amount of time it took for these companies to raise working capital, produce goods for export, and get the products distributed, there was a time lag between the onset of the crisis and when the effects of increased competition were felt worldwide. In the interim, U.S. companies, for example, wrongly concluded that because they saw no immediate change in competition from imports, none would ever arrive. Again, looking at past financial crises would have revealed in advance this likelihood of delayed competition. In making your analyses, you must be sure to consider the ripple effects of each event.

The effect of the Asian collapse on other non-Asian countries was also underestimated. The resulting economic crises in many other countries (such as those in South America) combined to impact all other parts of the world through reducing demand for commodities and finished goods of all kinds. The decreased demand for many third-world-produced raw materials caused reduced prices, which lessened the incomes of those who produced the commodities, which, in turn, reduced the demand for everything else these people buy. For many U.S. companies, this chain of events sent a false signal that the Asian problems were a benefit in disguise because costs immediately dropped for commodities. But the ripples of softened demand for goods and services eventually reached those U.S. companies as well, which then had to lower the prices they charged to remain competitive themselves.

Many commentators saw the decline in Asian currency values as a localized event, and predicted that it would be over in a short period of time. They overlooked the resulting series of vicious cycles that fed on each other. For instance, currency concerns caused savers to move their money to countries with sounder economies and currencies. Less money deposited locally tightened credit availability. Tighter credit meant even more decreased access to working capital, which resulted in further production slowdowns, which caused layoffs, which reduced income, which meant less savings, which tightened credit, and so on. In looking at ripple effects, be sure to consider how they can connect into related cycles of change that may be mutually reinforcing.

The movement of funds out of weaker currencies helped fuel an enormous boom in the U.S. and European stock and bond markets through 1999. This reaction also fooled a lot of people into thinking that even better times were just around the corner. Literally all the excess liquidity in the world was deposited in just a few places and created a temporary inflation in the financial assets in those currencies. The drops in the local economies that first collapsed eventually affected import demand for goods and services from the hard currency producers. Their stock values soon exceeded the earnings and cash flow performance the companies could deliver. Then most stock prices dropped. In such a circumstance, this cycle can take years to play out. Impressively, many Asian stock markets began to rally about 18 months after the onset of the crisis, fueled by a successful export boom based on lower prices. The rally, in turn, began to draw investment capital back into these countries and reduced liquidity in the hard currency countries. The big winners in this case were those who shifted their money into North American stocks prior to the devaluations and those who used hard currency to buy strong exporters in the devaluing currency countries after their devaluations.

The Asian example points out the complexity of such situations. Most people will overestimate the significance of immediate issues and underestimate the longer-term ones. Since situations like these can cause some immediate benefit and have delayed negative impact, the casual observer may misjudge the ultimate overall effects. The lesson of this example is that irresistible growth enterprises must understand the need to accurately assess the impact and timing of such events. They can learn to use capital flows and their application as barometers of potential change in a country's currency, investing, economic, and acquisition climate.

Timing Is Everything

When a company launches a new product or service, the usual approach is to put a lot of marketing support (more than will continue in the long run) behind the product during the introduction. For a typical consumer product, this extra marketing attention can translate into a schedule lasting six months to a year. What the company in this case may not realize is that forming a habit among customers usually takes about 30 repeat purchases. If the product is bought once a week, the 30 repeat purchases can happen in only seven months. If the product is bought once every six weeks, the same 30 repeat purchases require three and a half years to occur. Unless the company keeps a high spending level to reinforce the habit-building for that entire three and a half years, the product's customer base will be vulnerable to inroads from competitors.

Purchase frequency can vary greatly. Items like chewing gum may be purchased every few days by an individual, while equipment for new cement plants may be purchased only once a decade by a company. Whenever someone is about to buy something is the time when market share and habits can change. With frequently purchased goods, competitors have a chance at almost all of the customers right away, while with less frequently purchased goods most customers are out of the market at any given time.

Consider replacement auto tires, which are usually first sold when a new car has been operated for about 60,000 miles. The irresistible force here is that most people won't replace their tires before the old ones wear out, no matter how superior the replacement tires are. A replacement tire manufacturer can track new car sales and annual driving distance trends to predict future demand for its products.

You will almost always find such lags in effects from irresistible forces. You should always look for them in planning your marketing because it takes time and effort to form a lasting customer habit of buying your product or service.

Is Time on Your Side?

To get the most benefit from your leading indicators, or barometers, you need to know if the amount of advance warning you get from them is sufficient for your needs.

Returning to the oil rig example, if your longest lease is now out for 24 months, the optimum amount of anticipation you need would be something more than 24 months. The minimum will be quite a bit less than that. Suppose that only half of your rigs are under contract for 6 months or more. You can get a substantial benefit from having just over 6 months of lead-time warning of an oil price trend shift. In cases where you'll want to buy or build more rigs, the lead time must lengthen to allow you to take these capacity-adding steps.

Let's assume that your oil rig company has found leading indicators for the irresistible force of oil price direction that work well only two months ahead. Given the usual length of your leases, you need more warning than that. So you need to find better indicators. But you've already done a lot of work, and no better ideas have surfaced. How will repeating the process of finding barometers make a difference?

What you have to do differently when you repeat the process is to go back further in time or probe more deeply into the causes of the changes in leading indicators you have already located. In this case, you are looking for indicators far back enough in time to provide you with the length of warning you need. You might reconsider the discussion of oil demand. You had found a cause-and-effect relationship between the leading economic indicators for countries and the future price for oil. So you need to look for leading indicators of the leading economic indicators for these countries. Then test these once-removed leading indicators to see how well they predict changes in the direction of oil prices.

As you move further away from the event you are trying to anticipate, make sure that there is a logical reason why event A (a leading indicator of a leading economic indicator) should lead to event B (a change in the leading economic indicator). If you aren't sure, test the relationship you have found with experts for their reaction. They may be able to suggest other data series that are more likely to be causes, and that would, therefore, provide better advanced warning.

This iterative thinking involves looking for potential causes that act indirectly on what you are trying to anticipate, like checking the color of your grandparents' eyes to help you understand why your eyes are brown when your parents' eyes are blue and to predict what color your children's eyes may be.

Stallbusting

In this section, you can learn a process for finding proprietary barometers that predict changes in irresistible forces that affect your enterprise. In addition you can learn how to determine what amount of advance warning such barometers provide, compare the advance warning to your needs, and understand more about how and when to repeat the process in order to develop more timely anticipation.

Find a Proprietary Irresistible Force Barometer

Barometers that aren't available to others will be more useful to you than ones that everyone can access. If everyone learns how to forecast an event, behavior will change, and the event will no longer turn out the same way. So far we have limited ourselves to considering publicly available measures. Now we turn our attention to proprietary data.

What proprietary irresistible force barometers can you find that work better for your business than publicly available ones? The best barometers are those that measure events that occur within a business itself and are invisible to others. In your oil rig business, you might find that the number of requests you receive to bid on rig rentals from a particular set of companies for whom you are the dominant supplier may be a uniquely effective advance indicator of oil company perceptions of future oil prices. Notice that here we are focusing on oil company perceptions rather than actual oil price trends (oil companies historically have been bullish about upward oil price trends more often than those trends actually occurred). You might have shifted your focus in this new direction based on an earlier analysis that showed that oil company perceptions of future oil prices were a more powerful irresistible force for oil rig leasing than the actual trend in oil prices.

Start by assembling all the internal data that you have been keeping track of for a long time and compare those data to your company's later performance, paying particular attention to the time lag between events and results. In the oil rig example, the performance you want to predict could be defined as placing more rigs at higher prices for longer periods of time. You could develop an index that captured this pattern. Then you would use single variable statistical regressions to compare that success index to earlier patterns within the business, such as the number of requests to bid on rig rentals. If you don't know how to do these statistical regressions, chances are that some of the recent business, economics, or math graduates in your organization do. Work with them by showing them this chapter. The statistical relationships that emerge should be tested for the frequency with which they give accurate signals, as well as the logic of why the factors should be related.

Once you begin to identify some of these relationships as barometers for the success index, you may find it helpful to check if combinations of the barometers have worked better in the past than individual barometers. For example, if all of them give you the same signal, then the forecast's accuracy will usually be higher than if only a few give that signal. You can also employ multivariate regressions (using more than one variable at a time to create your barometer) to improve the weight you give to different factors. However, be aware that multivariate regressions can often produce some statistical relationships that are probably wrong (such as if the regression says that a faster growth rate of the economy leads to lower petroleum prices). If you are working with people who don't know the subject area well for these regressions, be sure to check that the relationships make sense.

Determine the Time Lags

Your selection of a barometer should be determined both by its accuracy and by how much advance warning of the change you want to anticipate the barometer provides.

How much advance warning does the barometer provide under various circumstances? Most barometers will work better in anticipating some changes in irresistible force direction than for others. Consider using several barometers simultaneously to test various possible changes in direction. The same applies in selecting barometers that provide the most advance warning. As in our dress length example, continuing the current trend in shortening or lengthening dresses will work fine until the dresses get to extremes of being very short or very long. In that business situation, at least two types of barometers will be needed.

In considering the time lags, think about if there is a reason why these time lags will change in the future. As information access and communications improve, there is a general tendency for time lags to shrink.

Compare the Barometer's Advance Warning to Your Minimum Needs

To evaluate the effectiveness of your chosen barometers, you need to determine how much advance warning of a shift in irresistible forces your organization needs to be ready to take best advantage of that shift.

What are the different, sequential needs you have for advance warning, and how much do they add up to in total elapsed time? First, begin by considering how long before everyone else would know the irresistible force has changed you need to be taking action in order to secure a significant advantage. Second, move backwards in time from the point where you expect that others will first perceive the changed irresistible force in order to estimate how long it takes your enterprise to implement the necessary action. For example, getting your proposal in good form to present to customers may require three months (including the time to get the appointments, create the proposal, and prepare the presentations). Third, move further backward to measure how long it will take your company to turn the information supplied by the barometer into a decision about what you want to do. In some cases this time frame may be only a few days, but for many organizations the time will be several months. Be sure to use an estimate that applies to the type of decision you will be making, because different types of decisions usually vary in the elapsed time required. Finally, add some contingency time for things to go wrong (such as the information coming out when many people are on vacation).

Repeat the Process to Improve Lead Time

If yours is like most businesses, the first barometers you find will provide lead times too close to the change in irresistible force direction to meet your minimum needs.

How can your barometers be improved to provide either the minimum or an economically attractive longer period of advance warning? If you have a few large customers or competitors, you may find it advantageous to consider developing specific barometers designed solely for making your most appropriate response vis-à-vis each of them. Another useful approach is to poll knowledgeable people in and outside your company. They might collectively provide greater advance warning by giving you more perspective on anticipating the future change. Since only you will know what the poll shows, it would also be a source of proprietary information for you.

In addition, some people within your company may have formal training and significant talent for identifying leading indicators. Be sure to utilize this resource. However, you can also outsource the task of finding barometers to get started. Without an internal capability, though, you'll probably miss many of the best opportunities to create proprietary barometers. By their nature, external organizations can never become familiar enough with your business to identify the richest sources of proprietary data.

Some future ways of locating, anticipating, and adapting to changes in irresistible forces will rise above others in effectiveness. You will want to start improving by identifying those most promising future methods.

13

THINK AHEAD TO PIN DOWN
THE RIGHT SUCCESS
PATTERN

STEP THREE: IDENTIFY THE FUTURE BEST
PRACTICES FOR LOCATING,
ANTICIPATING, AND ADAPTING TO
CHANGES IN IRRESISTIBLE FORCES

The secret of success is to know something that nobody else knows.

—Aristotle Onassis

Understanding what you need to do to be the first to locate, anticipate, and adapt to shifting irresistible forces will help you gain the competitive edge. This multidimensional approach will enable you to capture more benefits sooner and avoid delays and problems.

The Multidimensional Advantage

Weather or Not

At the 1998 British Open golf tournament, the weather conditions changed enormously from day to day. On wet, windy days, the golfers from England and Scotland (who are used to such weather) scored very well. On bright, warm, windless days (more usual during professional events in the United States), the Americans excelled. Anyone wanting to place a winning bet on a golfer (a legal activity in the U.K.) needed to be pretty sure what the weather would be during the tournament. With just the right balance of both kinds of weather and experience in both kinds of playing conditions, Mark O'Meara of the United States pulled off the victory by a narrow margin.

Here is a key point: Many observers feel that in most activities no newly developed competitive advantage will last for long. Either conditions will change unexpectedly like the weather, disfavoring those who can't adapt even if they have been on a winning track, or competitors eventually will find ways to maneuver around the advantage.

If this view is correct, your company will have to hold its lead by expanding the competitive gap continuously in some more dimensions to achieve a sustained competitive advantage. Even if this proves incorrect in your circumstances and you can achieve a dominant advantage from only one set of changes, you'll probably find the benefits from this insight to be motivating for your colleagues. This assumption will prepare you both for an environment in which conditions change rapidly and competition keeps up, as well as one in which your continued progress creates ever more significant competitive benefits for your firm.

The Irresistible Growth Challenge

In chapters 11 and 12, you learned about some successful methods that enterprises have been using to benefit from two dimensions of irresistible force management: locating and anticipating those forces. But what about the future? Will organizations remain satisfied with the current level of predictive skill? Probably not. The common desire to improve management processes is one of those irresistible forces that your company must take into account. This desire means that customers, competitors, suppliers, and others you interact with will continually try to gain an advantage over your enterprise with each new wave of irresistible forces, as much as you strive to gain on theirs.

Keeping ahead of the pack requires several interrelated activities:

1. Giving priority to building benefits for individuals (both outside and inside your organization) ahead of building benefits for your company or organization. As we saw with Habitat for Humanity, altruism can be a powerful force to harness. Equally remember that most people in an organization will act more from their perceived self-interest, than from the company's self interest. To capture both these powerful forces, be sure that objectives, rewards and recognition encourage the desired behavior. Let people do good for others while doing well for themselves and their families.

2. Building company or organization benefits and resources faster than any of your competitors.

3. Seeking out as many irresistible forces as possible and converting them into assets. Combining harnessed forces offers geometric gains in benefits.

4. Creating maximum adaptability to irresistible forces with minimal change to organizational structure and size. Adaptability needs underlying continuity. A sports analogy may be helpful: The teams that change players often during the season generally fail to execute well because their players don't play smoothly together. (You can learn more about how to apply this concept in chapter 17.)

Pursuing these activities and achieving the goals they're aimed at can provide the foundation for future success in engaging irresistible forces. Without the understanding that supports that perspective, you'll find yourself coming late to market with inappropriate solutions, and your organization will find itself in an unwinnable game of catch-up.

How Do You Keep Score?

The future best practice is simply the best way of doing something that another organization will achieve given the probable resources and environment that are and will be in existence by the time you can establish your new way to do it. (Bear in mind that the best practice for something isn't necessarily found within the same sphere of economic or social activity in which your organization is involved.) Determining the future best practices for locating, anticipating, and adapting to changes in irresistible forces is particularly challenging. You need to develop multidimensional skills. For example, if your firm is better at locating irresistible forces than anyone else's organization, but you cannot adapt to these forces, you will have gained no advantage from your insight. Conversely, if you are the best at adapting to irresistible forces but are slow to locate them, you'll also be at a major disadvantage.

In the Olympics, you can compete in individual events in track and field (the 100-meter dash, long jump, javelin throw, and so forth). You can also compete in the decathlon, which combines ten track and field events over two days. In the decathlon, you are scored based on your measured performance in each event, and the winner is determined by the combined score in all ten events. Determining the future best practices for locating, anticipating, and adjusting to irresistible forces is more like the decathlon than are individual track and field events. However, the standard is even higher. You'll need to be the best at all three activities in order to obtain the future best practice for your process. (Think about this: Even Dan O'Brien, the greatest decathlete of the twentieth century, didn't win every event of the ten he competed in.) Such a high standard is necessary because the three activities are so interdependent for achieving the ultimate result: sustained competitive advantages that leave competitors behind, gasping in your dust.

The Initial Dimension: The Future Best Practice in Locating Changes in Irresistible Forces

First Things First: Look Around Before You Leap

You should begin by being sure that you have identified all of the irresistible forces that you feel are influencing or could strongly affect your enterprise's effectiveness relative to direct competitors or potential substitute products and services. For example, if you produce steel for automobiles, in addition to your steel competitors you need to consider the possible threats posed by aluminum, other metals, plastics, or composite materials. If car use could be substituted for, in part, by improved telecommunications, home offices, and Internet shopping, you would need to consider the irresistible forces behind those trends as well. It is a common mistake to focus too narrowly. Call upon a wide range of expertise and backgrounds when building your team for locating forces. You only have to miss one key irresistible force to experience a severe disadvantage.

Measurements and Monitors: Become a Measurement Maven

Next, for each irresistible force you identify, you need to find out what measurements others have been using in the past and are using now to most predictably capture changes in its direction, speed, or character. Here is a key clue: You'll probably find the biggest efforts to understand irresistible forces where the stakes are largest. For example, if your operation is smaller than others who are affected by a particular force, be sure to contact the larger operations. But don't ignore those that are smaller than yours. If smaller firms are literally betting their entire existence on their ability to track a force, you may find that their need to survive has driven them to better solutions.

What you'll probably learn is that almost everyone does their trend checking in pretty much the same way, looking at the same data and interpreting them similarly. That perspective is useful because it can teach you how and when they'll perceive any switch in direction. For example, trends in consumer spending are usually monitored by looking at the latest actual sales trends in the economy, the ability of consumers to spend (income and costs), and the confidence that consumers have in the future (influencing their willingness to exchange cash or debt for a benefit now). However, you'll also find that some companies have been or are looking at the trends in vastly different ways, using hundreds of different perspectives and measurements; and it is these methods that will be most instructive.

You need to test these various ways of measuring change in irresistible forces by asking the following questions:

- Which ones are most often accurate in locating continuing shifts in the irresistible force?

- Which ones are best at the earliest identification of a shift?

- Which possible shifts in direction are all of these measures poor at identifying when they occur?

- Can you suggest which other measures would be better at locating these poorly-identified force shifts?

You also need to expect that others will be trying to improve their ability to monitor these same areas, are aware of the rate of improvement in these monitoring measurements, and are attempting to foresee new sources of information that could be useful in better monitoring practices. In making this assessment, be sure to consider how existing and new measurements could be made more accurate and timely by using them in combination with each other. You'll find that in most cases, a combination of at least three measurements will provide much more useful information than any single one or combination of two. And for the best results, one of the measurements should be based on current information about future plans. Based on the perspectives revealed in those areas, you can develop a composite picture of the most effective monitoring methods that could be in place over the next few years, as well as their strengths and weaknesses.

The Second Dimension: The Future Best Practice in Anticipating Changes in Irresistible Forces

Determining that a trend has changed is clearly much less helpful than successfully anticipating that change with a significant lead time. Your look at what other firms and organizations are doing to understand irresistible forces will also need to include an investigation of how these other groups are using measurements to anticipate changes in those forces. You should ask the same questions about these measurements as the ones listed in the previous section on locating changes in irresistible forces. You also need to add a consideration of causes and effects. If you have found accurate measurements for describing changes in directions, there surely are causes of the changes that themselves can be measured.

The Chicken, or the Egg, or the DNA, or the Intent, or the Impulse?

Although we took a good look at finding barometers of change in the oil rig rental example in chapter 12, our search for the future best practice has to take us further back toward initial impetuses in order to find the primary causes. Let's look at another example.

Imagine that you are a brokerage firm and you're planning for future staffing needs. You need to know how the securities markets will be performing in the future. When stock prices are rising, you can make money having lots of capacity to handle trading orders. When stock prices are falling for an extended time, you need to cut resources, including staffing. Anticipating the need to shift is very valuable because it takes time and money to add systems capabilities and to recruit, hire, and train new employees. Both starting and stopping large activities in this area require some advance notice for the best results.

In addition to adjusting the computer systems expansion and the hiring and training cycles in brokerage firms, the ability to anticipate the general direction of the stock market would have far more valuable applications. Studying more about the related irresistible forces may reveal insights that could be used to build other competitive benefits. For example, you might become effective enough at understanding the general trend of the stock market to be able to provide better advice to your brokerage customers so that they would make more money, spend more of that money with you, and stay with you longer.

When you ask people how they anticipate the direction of the stock market, you will hear answers involving measures such as corporate earnings, interest rates, investor sentiment, flow of investment funds, the value of your country's currency versus other currencies, and the level of the market compared to various measures. For your purposes, in addition to determining which of these measures is better for anticipating results, you need to develop a sense of what causes what.

Let's take investor sentiment. Many people find that investor sentiment tends to follow the market. If you've been enjoying steady stock-price gains, you are likely to continue to believe that steady gains will occur in the future.

After stock prices drop for a long time, you are likely to believe that recovery is far off. This historically dependent sentiment clearly has a real effect on the future of the market because it determines how much new money some investors put into the market. To work backward, we want to know what caused the market to rise or fall in the past that was independent of investor sentiment, because investor sentiment is a lagging indicator. We know that investor sentiment is important though because it will help us sustain the new direction once it has begun.

Now think about a measurement you may not have considered before: the effectiveness of top managements in running their companies to improve stock-price growth, independent of economic and financial market conditions. Even in the worst markets, some stocks will rise because managements are doing such a superb job of pleasing investors. Similarly, other stocks will fall even in the best markets because managements are unintentionally annoying investors. Our brokerage firm could develop some great insights into the future trend of specific stocks from looking at a measurement like top management effectiveness in improving stock-price growth. And that measurement could have other profound benefits, like helping the firm to know which stocks to recommend. If the brokerage firm used its own analysts to gather data for the measurement, the advantages of proprietary information could be garnered as well.

In this search for better and earlier anticipation, you can always look deeper for a still earlier cause. One of the factors determining management effectiveness in stock price improvement might be the source and quality of the education that some managements received about how to improve stock prices. Your brokerage firm could then monitor such educational efforts in companies.

This backward-looking search for causes can and should continue until useful insights are no longer available. In the brokerage example, the decision to pursue the education those managements receive could be inspired by articles and advertising in leading business publications describing the benefits of this education. Those articles and advertising could have resulted from the intent of editors (who plan their features for the issue) and education providers (who buy the advertising). Deeper research might even uncover the causes of the editors' intentions, such as missed revenue targets or the desire to improve sales to earn a larger bonus.

Identifying the future best practice in anticipating changes in irresistible forces, then, requires a process that uses many data sources and searches more deeply into prior causes. Employing that process should help you create many more 2,000 percent solutions.

The Third Dimension: The Future Best Practice in Adapting to Changes in Irresistible Forces

But I Don't Wanna!

Because so many businesses are essentially unable or unwilling to adapt at all, your search for the future best practice in adaptability will probably be the most valuable part of the three searches described in this chapter.

Further, of the three dimensions of irresistible force engagement we have been exploring, adapting to changes in forces is by far the most difficult to do. One reason for this difficulty is that many people need to be involved, each of whom can derail the operation. Here are additional contributing factors:

- Changed force directions can cause denial about the need to change ("If I keep doing the right things, I'll be all right.").

- Individuals may choose to ignore the new direction if their compensation is harmed (the bonus and quota systems will usually reward appropriate behavior for the old environment rather than for the new circumstances).

- People in your company may have no idea what to do (this is particularly likely when the circumstances have not occurred before and you poorly communicate what is needed now).

- Your enterprise's insight into the changed direction may not be well understood ("If you really wanted me to stop hiring brokers, you wouldn't have just promoted me to vice president in charge of hiring brokers.").

When people have little choice but to change, they will do so. Your search for the future best practice in adapting to changing forces will be most rewarding if you continually scrutinize organizations that routinely adapt to new circumstances when irresistible forces shift and thus avoid facing severely negative consequences. Don't be satisfied with the first practice that your company finds that creates any adaptability at all.

Thriving on Earthquakes, Fire, Flood, and Pestilence

A good place to find those who are at the cutting edge of this current best practice in adaptability is to focus on organizations that must be readily adaptable in order to fulfill their mission, because changed circumstances are their reason for being. For example, those who provide emergency relief supplies to victims of natural disasters in lesser-developed countries have to be adaptable at a moment's notice or they can never hope to do their jobs well.

Such groups are masters of contingency planning. Because they never know what terrible event will hit next and when, they are always planning for the widest possible range of disasters. To hone their skills in quick adaptation, they practice meeting disasters as exercises when no actual disaster is keeping them busy.

These organizations are usually open to access from outsiders. For example, you and your colleagues can volunteer with these organizations and develop firsthand skill in becoming more adaptable. From this direct experience you can also better understand the motivations necessary to create a highly adaptable enterprise. In these organizations, a strong desire to help others that transcends the need for one's personal comfort is often a factor. You may even find that committing your company to support one of these organizations will be a future best practice in learning adaptability.

Scavenging Adaptability

Like scavengers tracking predators to find the kills that will be their food source, many organizations choose to pay little attention to anticipating changes in irresistible forces, but do make being first on the scene their top priority. These companies often describe themselves as "fast followers." Their idea is to spot new, effective actions that competitors are taking, quickly improve on those actions, and be the first to make the benefits universally available to customers.

Manufacturers in Asian Tiger countries (like South Korea, Taiwan, and Singapore) often use this scavenger approach, sometimes placing their version of newly introduced products into the market within hours of when the product is first introduced by the innovator in another country. A good way to see how this process works is to select a design you were working on that you have abandoned for some reason. Take it to manufacturers who have a reputation for quickly copying and improving on designs, and see how long it takes for other manufacturers to launch variations on your now-improved design. Then backward engineer the process whereby your design spreads into manufactured reality so quickly among so many companies, and you'll discover a great deal about adaptability.

The Scenario's the Thing

Another source of potential future best practices is to study those who use scenario planning to be prepared to act in the event of a wide range of circumstances. These organizations typically understand that they can't predict or forecast the future with any certainty, but that they can be prepared to position themselves advantageously regardless. Advance thinking allows these organizations to become comfortable with the idea of change, see the ways that change can be an advantage, and create advance communications through business plans to direct their actions when the time comes. This approach obviously fits well with monitoring and trying to anticipate changes, as previously discussed.

A well-documented application of this approach was by Royal Dutch/ Shell after the Arab oil embargo in the early 1980s.* The company's corporate planners identified a large drop in oil prices from the $30 per barrel level as one of several scenarios they had developed. When the drop actually occurred, Shell moved well in advance of others to develop lower-cost ways of offshore drilling.

Scenario planning has come a long way since then, so you'll want to explore the best of what is being done now and how that will probably improve in the future. While other companies may not want to share the results of their use of such processes, they are generally willing to describe the steps involved to achieve the results. Knowledge management conferences and academic papers are other good ways to locate those who are doing top work in this fruitful area.

Stallbusting

In this section you will find the questions you need to answer in order to identify the current and future best practices for engaging irresistible forces. Although you might be tempted to answer only the questions pertaining to one of the three dimensions, limiting yourself in that way would be a mistake. You'll achieve far better results from this process if you look into all three areas (locating, anticipating, and adapting). Similarly, you may see some of these questions as only of theoretical interest, but that is a false perception. Working to find the answers to these questions is essential homework for you to be able to master the full potential of your enterprise's future.

Michael Dell put this subject into the properly important perspective in his speech at the 1998 World Congress on Information Technology in Vienna, Virginia. He said, ". . . [P]roduct differentiation is becoming harder to achieve. It will give way to *process* innovation as the fundamental source of competitive advantage." He went on to describe a trend that needs to be taken into account under these circumstances: the Internet. Dell stated that through use of the Internet, ". . . [I]t will be possible to revolutionize processes in a way

---

*See "Planning as Learning," by Arie de Geus, *Harvard Business Review,* March-April 1988.

that blurs traditional boundaries between supplier and manufacturer, and manufacturer and customer."

Dell's comment itself is a leading indicator of a shift in thinking among those who are trying to make best use of irresistible forces. They will not only emphasize making adaptation easier and more effective, they will encourage everyone else in and out of their enterprises to do the same. Thus the need to examine first causes is becoming ever more critical.

Find the Path of Least Resistance

Keep in mind that the processes you use to locate changes in forces, anticipate some of those changes, and adapt to changes have to be simple, fast, inexpensive compared to their benefits, and easy-to-use. Otherwise, you'll reap few benefits from your efforts and the expenses could be enormous. Working with these following questions is intended to help you determine the most efficient processes.

Who is getting the best results with the simplest process? Not answering this question can cost you enormously in lost opportunities such as foregone profits and cash flow because you did not act in a timely way. One of the most cost-effective routes for taking step three involves researching the answer to this question.

Consider that most companies have found that orders for one or more of their products or services are extremely good predictors of future economic directions that affect them. This may be the case because the product or service is tied into some essential precursor to increased or decreased economic activity. For example, most industrial processes rely on electricity. If no new electrical generating capacity is added, the economic growth rate of most countries will decline, even with rigid allocations of the existing electrical capacity.

One way to improve on these insights would be to pool information with customers or suppliers so that you can cross-check your insights very quickly from other perspectives. For example, in the early 1990s, Dell Computer built a simple model to anticipate and adapt to changes rapidly based on the orders it received for custom-built machines. However, Dell soon found that it couldn't rely solely on itself. If suppliers weren't attuned to the same issues, Dell might go off in the wrong direction or suppliers might not be able to support Dell. Dell moved early to making long-term commitments to its best quality suppliers, thus treating them as partners and sharing information and responsibilities for new product design in a way that blurred the normal supplier-customer relationship. The suppliers have their own engineers stationed inside the Dell facility during each new product launch. As e-mails and telephone calls come in to Dell that pinpoint problems, product orders and shipments using those components stop until the on-site supplier engineers solve the design flaws.

Because this Dell approach to locating, anticipating, and adapting to changes merely involves statistical regressions that you can do on computers, you can test thousands of alternative directions for each irresistible force in seconds after you have the data in electronic form. Since you probably keep your own records of orders, customer complaints and so forth in electronic form, this method can be the basis of a proprietary best practice of considerable value by drawing on your own firm's confidential data. Few today can hope to locate a simpler, faster, and easier process to use than this one.

Which organizations act as though they have mastered engaging irresistible forces ahead of others? Management and business publications are literally full of such success stories. While many claims are overblown, checking with the source is a way to start your search for authentic winners. Telephone interviews are often sufficient to determine if the people involved are using a process you should evaluate or if they simply believe their own press.

Who tracks this area? Academics and business editors often make a living researching such organizational processes. Ask these people whom you should investigate for best practices.

Who is the best in every country at these activities? Most people have a bias in favor of the way that people in their own home country do a process. Yet someone in another country will often have developed something a lot better. The odds that the future best practice for engaging irresistible forces will originate in your country are probably less than 10 percent, so don't be chauvinistic in your search.

Should you outsource locating and anticipating? Your company may find it easier, less expensive, and more reliable to hire an external firm or person to provide help with implementing whatever process you decide to use for locating and anticipating change. Management consulting firms, market research organizations, economic forecasters, and futurists now provide this kind of help in certain areas. Be sure to check with those who are most successfully outsourcing this activity to find out what aspects of these processes they are outsourcing. Beware of using standard reports that are available to anyone. Chances are that no future best practices can be built solely on such reports because the results will be too easy to duplicate.

Be Thorough and Continuously Farsighted

Most people stop their searches for the future best practices too soon. They think once they've found *a* future best practice that it is *the* future best practice in their industry or that their enterprises will use. Actually, what they've found is probably the best that any other organization will be doing in the next few years. To get the right answers you have to be thorough and constantly looking further ahead.

Can someone fit all the pieces together for the first time? In future best practice research, it is often true that many different companies and organizations will have useful practices that they are employing. You may find that most groups, however, are using only one or two of the dozens that you locate. It may be possible to combine almost all of these best practices into a new, future best practice. You can be sure that if you can figure that out, someone else will, too. Plan on that combination occurring to someone else, and plan on being the first to come up with and apply it.

Can you make a cherry pie simply by throwing together a lot of cherries? In answering the preceding question, you were encouraged to combine individual elements of current best practice in new ways. However, you need to use that approach carefully or you can end up with a process that is ungainly and inefficient. To avoid unnecessary complexity, take the following steps: First, eliminate any duplicate elements. Second, take out anything that adds relatively little incremental benefit. Third, simplify what remains. Fourth, consider how what remains could be made more valuable by adding elements that no one has ever used before. Fifth, work with information technology professionals (internally and externally) to create an automated way to do what remains using off-the-shelf software that is cheap, easy to use, and fast to install. Whether you create your own solution or outsource the search for future best practices, you should keep involved to be sure that you avoid inefficiency.

In identifying future best practices, how can you anticipate problems that may not arise for years? Simply by thinking further ahead. The classic example of not thinking ahead is the Y2K problem that many computer and electronic device users could have suffered from at the end of 1999. Earlier generations of computer programmers had allowed only room for the last two digits of calendar years to save space at a time when electronic memory was expensive and bulky. They assumed that someone would find a way to add the other two digits down the road. Of course, with the year 2000 came a risk that computer programs would recognize "00" as 1900 rather than 2000. Tens of billions of dollars were spent around the world fixing a problem that could easily have been anticipated and solved in the beginning at a far lower cost.

Some examples of problems you should anticipate include: poor quality data being introduced; the loss of data elements due to the government changing its definitions; changing suppliers so that data series are no longer available to you; accidental errors in calculating with the data; new relationships arising between causes and effects; and misuse of the output by people who were not involved in developing the original process. See *Quality Information and Knowledge* (Prentice-Hall PTR, 1999) by Kuan-Tsae Huang, Yang W. Lee, and Richard Y. Wang for these and other useful perspectives on quality problems you can expect with computer-processed information.

How can you improve your process for determining future best practices for engaging irresistible forces? In a sense, every new process becomes obsolete the day you stop improving it. Improvements are no longer added, and the process gradually becomes less and less relevant. Be sure your process includes methods to keep it up-to-date and constantly more effective.

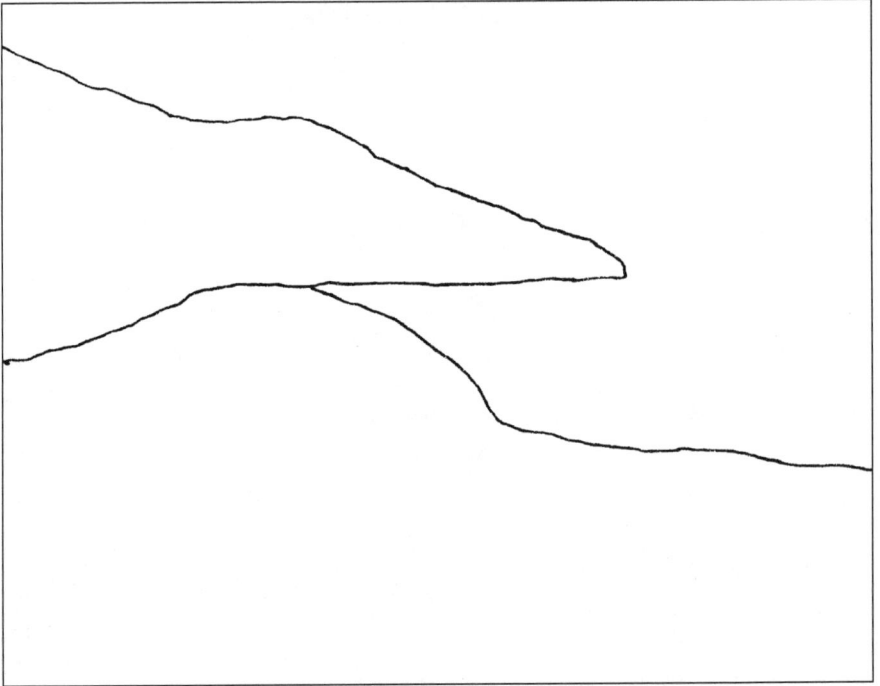

Surpassing all others in using irresistible forces to your advantage requires having a superior vantage point for surveying what is ahead.

14

WEAVE THE THREAD OF SUCCESS INTO YOUR FABRIC

STEP FOUR: EXTEND YOUR VISION TO ACCOMPLISH BEST PRACTICES BEYOND ANYONE ELSE IN THE FUTURE

You have to kiss a lot of frogs to find a prince.

—Various

Chapter 13 introduced the process of estimating the future best practices others will achieve for locating, anticipating, and adapting to changes in irresistible forces. In this chapter you can learn how to extend that process for the purpose of seeing advances beyond that level into the future. Suggested methods include developing proprietary data that others cannot duplicate, faster ways to shift internal rewards and recognition, and in constantly combining these techniques in new and improved ways.

When the Players Take the Field

A good way to think about extending beyond the future best practices for engaging irresistible forces is to liken that activity to what football coaches and their staffs do during a game. Coaches start with a game plan that builds on analyzing the history and potential of each team versus each other (offense versus defense, defense versus offense, and special teams against each other).

However, as play starts, many things can change and affect those plans. Key players may be injured early in the game. Your opponent may surprise you with new tactics. Weather or field conditions outdoors may change unexpectedly. And the field may be in worse or better shape than you anticipated.

You need to adapt quickly to these circumstances as well as anticipate what will happen in the future. The field may become wet and slippery. Injuries may occur unless you change the spikes on the players' shoes. If you make your players less maneuverable than your opponent, they may run around you (literally) and you will lose. So you have to balance safety and maneuverability to reflect what the current conditions are. And you should have a lot of people who can quickly change the spikes because you may have to do it more than once.

You will probably find that you'll want to call the plays from the sidelines so that the latest thinking about the changing conditions can be fitted into the revised game plan. You may want to have a lot of data loaded into a computer ahead of time so you can produce adjusted game plans to reflect the conditions in seconds. Turnovers and touchdowns happen quickly in such situations, and one or two such turnarounds can determine the final outcome of the game. If conditions change a lot during the course of the game, you'll probably have a big advantage because of your flexibility. For example, sometimes you'll have the right players in with the right spikes and the right play while the other team is falling down (literally) with the wrong personnel.

In this chapter, then, we provide techniques for perfecting your game plans for looking further ahead of the future ways others will engage irresistible forces. By pursuing this activity you can create a sustainable competitive advantage because few operations pay much attention to the whole idea now, and those who are using best practices in this area are employing only a fraction of all the currently known best practices. In addition, many companies won't allocate the time, money, and effort needed to develop new combinations of best practices. By taking advantage of these weaknesses and adding proprietary sources of data, you can achieve lead times for engaging these forces that will take decades to surpass.

Locating Changes in Irresistible Forces: Monitors, Measures, and Making Decisions

Like an Eye in the Sky

Although traffic reports may sound the same from day-to-day, the ability to report the exact condition of traffic has reached a high level in many places

(New York City, for example). Some cities have cameras operating 24 hours a day at the usual choke points and a traffic helicopter with a camera in the air to see the other areas. Other factors, like weather, special events (such as the president visiting the United Nations, parades, sit-ins, and strikes), curiosity-drawing occurrences (people getting traffic tickets, accidents, and road construction crews), and the conditions of the road (wet, snow-covered, etc.) can all be noted and reported simultaneously. By measuring these factors continuously, radio reports provide precise information about delays (for example, a 25-minute backup at the Lincoln Tunnel).

As a result, drivers have almost all the information they could wish for to be able to pick the fastest route to their destinations simply by listening to a radio station. Think about improving this capability further by allowing the driver to actually use all of the information that the radio station has to plan a route. An ultimate goal could be to let a car computer plot the best route for minimum travel time after interacting with the radio station's computer. The car computer's calculation could then reflect both current and anticipated driving conditions on all of the routes in the metropolitan area. This optimal routing could be continuously updated as the trip ensues, much as the current GPS car navigation systems allow you to do after making a wrong turn.

By analogy, your enterprise can achieve optimal routing to competitive advantage with irresistible forces if it continuously measures what is going on with your customers, employees, distributors, partners, suppliers, shareholders, competitors, and the communities in which you operate. To stretch that advantage, you'll probably have to take an additional step to measure the factors that in turn influence the consequences for these key constituencies. For example, families, friends, and home conditions affect employees. Simply observing someone at work will provide a limited perspective of what is happening in that person's life. Similarly, customers often reflect what is happening with *their* customers, employees, distributors, partners, suppliers, shareholders, competitors, and the communities in which they operate. These influences, in turn, are also heavily affected by their immediate environments, and so on. Thus the need for constant and constantly expanding vigilance should be obvious.

"Paging Dr. Kildare"

In a hospital intensive care unit, the key measures of health for a patient's particular condition are continuously monitored. If a measure falls outside the normal range, an alarm goes off so that the patient gets immediate attention, even if no nurse or doctor happens to be watching the monitoring unit at that time. These monitors don't indicate the cause of the problem but do focus attention on the symptom that indicates help is needed. By having a medically trained person then look at the patient, the appropriate action can quickly be diagnosed and taken.

Obviously, then, the most useful monitoring incorporates several elements:

1. A mechanism to track important trends
2. An alert to indicate a change in conditions
3. An expert able to interpret the situation
4. Communication to translate the interpretation of the situation into the appropriate action

The monitoring system in an intensive care unit is substantially more sophisticated than the traffic monitoring done by a radio station. The driver has to do the second, third, and fourth activities from the preceding list without further assistance from the radio station. In the organizational setting, you need much more assistance than just having the shift in trends be identified, which is where most people stop today. That's a big mistake. You need quick attention from knowledgeable people who are in a position to take the appropriate action as soon as possible. An effective way to speed the process is to link the information directly to those who must take action, and to assist them in learning how to effectively interpret and respond to the timely information through simulation-based exercises.

Automatic Advantage

The airlines sell a wasting commodity: airline seats. If a seat isn't occupied by a paying customer when the plane takes off, the potential revenue is lost forever. To combat this wastage, American, United, and some others instituted a system of continuous monitoring a number of years ago when they began offering computer-based reservation systems to travel agents.

These reservation systems greatly eased the travel agents' work, but also conferred large advantages upon their airline sponsors. Originally, the airlines supplying the systems made it easier to book on their flights than on those of competitors. Government action subsequently changed that tactic. However, the airlines were able to continue to maintain a large base of understanding about the seat-buying market. They created computer programs that decided minute-by-minute how many seats to offer at different prices and to frequent flyer award users. The profit effectiveness of these decision-making programs is constantly monitored for potential improvements. Programming changes are made to reflect new market trends.

Such a setup is like having a computer not only to pick the best route for the driver, but also to drive the car. Creating such a system of automatic, intelligent response obviously puts the identification of and response to trends, and shifts in trends, at a more effective level. The key challenge is to constantly revisit the assumptions built into the automatic response to be sure that they constantly evolve into the best alternatives.

Anticipating Changes in Irresistible Forces: Secrets, Standards, and a Head Start

Confidential Sources Are Cooperative Sources

Under American law, reporters aren't usually protected from legal processes ordering them to reveal their sources of information. Yet hardly a year goes by without a reporter being sent to jail for contempt of court after refusing to reveal his or her sources. What makes reporters so protective of their sources?

Think about the last time you shared a secret. It's probable that how much you revealed depended on how much you thought you could trust the other person to keep the secret. In fact, if you doubted the person's ability to keep silent, you may have even told a slightly different version of the secret, perhaps having left out the most sensitive details. This selective telling would also let you know who had told it if you later heard that version repeated by someone else. On the other hand, if you absolutely trusted the person, you probably told her or him everything you knew and everything you guessed, and helped them to interpret what the information meant. Reporters depend on that kind of candor to get great news stories, and to get them right.

Likewise, if you enter into mutually exclusive, mutually beneficial, and confidential relations with those you want to monitor, you can accomplish a great deal more. You can exceed what will probably be the future best practice in anticipating shifting irresistible forces by gathering insights unavailable to those who only use public sources.

Standards of Comparison Make a Difference

To appreciate the advantages of having standards in place for purposes of comparison, consider the consumer packaged goods arena. In that business, the expense of launching a new product is enormous. Most new products fail, and the longer you wait during development and introduction before pulling the failures, the more it ultimately costs you. Clearly, understanding how the new product is doing throughout its development compared to some norm or standard of success would be very helpful.

As consumer packaged goods companies have become larger through internal expansion and acquisitions, some have been able to assemble an enormous quantity of information. Some of the most valuable data concern the customer and consumer reactions that occur at all of the various stages of the development and testing process for successful versus unsuccessful new products. Where enough information is available, some manufacturers can go so far as to factor in the effect of different irresistible forces (including the environment for consumer spending, competitive reactions, and how the product is priced and consumed). For any such company, the savings from earlier terminations of unsuccessful products can be measured in hundreds of millions of dollars a year.

Imagine the increased advantages of going one step further. You assemble all of these data not only for your own company, but also for every noncompeting company you can find who will cooperate with you in the task. Having this information would allow each of you to know more about the likely success or failure of a new product in advance of investing large amounts of time and money in it. It would be to your advantage to initiate this service because of the proprietary advantages you would gain in creating standards for making the comparisons. (Naturally, you'll have to be good at keeping a secret to keep your allies' data confidential.) You may decide to provide the simpler applications of this information for free if necessary to attract users. By spearheading the task, your organization will have the most exposure to the data and thus be able to derive the most insight from the information about irresistible forces. Everyone else with access to these data would probably focus on using them only to evaluate new products in the absence of irresistible forces.

You could even go another step further and, over time, create a database on a country-by-country basis. Having this information would make developing new global brands enormously easier. Notice, too, that taking this step would make it hard for competitors to overtake you in setting a better future best practice for anticipating how new products will do. They could never know as much as you do about patterns of success and failure unless you shared your data and analyses with them.

Moore Lead Time

For the past several decades, the number of transistors on a semiconductor chip has doubled approximately every 18 months at more or less constant cost for the chip. The observation of this trend, made by Gordon Moore, Intel's cofounder, is the basis of Moore's Law.

Those who are interested in exceeding future best practices for anticipating future events have often been slow to see the applicability of Moore's Law to their own situations. To help you in this regard, we propose a corollary to Moore's Law and call it The Irresistible Force Data Breakthrough Corollary: The ability to process data will expand by 128 times every ten years. One reason we feel we can safely make this statement is that unmet needs and rewards for such processing capability will stimulate its development. Those needs arise partly because the sought-after creation of new molecules through chemistry or biotechnology requires the simultaneous calculation of tens of trillions of equations. If that sounds far-fetched, realize that some scientific problems now require simultaneous solutions for a billion equations.

Therefore, you should be collecting proprietary data now for anticipating changes in irresistible forces that it will only be practical to calculate and use years from now (perhaps as many as ten). By taking this step, you can probably achieve a multiple-year lead on most competitors who will only begin assembling data when they can be immediately used.

Adapting to Changes in Irresistible Forces: Guerrillas, Games, and Drills

Revolutionary Tactics

During the Revolutionary War in which the new-world British colonies broke free to become the United States, the colonists in areas outside the main battle zones usually did not rely on a standing army of the sort that exists today. Forces assembled in many cases just as needed, a just-in-time army, as it were. On receiving a summons (such as seeing a light in a tower, or hearing Paul Revere or someone else cry "The British are coming!" or a bell ringing), the Minutemen grabbed their muskets, ammunition, and powder and were on their way within a minute or two to a predetermined assembly point. (Volunteer fire departments in small communities often work this way now, responding to pagers and cell phones.)

Through losses in the early days of the war (for example, at Lexington where the Minutemen stood their ground against a vastly larger British force and were routed), these scattered colonial forces learned to observe the British, pick their tactics to fit the circumstances, and adapt as the situation changed. Minutemen who were not with General Washington's standing army often avoided fighting a battle out in the open. They didn't always use European-style ranks of riflemen either. What worked best for them was what we now call guerrilla tactics. They fired at the more numerous British troops from behind stone walls and trees. On the march back from Concord where the Minutemen successfully held their ground, the British Army sustained significant losses because of this tactic while the colonists had relatively few. The British had only one way of conducting a battle, regardless of the circumstances, and were at a great disadvantage against an adaptable foe.

Your enterprise needs to have the same flexibility of response as the Minutemen did. In fact, a drawback in using automatic responses through computers (such as those described for the computer reservation systems) is that they can become too predictable and thus allow a competitor to outmaneuver you. For instance, the computer reservation systems seek to generate more revenue per flight mile. Yet, leisure passengers are almost always more sensitive to price than anything else, creating an irresistible force to drop prices. Airlines like Southwest that have focused on having the lowest possible costs can outmaneuver such a reservation system by almost always pricing their fares below the major airlines. Southwest is still able to earn a higher profit by attracting more leisure customers per flight (achieving lower costs in part by avoiding the higher expense of such a more complicated reservation system).

Games, Not Guessing

Arie de Geus points out that people learn much faster through play than through actual training on-the-job or classroom education.* He ascribes several reasons for this success: In play, our minds are more open to experiences because we have nothing concrete to lose; we also learn best when we enjoy what we are doing and, by definition, play is fun; and since play has few or no future consequences, we are less inhibited about trying things.

Simulation-based training, which helps employees become more effective in many fields, can be improved by putting it into a "game" or "play" setting to prepare people for adapting to irresistible forces. In addition, you can use games to anticipate how your enterprise will react to changes in irresistible forces and to the arrival of new irresistible forces. The outcomes will give you a clear view of what your stalls are likely to be under various circumstances. Then you can create simulations that use different methods to overcome the stalls. Similarly, this play or games approach provides enormous advantages in such areas as deciding how and when to modify compensation and recognition to reflect shifts in irresistible forces. Otherwise, you're just experimenting

---

*See "Planning as Learning" by Arie de Geus, *Harvard Business Review,* March-April 1988.

based on the best guesses of your staff and whichever advisors and consultants you happen to use. Such analytically driven experiments are seldom as successful as what can be learned in a few days of simulations, and the simulations cost much less to conduct.

Attention All Hands: Battle Stations!

Throughout the cold war, United States forces were constantly ready to launch a nuclear attack on the Soviet Union. Fortunately, there was never a real need to do so. However, the threat of such an attack wouldn't have been a very useful deterrent to a nuclear war if the forces weren't actually able to deliver. Using constant training and exercises to go partially into attack mode kept the forces at the appropriate state of readiness.

Your business or organization likewise can use drills to improve its readiness for adapting to changes in irresistible forces. It's best to conduct such drills before an irresistible force has actually shifted, but when you expect that it might shift. One good way to determine the timing is to find a limited geographical area where the irresistible force shift has already started to occur and to implement your adaptation approach in that locale. This activity will also give you a chance to shake out the bugs in your approach so that when the whole organization has to make the overall change, it can do so more effectively. Many companies and communities did just this during their Y2K planning by moving dates forward in computers past the year 2000 in isolated installations to see what would happen. This simulation helped them anticipate many problems that would otherwise not have occurred until months or years later.

Stallbusting

The following questions are designed to take your thinking beyond what your company has ever considered doing before in regard to irresistible forces, and to seek out best practices beyond what others will be doing in the future. Although the questions are grouped under three different topics—locating, anticipating, and adapting to changes in irresistible forces—you may find that a question strikes you with an idea for application in another area. If that happens, so much the better. You'll be even more likely to push the envelope beyond others' future best practices.

As noted in chapter 13, you may be tempted to answer only the questions for one of the three areas covered. Avoid that temptation because giving in to that inclination is a mistake. You'll achieve far better results from this process if you equally examine the three dimensions of irresistible force engagement.

Being deficient in any of the three areas can reduce your overall effectiveness from high to average. Think about these areas as multipliers. Suppose you score a perfect 100 in all three areas. The result would be $100 \times 100 \times 100 =$ 1,000,000. If you had 100 in each of two areas and a 21 in the third, many people would average this result to get 73 and assume that this score placed them well above average. However, the multiplied result would be 210,000 ($100 \times 100 \times 21$), or only 21 percent of the potential 1,000,000 score. You multiply rather than average these areas because the effectiveness in one area has 100 percent impact on the overall effectiveness in the other areas. If you don't anticipate, you can't locate as well. And any delay in anticipation or location has a big impact on adapting. Conversely, if adapting is weak, it matters little what happens in locating and anticipating.

Develop Irresistible Force Detectors to Locate Buried Treasure

Everyone has seen people walking along with metal detectors, hoping to find valuables that are lost in the grass or buried underground. Usually these people find enough to pay themselves about double the minimum wage for their effort. However, every once in a while they find something really valuable. You want irresistible force detectors to do the same for your organization. The locating process should always more than pay for itself in modest insights, and every once in a while it should unleash a bonanza, a breakthrough gain. Otherwise, you won't be effective in the marketplace, and you won't be able to afford the right level of effort in this area.

How can you monitor stakeholders (customers, employees, suppliers, partners, distributors, shareholders and the communities in which you operate) in proprietary, inexpensive, simple ways that competitors will have great difficulty matching or exceeding? This question may sound like an oxymoron (a contradiction in terms) to you, but that's one reason that the question is so valuable. Few people will think to ask it.

Begin by posing this question to the relevant stakeholders and seeking their help. Often there is something stakeholders need from you that you don't currently provide but that would be relatively inexpensive to offer (such as converting your intranet-based, customer service computer system into an Internet database that customers could directly access to check on the status of their orders). You can offer them one of the inexpensive things that they want in exchange for an inexpensive form of their cooperation (perhaps sitting down for an hour once a quarter to discuss their relationship with everyone involved).

How can you automate the evaluation of the data you have for locating irresistible forces? This is an important consideration because most managements either under- or overreact to changes in data. By automating the analysis of the data in ways that don't obscure what is going on for those who will use the analysis, you can minimize inappropriate responses. A good analogy is to the kind of internal diagnostics that many new pieces of equipment have in them to anticipate the need for parts to be changed, for routine maintenance to occur, and to correct errors made at the factory without the customer being troubled.

Many people will see the answer to this question as a software problem. Actually, it's a decision-making problem that management should participate in alongside those trained in decision-making techniques and statistics. Once the parameters are set, then the software writers can make their contribution.

Be Ready to Anticipate Now and Later

Many irresistible forces will arrive unannounced. Your best weapon in defending your business is to have a thorough understanding of what *should* be happening with your stakeholders if the irresistible forces are acting as you believe they are. When you notice that something new is going on, that can be your clue to look for a new or an impending shift in irresistible forces. These new influences usually affect some parts of the stakeholder universe first and can be leading indicators of the future impact of the irresistible force. With that model in mind, consider these questions.

How can you develop proprietary insights into what is happening with your stakeholders that allow you to compare them to a control group (so-called normal circumstances)? The chapter has already provided you with one idea: become the data warehouse and analysis functions for those who are like you but are not your competitors. Another way is to form mutually exclusive data-sharing agreements with your stakeholders who have private or semiprivate data collected from others that they can ethically and legally share with you. A third option can be to help launch a new company to collect data and receive a preferred relationship on a permanent basis for your initial help. You could also develop a new measurement that is easy to do and to keep private, but that others couldn't easily duplicate. For example, if you are the largest service provider in the industry, this information could be something that is collected by your service people when they are visiting customers.

How can you begin to inexpensively collect data now that will be critically valuable in the future, but that are impracticably expensive or complicated to use now based on the current level of information technology? In organizational environments, real-time survey information fits this description. Someone ten years from now cannot know "why" someone did what they did before unless they collected the information as the actions happened. An example is determining "why" customers switched from one supplier to another. Another example is capturing what such switching customers would have preferred that suppliers provide, that no one provided at that time. Documenting similar information in the context of acquisitions during an industry consolidation can provide excellent guidance for evaluating your potential to make future acquisitions and do better with customers in the process. By tracking this information over time, you will increasingly be able to anticipate shifts in customer preferences, even before the customers are aware that they are shifting their focus.

You can do similar things with each of the constituencies you serve, as well as profiling behavioral patterns of your competitors. In technical areas, you can accumulate experimental data that may be used for new types of analyses that will become feasible in the future. Concerning government policy changes, you can map out precursors to the changes to improve your ability to anticipate change using a wide range of factors. You will find it most helpful in each case to capture proprietary data where no one is measuring now.

You can collect the data, keep them in electronic form, and simply begin to use them when it becomes practical to do so. In the meantime, you can run small experiments to test the usefulness of the information. Such raw-form data collections can often cost as little as 5 percent to 10 percent of what the ultimate cost to use them will be. Since the long-term benefits can be staggering, this is an inexpensive way to extend further beyond the future best practices of others.

Be Flexible and Adapt, or Break in the Process

In New England, windstorms can be intense, especially when hurricanes come through. During those storms, the maple trees and pines withstand quite well because they bend in the wind. The oaks, however, don't bend and sustain a lot of damage as a result. When it comes to exceeding the future best practices of others in adaptation, you should go a step further than even emulating the maples and pines, and be like the dandelion. The dandelion isn't harmed at all because it totally flattens out in the wind and quickly rebounds to stretch for the sun when the wind is gone. In fact, if the wind blows while its seeds are ready to be released, the seeds may even find many more hospitable homes than would otherwise have occurred.

What games and simulations do you currently use to prepare people for volatile situations, and which ones work best? Very few enterprises have no experience at all with learning based on games and simulations. If for some reason yours has had little exposure to these techniques, arrange to experiment with some games and simulations so that you can see, hear, and feel which ones work best for your people. As part of this activity, ask people what a useful and fun experience would be like for them. Soon you'll have parameters you can use to create custom games and simulations to prepare your company for rapid adaptation.

What kind of preparatory drills would pay off for your business? Advance experience in adapting is very useful. Find out in which areas there is a lot at stake and in which your people would be prepared to run controlled experiments. Companies that acquire others often uncover much more difficult computer conversions than expected, which then have enormous consequences on business results and costs. During the "due diligence" prior to making the acquisition, simulating how to do the conversions could provide a lot of information about whether to acquire and how much to pay for the acquisition. These circumstances especially apply when acquiring service organizations.

What stalls do you most need to avoid? As discussed earlier in the chapter, these stalls can be determined by analyzing the behaviors exhibited during the games, simulations, and preparatory drills you provide. If you do enough of these, you can also make each person in your enterprise aware of their own stalls and see how these need to be adjusted during adaptations to irresistible forces.

How can you measure your effectiveness in adapting to irresistible forces so that you can locate your best opportunities to improve? In this area, it's important to measure overall effectiveness and how each organizational unit performs. Many operations will find that most of their lost effectiveness is evident in one or two places. Some companies have had wonderful market research departments that were very good at locating irresistible force shifts, but ineffective in communicating that information to the rest of the company so that timely action could occur. This communications challenge can be even greater if you use outside organizations to help you anticipate and locate changes in irresistible forces.

Understanding the most that anyone can possibly know about irresistible forces provides the broadest possible perspective for seeing opportunity.

15

CREATE THE PERFECT PATTERN

STEP FIVE: IDENTIFY THE IDEAL BEST PRACTICES FOR BENEFITING FROM IRRESISTIBLE FORCES

We are all prisoners of our past. It is hard to think of things except in the way we have always thought of them. But that solves no problems and seldom changes anything.

—Charles Handy

The pursuit of the ideal requires perceiving potential well beyond anything previously considered. You can use what you learned in chapters 13 and 14 about future best practices as a mental trampoline for now springing far higher in that pursuit. This chapter emphasizes the importance of identifying the organizational near-perfections all around you and drawing out their lessons for your own enterprise.

Strategic Repositioning for Ideal Flexibility

Concentrating only on where your enterprise has been and where it is now can obviously keep you from perceiving your best opportunities to use irresistible forces. And even looking beyond this scope to examine the future best practice often falls short of discovering the path to irresistible growth. To close that gap, you need to apply the concept of the ideal when it comes to the best practices for locating, anticipating, and adapting to irresistible forces.

At this point we need to make a distinction between what we term future best practice and ideal best practice. The distance between them is greater than that between the effectiveness of the best performing enterprise in its sector and its least successful competitor. A company that masters future best practice in dealing with irresistible forces will do a better job of anticipating them through forecasting. If you think about a business that always strives to position itself to keep the wind behind, it will, even with good forecasting, constantly have to alter direction to capture the tailwinds. Making those changes takes time and effort, and you can be error prone.

Ideal best practice goes beyond forecasting, and making constant changes of direction. By doing this you eliminate the time, money, potential errors, and effort involved in those activities while accomplishing much more. An ideal approach is to benefit immediately from all of the winds that blow, whenever and from wherever they do so, as a pivoting windmill does.

The ideal best practice is the best way to get the greatest benefit now and in the near future by applying knowledge gleaned from observations of examples of near-perfect use of changing conditions. Consider the bee and its hive. Bees always have scouts out looking for opportunities and enemies. When the scouts return to the hive, they communicate perfectly with their dances what they found. With that information, the hive quickly takes the appropriate action. The bees have the ability to change the sex of the larvae being hatched by changing the food so the population can quickly shift to the right mix of workers. If they lose the queen, they can make a new one quickly. They even have ways of deciding to move the whole population. As a result, it is very hard for an irresistible force to wipe out a beehive population. Given favorable circumstances, the hive's population will soar as the improved resources are quickly exploited. And bees always save for a rainy day by storing honey. In the biological world, the beehive exhibits nearly ideal practices for both irresistible growth and survival, and provides lots of lessons for the astute observer.

Be aware, however, that the ideal best practice is to some extent a moving target. Today's conception of an ideal best practice will turn out to be hopelessly limited compared to tomorrow's solution to the same concept. The important point is to keep pushing forward to find ever more ideal best practices (something you will learn more about in chapter 18).

Let's use the weather, once again, as the basis for additional examples to help bring the concept of ideal best practice into better focus. For industries such as natural gas utilities, propane and oil dealers, and heating oil refiners (the producers of the raw materials or the providers of the services used to heat homes, offices, and other buildings), good weather is "bad weather." They make their profits from inclement weather and benefit more the longer it lasts. Even under those circumstances, high profits are only possible if they have enough low-cost energy resources to supply most of the demand. If weather conditions deteriorate too badly, they may disrupt the supply and deliveries needed to meet the increased demand. How can these companies determine their ideal best practices for adapting to the weather?

The heating companies can start by looking outside their industry to find anyone else similarly affected by weather conditions to see what effective strategies already exist. They might even look at the behavior of football fans who prepare for cold January games in outdoor stadiums, like the conditions often found at Lambeau Field in Green Bay, Wisconsin. A January game means that their team is in the playoffs, so weather conditions aren't going to deter them from attending the game. Despite conditions that might discourage an Eskimo from going hunting, the local football fans go to the game and have a wonderful time (especially when their team wins). While the weather may be a big factor for the visiting players, it's not much of an issue for the fans.

Why? Because they come fully prepared for whatever weather conditions they may encounter at the game. Experienced fans know that weather forecasts can be wrong and that conditions can change after they've left home for the stadium. The cold-weather football fan comes prepared for *all* weather conditions, even conditions that might be more extreme than they have ever experienced before. They come ready for dry conditions, wet seats, sleet, snow, rain, or freezing rain in addition to wind, glare, fog, and whiteout conditions. Electric socks, chemical foot and hand warmers, ski masks, and many layers of weather-resistant clothing form a foundation of protection. Fans cover the seats with specially insulated materials. Wraparound sunglasses help protect the eyes against the glare, wind, and dirt. Those not inclined to sit out in the weather will have arranged to view the game from luxury boxes in fully heated five-star comfort. But even they need clothing and gear to travel safely and comfortably to and from their means of transportation and to protect them should the stadium power fail.

One way the heating-related utilities mitigate the effects of weather vagaries on their profits is to negotiate a pricing structure with the utility commissions that ensures a reasonable return on investment, regardless of how much natural gas customers use. The utility's customers benefit in that they, too, don't have to worry as much about unpredictable heating bills. So both sides find a benefit that allows them to locate, anticipate, and adapt to irresistible force weather changes in effective ways. This structure is certainly a 2,000 percent solution arrived at through the pursuit of the ideal best practice.

Be sure not to limit your thinking. You should be able to improve on these examples with your own. The object of strategic repositioning is to identify and take actions that will leave you vastly better off, regardless of which irresistible forces arrive, when they arrive, and from whatever direction. The idea is simple: Find a way of operating that is always aided by your irresistible forces.

Using the Nth-Degree Perspective
Ideal Dreaming

Any irresistible force provides substantial positive potential, but you and your enterprise won't see that aspect of the circumstance at first. All you will initially see is the disruption that the irresistible force makes in your usual plans and procedures. To get past that initially negative perception, it helps to start by thinking the unthinkable.

For example, imagine that you manufacture a product whose price is now in a down cycle. Perhaps the current price in constant dollar terms is back to 1968 levels. What if the price were to drop further to reach 20 percent lower than ever before, measured in constant purchasing power dollars? Your initial reaction may be that you should quickly find a new job while the company retains a bankruptcy lawyer.

But wait, what could be good about such a situation? You may have some high-cost competitors that would be unable to continue under the circumstances. Perhaps they would have to shut down before you do. You might have some lower-cost competitors who sell their businesses to you at very low prices. Would your industry be more attractive if it had fewer competitors, and you had created a new, more efficient combination of the best manufacturers? The answer is probably yes. Because of the lower price, would you be able to expand into new markets previously unavailable to you? Probably yes, again. While the prices are low, would you be able to buy in your own company's stock at a low price? Also probably yes.

Now, where could the money come from to make these purchases? If they face disaster, the low-cost competitors may be willing to sell out for your stock. If you operate another business in a different industry unaffected by the depressed prices, you could sell shares in that business on the public market. Maybe your stock will always sell at a premium multiple to others in the depressed industry. You might have excess assets such as unused land and buildings that could be sold, or you may have untapped debt capacity.

Utilizing this perspective on the lowered product prices, other advantages and winning strategies should become apparent. You could realize that the irresistible force facing your company isn't low prices, but, rather, the need for an efficient consolidation of low-cost manufacturers through acquisitions and joint ventures. The low prices are the result of the irresistible force of incomplete consolidation. Consolidation into fewer, more efficient competitors with some high-cost capacity being eliminated would solve the profit-pressure problem. Notice that this thought process can be helpful to you regardless of what happens to the variable (the product's price, in this case). This train of thought can identify a real irresistible force, rather than merely the consequences of one. You have succeeded in locating the irresistible force through the ideal best practice of analyzing an extreme (Nth degree) scenario.

By looking at the extreme version of what you perceive as your irresistible force, you can identify the benefits that will follow from that force's direction. From those benefits, you will usually find one or more causes of what you perceived as your irresistible force. Be sure to look at extreme directions, up and down, in testing for actions that always leave your organization in an improved position.

Anticipation Above and Beyond

Many businesses incorrectly assume that anticipating irresistible forces is only a forecasting process. Thinking that way will only keep you confused. An ideal best practice is using the Nth-degree test (looking at the consequences of an even more extreme change) for locating forces as a starting point for identifying what you should anticipate.

In the preceding example about a low product price, the organization might have decided to focus its attention on forecasting prices. It should focus instead on dealing with the *causes* of the low prices in a way that would be helpful in *all* price environments. What should be anticipated in this example are the circumstances that could lead to an industry consolidation. Let's assume that one reason that profits come under pressure in the industry now is freight costs. The producers pay for shipping, sometimes for great distances. Mergers with companies in other geographic areas could reduce freight costs. Or suppose one company in the industry is having problems making its critical computer systems work. That circumstance could also encourage a consolidation with someone whose computer systems work very well and are expandable. And if a company lacked appropriate successors for its CEO position, the board would be inclined to support a merger with a company that has an outstanding CEO.

As you can see, when you locate the right irresistible force (the cause of what you fear), the factors that should lead you to anticipate the needed actions are already likely to be in place. You and your business are likely to have missed them in the past, however, because of focusing on the consequences of the irresistible force (low prices in our example) rather than on the need for industry consolidation as the irresistible force. (Learning to overcome that tendency to look at outcomes rather than causes will help you develop a capability to apply the ideal best practices, the subject of chapter 16.)

Always-Win, No-Lose Adaptability

From the football fan example, you can see how useful it is to anticipate so many circumstances that you're ready for almost any conditions. Such preparation assures you of being able to enjoy being at the game, or to deal with whatever comes next. In the low product price example, if your company leads a successful industry consolidation, profits will be higher regardless of the overall price level due to efficiencies of the newly combined entities. The new, more adaptable organization will thrive whatever direction prices take.

Let's consider another example: a business in an industry where the firm's best customers are so satisfied, that the customers actually resist new and better products as unnecessary. Without the demand for improved products, how can this enterprise pursue the ideal best practice for adaptability? Here are some possibilities:

- Find new customers who need improvements located in other parts of the world, and preferably where competitors would have trouble following your lead.

- Develop new types of customers who could use your organization's expertise to solve different problems.

- Educate other executives in the customer organizations, who are open to improvements, about the benefits of potential enhancements so that these executives will want to sponsor the changes.

Notice that these are all good things to do even if the existing customers were demanding improvements instead of preferring to maintain the status quo. So, for best positioning regardless of customer demand, it's a good idea to allocate resources to work in these new areas.

What each of the preceding examples has in common is the pursuit of always-win, no-lose options that permit increased benefit regardless of the irresistible forces encountered. To better understand this kind of circumstance, imagine that you are developing a new medical test costing $25 that will diagnose the need for pharmaceuticals costing thousands of dollars per treatment. The pharmaceutical companies are often wealthy compared to your organization, and looking for new opportunities. Without your company's new diagnostic, the new pharmaceutical markets will not develop nearly as well. Perhaps some of the pharmaceutical companies would be willing to pay 90 percent of your development costs and leave you with 90 percent of the diagnostic profit. If such an arrangement could be made, your company would have plenty of resources, would grow much more rapidly, and be much more profitable. If implemented successfully, it seems to be an always-win, no-lose option assuming that more than 10 percent of the efforts bear fruit for successful new diagnostic test products. Thus, by working with complementary companies (those whose economic success results from what you are doing, but are not customers, suppliers or competitors) on a shared-benefit, shared-cost basis, you have found an ideal best practice for achieving optimal adaptability.

Utilizing always-win, no-lose options is like being a pivoting windmill. No matter which way the wind is blowing, you will win. There is no way to lose unless the wind is so strong that it breaks the windmill or the equipment isn't maintained properly. Such options provide 360-degree flexibility in harnessing the full benefit of any forces that come your way.

Stallbusting

Start-ups are often close to perfectly aligned with irresistible forces because the founding entrepreneurs feel free to disregard the obsolete lessons of the past and present. Your enterprise should temporarily cut its ties to its old thinking as well in this important step by conceptualizing model performance for the future. Look for examples of perfect alignment with irresistible forces wherever you find them to serve as analogies for opportunities that your irresistible growth enterprise can pursue. Working through the following questions can help you use new ways of thinking to identify the ideal best practices for locating, anticipating, and adapting to changes in the irresistible forces that your organization encounters.

What are the forces that, if they moved in the wrong ways now, could create significant adverse results for your company? Make a list which includes such factors as lower prices for your goods and services, higher costs from your suppliers, decreasing orders from your customers, greater difficulty of providing goods and services, and an adverse governmental environment. Add anything else that may apply, such as being overwhelmed by unpredictable new technology that changes the way that you have to operate your company. Make the list as long as you can. Fill it with your firm's worst current and potential nightmares. Then go on to the next question.

What would be the consequences for your enterprise, competitors, current and potential customers, employees, suppliers, distributors, partners, shareholders, and the communities in which you do business if you imagine these forces at the worst possible levels that would still allow your industry to survive (although in a much changed form)? In a worst-case scenario, many competitors would go out of business, customers would be scrambling to be served, layoffs would be large-scale, and so forth. In focusing on these circumstances, you should immediately start to think about those for whom such conditions would be unacceptable. Their behavior would probably change in some way that could help to alleviate the situation. For example, customers who really need what you have to offer for high-value applications would be most anxious to have reliable suppliers who would protect them from the disruptions that these events would bring. Some competitors would be willing to merge before going out of business. Some suppliers would be willing to make concessions to help you be more effective before they lost too much business, and so forth. Find out what to do with these ideas by answering the next question.

What irresistible forces are causing these responses? One possible answer could be that there are two parts to the market, with customers falling into either a high-value or a commodity segment. Trying to serve both segments may be economically insupportable in adverse circumstances because of excess competition. This factor raises a question of whether or not you can refocus your attention on the high-value segment in such a way that precludes the commodity competitors from being effective against you in that segment. Alternately, you should also consider whether or not you can achieve such a benefit from being the low-cost supplier to the commodity segment, and automatically inherit the high-value segment in a severe shakeout. Once you know the answer, you can decide which irresistible forces you want to align with.

Which of the conditions that lead to this irresistible force are already present and require action? Continuing with the example, let's assume that there are shared economics whereby it would be most efficient to have one, very large supplier for both the commodity and the high-value segments. This circumstance would mean that the irresistible force is the need for industry consolidation. If those potential economics exist and there are financially feasible ways to begin the consolidation, then the necessary conditions are already present. You should simply list them here. You would probably find that these conditions include ineffectively configured competitors, costs in the industry that are too high, pricing that should be lower, and the need to have a firm that further differentiates its product and service offerings between the high-value and the commodity segments. The actions needed would probably include changes in how your organization operates to better serve the high-value segment, possibly acquiring or merging with others, and lowering prices for the commodity segment.

What are your no-lose options? In this example, standing still is probably not one of them. At a minimum, you have to make the operational changes needed for the high-value segment, and do them better than anyone else. You'll probably find that this action will at least leave you as strong as you are now. Going after the commodity segment without the requisite cost position would probably be a losing option. You might be able to find some combination of acquisitions and mergers, or changed operating practices, that would first have to occur before your pursuit of the commodity segment would be a no-lose option.

What are your always-win, no-lose options? Working with your current and potential customers, employers, suppliers, distributors, partners, shareholders, and the communities in which you operate is probably critical to developing these options. Basically, you are looking for cooperation from some of these groups who perceive an advantage for them to your moving in the direction of being well aligned with the irresistible force.

For example, adding the capability for the high-value segment's needs is an always-win, no-lose option if enough customers will give you long-term contracts at a profitable level for adding these customer benefits. To get your costs down for the commodity segment might require work rules that differ from the current union agreements in your plants. The union might be willing to renegotiate on these points in exchange for somewhat greater employment stability for existing employees (which you could offer if you are about to gain a lot of market share as a result).

Be sure not to stop when you have found one always-win, no-lose option. There may be others that are more attractive to your irresistible growth enterprise. Be sure to check how well the options hold up under average and positive conditions, as well. Otherwise some competitor may grab a better opportunity and drastically reduce your potential benefits. And be sure to evaluate always-win, no-lose options from the perspective of your competitors, partners and those you serve.

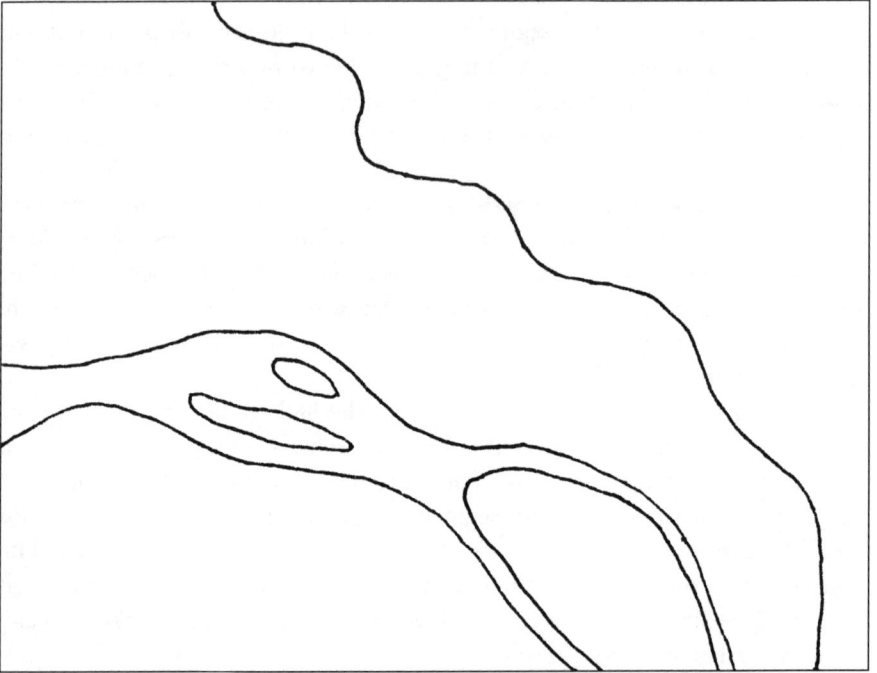

To approach the ideal best practice for locating, anticipating, and adapting to your irresistible forces, the irresistible growth enterprise will broaden its perspective across the dimensions of space and time, effect and cause. This will mean looking narrowly, like through a microscope at a biological sample, as well as broadly, like through a space telescope at a section of the Earth.

16

GO FOR A PERFECT FIT

Step Six: Determine How to Operate Close to Ideal Best Practices for Locating, Anticipating, and Adapting to Your Irresistible Forces

Companies should measure their success not by the fact that they are still around and making money, but by how many opportunities they have missed.

—Gary Hamel

This chapter contains practical advice for coming as close as possible to achieving ideal best practices as introduced in chapter 15. You will learn how to think about your irresistible forces in order to ensure timely use of the ideal best practice concepts. You will also learn about other important facets of successfully dealing with irresistible forces: initiating them or creating changes.

Fashionable Flexibility

Regardless of the ideal best practices you choose to pursue, you will build far more breakthrough gains by first aiming for ideal flexibility. For example, to achieve irresistible growth, an enterprise needs flexible capabilities and options for more and faster ways to change, for causing less disruption to the organization when pursuing options, and for creating or changing irresistible forces to its benefit. To illustrate, let's begin by considering a personal analogy. Many people gain and lose weight often enough that they either find themselves with more than one wardrobe or just buy baggy clothes so they can look about the same across a wide range of weights. By considering the irresistible force that affects your wardrobe requirements, you have two different options:

1. Adjust your eating, drinking, and exercise habits to reflect variations in the conditions that normally cause you to gain and lose weight, or change shape, so that one well-fitted, attractive wardrobe will work for you all the time. This approach is desirable because it means that you are always at your best.

2. Acquire clothing that attractively adjusts to fit your changing shape when that occurs, and remains stylish over time. This option is appealing because it corrects for errors in the first approach while allowing you to rapidly adjust to unexpected changes.

Notice that these two options address the problem of adaptability for a changing shape from opposite directions. The first requires flexibility in your behavior in order to keep your body constant so that the clothes can be the same size over time. For an organization, this first approach would be like maintaining the same level of resources and effectiveness in relation to irresistible forces, regardless of force conditions. The second option requires flexibility in your clothes to adapt to a changing body shape. For an organization, this approach would often mean having external partners and suppliers who adjust to your needs and provide you with adaptability beyond what you could do for yourself. For some, the second option seems impossible because styles of clothing change so much. To take best advantage of this direction, therefore, you would have to be able to create new irresistible forces, such as fashion preferences, that will support your wardrobe's flexibility.

The ideally flexible solution is to implement both options simultaneously because each one will cover for a breakdown in the other. As a result, you will have enormously increased your likelihood of always having a good and fashionable fit for your clothes at low cost. Also, since you may change your mind at some time in the future about what weight and shape you want to have, employing both options creates the ideal flexibility for you also to make that adjustment effectively and inexpensively as well.

The credit card enterprise VISA provides a good organizational model because it combines the elements of constancy and adjustability. The organization is governed by a constitution, which each provider of credit card services must sign and abide by. The constitution creates the equivalent of permanency in size and shape that makes the central organizational structure an unchanging one. Yet each member organization is completely free to adapt to local market conditions in any way that it chooses, subject to the limitations of the constitution.

VISA can also grow and adapt by adding new members and services, like an adaptable garment that keeps the wearer in fashion. These members can also interact with the governments in their respective countries to seek legislation and regulation that will create more favorable irresistible forces for credit cards to help keep the VISA approach in style. It's not surprising that VISA was one of the fastest growing large organizations in the world at the end of the twentieth century.

Continuing with the clothing analogy, many organizations constantly change their size and shape to adapt to irresistible forces (such as ones that cause large changes in demand for the organization's goods or services). For enterprises, cycles of hiring and layoffs (and of acquisitions and dispositions) are the equivalent of personal weight gains and losses. Such fluctuations in response to irresistible forces creates a lot of waste because they are costly, time consuming, and difficult to implement well. Organizations taking this approach will always find themselves behind in adapting to irresistible forces because it is simply too slow (particularly when rapid expansion is needed). What's needed instead is a size and shape (and access to other organizations that can expand flexibility) so that accomplishments can be adjusted without changing the organization. Such a configuration can avoid the most costly, difficult, and ineffective elements of the change process.

Locating Changes in Irresistible Forces: Sensitivity, Selectivity, and Extrapolation

Sunshine on Your Shoulders

Irresistible forces can't be studied if the changes they cause go undetected. Many organizations aren't very good at noticing anything new and need to develop more sensitivity in that area. Imagine wearing a blindfold and facing the horizon at sunset. By using all of your available senses you can tell when the sun is setting by noting clues such as losing the feel of the sun's warmth on your skin, the little rustle of wind that often comes then, and the changes in animal sounds. By using all of your organization's senses—each person and each dimension that they are sensitive to—you can overcome any blindness that your organization may now be experiencing and begin to feel the changes in your irresistible forces.

The blindness that almost all organizations experience causes missed opportunities. For example, if your key competitor has a large layoff and many of its most effective salespeople leave, you have a chance to get business in accounts that had been closed to you until now. Unless you are paying attention though, another competitor will notice the situation first, hire these salespeople, and capture many of the accounts for itself. Although your sales and profits won't drop as a result of missing that opportunity, they'll certainly fall short of their potential.

You need to develop increased sensitivity to locating irresistible forces. A good starting point is to teach everyone in your organization to notice when the unexpected happens, either positively or negatively, to you, your competitors, partners, suppliers, customers, distributors, shareholders, and the communities in which you operate. Each person must then *share what they noticed immediately* in some way so that it can be considered in the context of other unexpected occurrences. For example, if a customer who is normally a tough sell suddenly becomes easy to sell to, something may have happened to affect that customer's mood and orientation. Or if a supplier suddenly can't meet your delivery standards, there may be unexpected excess demand for the supplier's products or a shortage in needed materials. When enough unusual circumstances are evident that could have the same or similar causes, you need to begin looking into why these things have been occurring. Since you may only be noticing a small percentage of the clues, you can probably assume that something significant is happening whenever your organization becomes aware of at least three indications of mutually consistent changed behavior.

To make the best use of increased sensitivity, you need some simple way to collect and work with the information collected. If everyone in your company is on an intranet, you can use some form of group software both for reporting the circumstances and inviting comments on what might be involved. Or you can use voice mail or paper forms to do the same thing. The important thing is to foster a heightened awareness of your organization's environment and to encourage effective communication of the resulting observations. Your initial reaction may be to consider this change monitoring activity as an immense task. However, you need to remember that while tracking must be continuous, actions aren't required until a significant change is noted and confirmed. As a result, each individual may only be noting a few things and reviewing what others have been noticing, which is hardly very time-consuming. If your notational system is taking too much effort for the benefits, you should have someone review and winnow down what your organization is reporting to make the data more relevant and useful. On the other hand, if it is time-consuming but you are getting a lot of benefits, it makes sense to make the necessary commitment. If the latter is the case, be sure the process and regular workloads allow enough time for prompt and thoughtful attention by each person involved.

Static or Important Statistic?

Like static heard on a radio during a passing thunderstorm, some random events will always be occurring. If these events don't constitute a shift in irresistible forces, nothing need be done. When you gather a lot of reports that could mean something, you need to be carefully discriminating in interpreting the data.

By being aware of two dimensions—the degree of shift and the duration of shifts in behavior—you can more easily develop ways to approach the ideal best practice for locating changes in irresistible forces. If the degree of shift is great enough, it can be an irresistible force even if it doesn't last very long. For example, suppose you announce a new service to begin in six months, and then orders suddenly dry up for your existing service. Unless you do something now, your announcement will have a large, negative impact on your organization. On the other hand, the degree of shift can be modest but by continuing over a long period of time, the shift can become very significant. For example, customer loyalty (continuing to be a customer with the same or a higher level of purchases) dropping by only 1 percent point a year becomes a crisis if it continues long enough, because keeping an existing customer is usually at least four times more profitable than adding a new one. If you have to replace too many customers, your profits and cash flow will all vanish at some point.

You also need to consider how you can gain benefit from varying conditions when they occur. For example, if competitors' customers start buying twice as much, and no more from you, this change won't affect your performance versus budget, but your share of industry profits will become much smaller. Presumably, there would be some profitable way that you could capture some of this increased volume for your organization.

A great help in selecting data that are important versus data that are not is to identify areas that have large economic significance and to track them in some visual way (like a graph). Such visuals are even more effective if they have an historical trend line or the extrapolation of that trend displayed on them. New data plotting significantly above or below the trend line can be the first sign that change has arrived.

To Infinity and Beyond

Yet another technique for approaching the ideal best practice for locating changes in irresistible forces is to become expert in the use of Nth-degree searches. As we explained in chapter 15, an Nth-degree search is simply a way of extrapolating the new irresistible force condition to an extreme level to make the irresistible force's causes easier to see. When you start to work in this area, your organization will tend to make two mistakes. First, in pushing the condition to an extreme, your organization probably won't go nearly far enough. For example, if the repeat customer buying percentage is dropping by 1 percentage point per year, you might choose to look at the implications if the percentage drops by 3 percentage points a year instead. Actually, a better way to look at it is to assume that the drops that are likely to occur over the next 20 years occur overnight (20 percentage points of drop all at once). In choosing the degree you look at, remember that you aren't trying to forecast the future. You are just trying to understand the causes and consequences of the current trend. The more you exaggerate the condition, the more important aspects of the condition will become obvious and the less time and effort will be required to understand them.

In chapter 15, we also explained that many organizations fail to consider causes, preferring to treat symptoms instead. Having now started to look for causes, you may make the second mistake of not being disciplined to look far enough toward the ultimate causes. For example, if you find a new direction in the buying habits of competitors' customers, you may be tempted to stop looking when you find that these customers' own customers are not buying as much. However, there is some reason why those customers' customers aren't buying. You need to look further until you reach the ultimate cause.

While you may still be concerned about how complicated and time-consuming monitoring activities will be, you'll probably find that the more deeply and broadly you search, the simpler the task becomes. Consider that you may be seeing dozens of variances from historical trends going on, but, on closer examination, they will often turn out to all be related to exactly the same irresistible force. For example, everyone is aware that there are tremendous pressures to reduce costs in the health-care area. Health-care costs are simply rising too rapidly for what is affordable. That single irresistible force, however, can have hundreds of different specific impacts, each of which could be considered an irresistible force. For instance, a declining bed utilization rate in hospitals could be viewed by a hospital administrator as an irresistible force all by itself, yet it is clearly driven by the overall force of pressure to reduce health-care costs from insurers and the government.

Anticipating Changes in Irresistible Forces: History, People, and Precursors

A Backward Look

As we pointed out in chapter 15, when you locate the actual irresistible forces (such as pressure on health-care costs in the preceding example) that cause the conditions or forces you are experiencing (such as declining bed utilization in hospitals), you'll usually find that the causative force has been in place for some time. To approach the ideal best practice in anticipating changes in irresistible forces, look at the history of the original force to see what conditions are associated with its direction, rate of change, and significance. Simple statistical tests are adequate for this purpose. (If you don't know how to conduct the tests, arrange to have someone help you who is familiar with the process.) Basically, what you want to do is to determine what preconditions are usually associated with changes in the factors that are of interest to you. Research this aspect by comparing data series from earlier time periods that precede the changes you are studying to discover precursor events.

Those in the Know

Statistical tests will rule out some potential causes, but you'll still have a long list of possible causes to check. You need to find people with the knowledge and experience with the specific forces being studied by the statistics tests to tell you which ones are more likely to be the actual causes. Focus first on those closest to the problem or who have outstanding expertise on the subject. If the forces are affecting customers, talk to customers. If they affect shareholders, talk to shareholders. If they come from government policy, talk to those who create and implement government policy. In each area, these people are the experts who can help you to link cause and effect. You'll get even more help if you show them what you think you have learned from the statistical analysis because some of them will be able to spot the potential influence of other factors that you may have ignored. And don't forget to get ideas and help from those who may have been studying the subject matter for some other purpose.

A Forward Look

You will often draw the wrong conclusions about irresistible forces if you only review historical relationships. For example, when oil-exporting countries were discouraged by low prices prior to the Arab oil embargo of the early 1970s, they complained but took little action. OPEC's efforts through the embargo and reduced production to cut the supply then proved to be a very effective way to raise prices. In the late 1990s, oil prices were again relatively low in constant dollar terms, but the cartel-led reduction in supply did not raise oil prices as much that time. It would be easy to totally dismiss the consequences of higher oil prices in constant dollars because the likelihood of this recurring seems remote. But that viewpoint overlooks the fact that certain kinds of military action could create a price effect similar to the Arab oil embargo by damaging the world's major oil fields so that large amounts of current and future production would be curtailed. Many oil fields, especially those located offshore such as those in the North Sea, are vulnerable to sabotage as well. Although invasion or sabotage would be unfortunate and few would wish that either happens, either occurrence is one that would make a lot of sense for certain political interests to pursue.

From this example, you should be able to see why your organization should develop scenarios for such kinds of irresistible force causes. (See Getting It All Together to Go the Distance, in chapter 3, and The Scenario's the Thing, in chapter 13.) In addition to being better prepared to deal with the consequences, should they occur, you can learn what the precursors of such an event would probably be and thus be better able to anticipate it. For example, increased reports of dissident terrorist groups operating in or supported by oil-rich countries would be one sign to look for. Notice that the only action you may need to take, unless you are in the petroleum industry, is to secure a long-term price contract not subject to a war clause for your petroleum and petroleum-based product needs. Yet, by taking only this action, the savings over several years could be enormous.

If oil prices should rise for some other unexpected reason, a long-term price contract would still protect you. In fact, studying the history of petroleum prices would have shown that whenever the prices reach a new low in constant dollar terms, it's a good time to secure a fixed-price supply. Any organization that took that action in 1998 would have cut its petroleum costs in half by the beginning of 2000. Thus, flexible arrangements can create benefits regardless of future circumstances.

Adapting to Changes in Irresistible Forces: Optimism, Options, and Open-Mindedness
The Pot of Gold at the End of the Cold Shower
To approach the ideal best practice for adapting to irresistible force changes, the biggest challenge to you and your organization is to view the consequences of such trends optimistically (although not overoptimistically). You need to see the many ways they can be turned into a delightfully supportive environment

for your organization. Most trends will initially seem to be about as desirable as a cold shower after being outdoors in cold weather all day. But that cold shower does have benefits. It can keep you from wasting water by shortening your shower, reduce your utility bill for heating water, make you more alert, and help you stay used to cold conditions for other times when you'll be outside in the cold all day.

A good way to start retraining your outlook is to ask yourself, "What is totally positive about these new circumstances?" Then each time you come up with an answer, ask the same question again. You may have trouble finding answers at first, but with practice you'll come up with quite a few. The more frequently you answer this question about some circumstance, the more likely you are to hit upon a valuable opportunity that will help you in both the current and alternative environments, regardless of what comes next.

An exercise in this area works best if a large number of people in your organization consider the question in small groups, using classic brainstorming techniques. In fact, some organizations have found it helpful to split the entire company into small study groups on the same subject. Each group then reports what it learned to the other groups. Stimulated by the new thinking, the brainstorming subgroups meet again and find even better ideas. Then the results are shared again. This procedure can be repeated, each time getting closer to the ideal practice, until this thinking is no longer productive. At that point, you can expand the number and types of people involved to include users, customers, partners, suppliers, distributors, shareholders, those in the communities you serve, and even experts from seemingly unrelated fields. They will help you see, feel, and hear more benefits from the new circumstances, thus providing more attractive opportunities for adapting to them.

The Choice Is Yours

When you have many choices to consider, you need first to determine which of the choices or combinations of choices exhibit no-lose or always-win, no-lose characteristics. (In making this determination, you need to be particularly careful of the overoptimism stall discussed in chapter 8.) It's best to have someone other than those who generate the ideas do the evaluation. In fact, the more picky, fault-finding, never-satisfied people you can locate to review your options, the better. Then once the evaluations have been made, send the options back to those who came up with them for revisions based on the new issues that have been raised by the picky people.

When you select the options to go with, favor those that look safest on the no-lose grounds over those that look best on the always-win grounds. Organizations seem to be better at finding ways to avoid loss than in finding ways to always succeed. In this way, you can further hedge your bets while you are developing a higher level of skill in locating and implementing the always-win, no-lose choices.

The organizations most innovative in seeing better options will be the most successful in the environment we are postulating of ever-volatile, and increasingly unpredictable, organizational conditions. This viewpoint has another fundamental advantage: It becomes a way to force the abandonment of your current organizational direction before conditions intercede to require that change in direction for merely achieving survival.

To truly approach the ideal best practice for adapting to irresistible force changes, never consider your work in this area completed. You need to keep an open mind to be able to see that the adaptations you've generated are simply the best options you've identified so far, and that there are far better ones you haven't yet uncovered or considered. You want to keep finding these better choices continuously, and smoothly substitute them for the ones you are pursuing now by being prepared to shift directions in a heartbeat when something better is identified.

Creating Changes in Irresistible Forces: Now You're Cooking!

Writing about this subject could encompass several entire books, so for the purposes of this chapter, we simply present one quick-to-make basic recipe for creating irresistible forces. Having learned a basic recipe, you can then go on to try others from the various cookbooks on influencing public opinion and attitudes.

A Dash of Demand

Whereas governments have long been interested in shaping public opinion for political purposes, formally doing so for commercial purposes is fairly new. Demographics, money flows, the weather, and many other large irresistible forces are mostly beyond the ability of one organization to influence, although some do try. The Chinese government has been changing family structure for some years now with its policy of one child per family. The U.S. Federal Reserve coordinates financial policies such as interest rates with countries around the world in an effort to affect global economic activity. Manufacturers are constantly making innovations in housing and clothing that permit everyone to be less affected by extremes in weather conditions.

Perceptions are easier to influence than many other areas of irresistible forces. Current popular trends will inevitably become unpopular. But can the unpopular be made popular? Edward Bernays, the founder of modern public relations, once told a story about having a client who had bought too much red fabric one year and sales were poor. Undeterred, Bernays invited the most fashionable people to a special party where the women were to all wear red dresses. Amid much newspaper publicity generated by Bernays, red soon became the rage for dresses and the client was saved.

In his excellent book, *Influence: Science and Practice* (3rd edition, Harper-Collins College Publishers, 1993, page 97), Robert Cialdini of Arizona State University pointed out that social proof often guides behavior. For example, at the height of the disco craze, some club owners delayed admitting customers, creating long waiting lines on the street even when there was plenty of room inside. The purpose? To benefit from Cialdini's observation: "Since 95 percent of the people are imitators and only 5 percent initiators, people are persuaded more by the actions of others than by any proof we can offer." If lots of people are waiting to get in, then most of us would conclude that this must be a trendy club that we should go to.

In a similar way, you may be able to create demand among those who set the trends of irresistible forces and thus influence many others. Manufacturers often provide their new products for free to prestige accounts, hoping to get those accounts to provide testimonials for the products. Publishers send free galleys of their books to periodicals, hoping to garner favorable reviews that will later appear in advertisements and on the jacket covers. Companies use public relations and advertising all the time to shape public opinion about what is "in" and what is "out," and even the smallest organization can use these tools to help create or shape irresistible forces.

A Pinch of Prototypes

Smart salespeople have known for a long time that determining the specifications that will be used in purchasing for an industry will have a large positive impact on their sales. For this reason, companies often charge very little compared to their costs to develop prototypes that will be used to help establish an industry standard. These prototypes will provide them with large advantages should they become the industry standard that everyone must meet. Shrewd companies make the prototypes in ways that will be much more difficult and expensive for competitors to copy.

This process of setting standards usually begins by finding a technical person in the purchasing organization who is sensitive to little details. The customer's supplier is willing to provide unique solutions to those little details that a competing supplier would have a hard time duplicating at the same or lower cost. If the technical person is delighted with the product results, that's good for the supplier. The purchasing agent will find that the recommended specifications for buying new products include many of the delightful little technical details so prized by the technical person. Competitors then have little time to respond. Without a way to earn a decent profit margin on the new business, competitors may even decline to bid. A process like this has often occurred in government procurement for weapons systems, for example.

A Cup of Celebrity

It's not uncommon for shrewd marketers to spice up their product campaigns by hiring celebrity spokespeople for their products and services. When Michael Jackson was at the height of his popularity in the early 1980s, Pepsi-Cola saw its market share rise in part through extensive concert-type advertising featuring this performer. Robert Young, the actor who appeared as the doctor in the highly rated television show, *Marcus Welby, M.D.,* became so credible to the millions who admired and liked him that manufacturers of over-the-counter medicines hired him to appear in their advertisements. In the 1990s, Michael Jordan, the basketball player, enjoyed the same kind of appeal and generated an enormous income solely from being a spokesperson for a variety of products, including basketball shoes.

Similarly, start-up organizations will often salt the board with celebrities and soon enjoy a high-profile level of influence. Almost overnight, the Drucker Foundation became a major factor in the development of thinking about the nonprofit sector through the prestige that Frances Hesselbein provided as head of the foundation. She is the former head of the Girl Scouts and one of the most able and admired nonprofit executives ever. She then persuaded Peter Drucker to lend his name and advice to the foundation. Using their combined influence, the best thinkers in the world volunteered their services in exchange for the recognition that being part of Drucker Foundation activities could provide. This popularity drew success much more rapidly than mere quality and marketing could have done, allowing the Drucker Foundation to approach more closely to an ideal best practice.

Stallbusting

Your key challenge in approaching the ideal best practices for locating, anticipating, adapting to, and creating or shaping changes in irresistible forces is to create a mindset in your organization that sees the full positive potential for your organization in every force change, and is excited and energized by the occurrence of these changes. Working through your answers to the following questions can get you started in the right direction.

Examine How Approaching the Ideal Best Practice Will Challenge Your Organization

If you stop to think for a minute, you may realize that your organization almost always responds to any problem or opportunity in a limited number of ways. You may also notice a great sensitivity to some kinds of external changes and complete deafness to others. In this section, you will find questions designed to help you locate areas of insensitivity and unresponsiveness that keep you from enjoying the benefits of operating close to the ideal best practices.

What aspects of approaching the ideal best practices will be new for your organization? New activities are hard to understand, hard to see as advantageous, and hard to learn how to do well. Being aware of these difficulties can help focus your attention on taking more time to explain what is involved and providing relevant resources and experiences.

What aspects of approaching the ideal best practice will cause resistance in your organization? New processes automatically create powerful critics because they are so different from the way the organization has proceeded in the past. Since the organization is still operating, you and your colleagues probably consider yourselves a success. In fact, you may attribute some of that success to things that this process will change, and you may well be right in that assessment. What you need to determine is if this process will allow you to be even more successful.

The areas that violate your instincts should be openly identified for rigorous testing with the most difficult problems you can find. Include people who are most critical of these ideas to help evaluate their effectiveness. Be careful that your experiments are done well so that the new practices have a chance to show their benefits. Keep repeating the experiments until you have at least one significant success. Then you can begin to properly evaluate what you will gain and compare that with the difficulties of making these changes.

Because of the geometric advantages of being better aligned with irresistible forces, a little improvement in alignment greatly outweighs a lot of cost and difficulty in getting there. You'll probably decide to go ahead with the elements of approaching the ideal best practice that originally created discomfort, unless the deck is hopelessly stacked against you because the CEO, for example, doesn't have an open mind. Naturally, if you still believe in the new approach, you can practice it privately, even if no one else agrees. The good ideas you generate will often run circles around the alternatives.

If you anticipate strong resistance to introducing a major program, you can use careful questioning to trigger the needed changes through the power of the insights that they elicit. Use the questions in this book as a starting point, rephrasing them so that they have more relevance and meaning to the people in your organization.

What aspects of approaching the ideal best practice will be most difficult for your organization to implement well? The answers to this question will vary greatly from organization to organization. For some, it may be operating in a more openly communicating environment. For others, it may be generating always-win options. For still others, it may be seeing heightened opportunity in the face of every change. Whatever your answers are, you'll need to provide the most support and practice in these areas. Be sure to measure how you are doing so you can help your organization see how it's progressing and how it can improve. (The techniques developed in chapters 11 and 12 are helpful here.)

Make Implementation of Approaching the Ideal Best Practices Seem More Like Play than Work

Organizations do better at dealing with a new process when they are playing than when they perceive themselves to be "working," "being trained," "studying," or "being lectured to." By turning the process into "play," you can unleash more interest, creativity, and effective thinking.

What forms of play does your organization enjoy the most now? In this regard, you can consider what games people in the organization like to play now. Is there a company softball team, or do you have competitions to name new products? Particularly note if these are team or individual games, and see which ones create the most happiness and satisfaction. Some games create more frustration than happiness and should be avoided. For example, golf can be frustrating for those who overly focus on the score, rather than on the fellowship and surroundings.

What forms of play are the most useful to helping your organization succeed now? Almost all organizations have held development conferences, seminars, training sessions, picnics, or family outings. Ask others in your organization which such group activities worked best and what each was good at accomplishing. The response will give you ideas of formats for the play you wish to create.

How can this process be reformulated to have the context of playing that will work best for your organization? If, for example, your company makes bowling equipment, chances are that many of your employees have an interest in bowling. You can start by reframing the process to use bowling examples. You can then create your teams to develop ideas so that the idea generation is relieved with some time off for bowling. You can put names on bowling pins for the irresistible forces you are considering so that people can take turns knocking them down for the benefit to their score. And so on. In each case, just ask how it is going, watch whether people are happily engaged or not, listen to what the people are saying to be sure they are really having fun, and that they are thinking and learning while playing. If you're not having much luck with your approach, let those who will be doing the thinking pick their own forms of play. They are bound to think of something they know they'll like better.

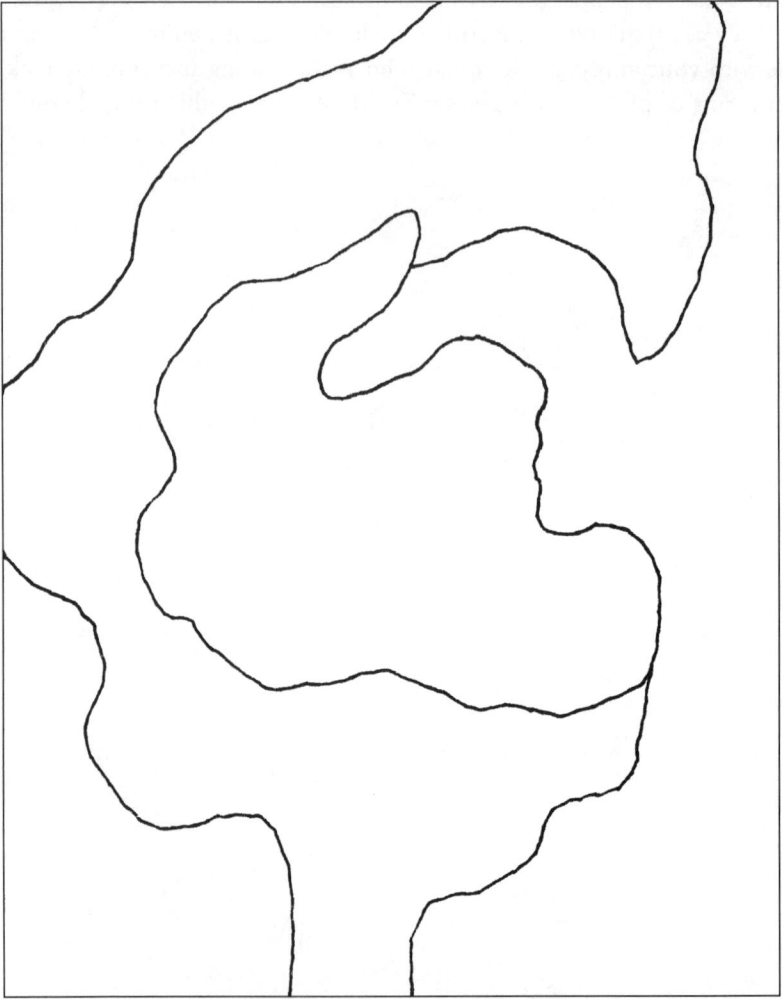

Establishing a close and effective relationship among those dealing with irresistible forces in your enterprise will reduce the chances of being caught unprepared. Like a close-fitting mosaic, there is no risk that a hostile irresistible force can intrude and tear the relationship apart.

17

ASSEMBLE A
TAILOR-MADE TEAM

STEP SEVEN: ENHANCE YOUR PEOPLE'S ABILITY TO ACHIEVE THE BENEFITS OF IRRESISTIBLE FORCE MANAGEMENT

You bet on people, not on strategies.

—Larry Bossidy

Building and motivating your organization are key elements in achieving the full benefits of irresistible force management. This chapter points out that critical skills are probably missing in your organization, and that they must be quickly added through learning, hiring, and adding partners and suppliers. In addition, it can help you diagnose whether your current recognition and reward structures are undermining your irresistible force efforts, and how you can realign these signals with your new organizational focus on ultimate flexibility.

Recognizing the Importance of Teamwork

Your goal is to always get the best results from irresistible forces, regardless of their direction. Imagination, when used to create flexibility, can allow you to experience favorable irresistible forces even when the effects come from a variety of directions. Sailboats provide a good analogy. Although a sailboat's design is not as effective in dealing with changeable wind direction as the pivoting windmill, they still allow the captain and crew substantial flexibility. A sailboat can move forward with the wind coming from virtually any direction except a few degrees of directly head on. For those circumstances, a motor is a handy adjunct to create perfect flexibility.

To take full advantage of the winds, you need to understand their effects. Common sense would make you think that a sailboat can travel faster with a following wind rather than with headwinds or side winds. But, as it often is with irresistible forces, common sense is wrong in this case. For unlike airplanes, most sailboats actually go fastest with a side wind. With a wind perfectly behind the boat, the back sail inevitably diverts some of the wind from the front sail or sails. In a side wind from either direction, a course can be set and the sails can be angled so that all of the sails are used to their fullest potential. Utilizing the sails this way is a substantial advantage for sailors because winds come from the side (there being two sides) much more often then they come from behind. But the potential can be wasted if the captain and crew don't make timely adjustments to turn the side winds into a favorable irresistible force. You can keep your organization beneficially aligned with irresistible forces if you too execute your new direction properly.

In sailing, the best results come from having both a captain who is good at reading the waves to spot shifts in the wind so that the course and sails are set optimally, and a crew that can get the job of setting the sails done by working in quick, careful coordination. All hands must be alert and the crew in top physical condition. Most importantly, the crew must cooperate in a timely way with one another when the order comes to make a change in the sails. This teamwork takes time to develop. As the crew practices, it gets better at doing things right the first time, and in less time. As the captain better understands what the crew can do, she or he can do a better job of timing orders to take best advantage of the shifting wind. Also, the captain and the crew will develop ways of sharing information about the upcoming wind conditions that improve anticipation.

The same circumstances are true for your organization as it seeks to get the most benefit from irresistible forces, but with one difference: Whereas the ship's captain must be an effective dictator, your organization must have continuing help from everyone in it to spot shifts in the irresistible forces and design effective ways to adapt to them. The need for coordination and cooperation is much more critical than on even the most effective sailing ship because there is so much more to be done.

However, when it comes to working with irresistible forces, many organizations might as well be in dry dock. Their captains are wearing blinders and are hard of hearing, and so have little sense of the future shifts in the irresistible force winds. Some of the positions in the crew have no one in them, and so some key tasks aren't getting done. Coordination and cooperation are at a low level, so errors and slow progress occur when an order does come. The crews are timid about telling the captains what they need to know in order to choose the right course with the proper sails. Each person gets most of her or his annual compensation for maximizing individual personal performance rather than cooperative effort, even when the organizational boat will go slower as a result. In such situations, getting people to understand about using irresistible forces is only the beginning of the task of capturing the irresistible force benefits of having continuing favorable wind conditions for the organizational boat.

Organizations are more like the crews of sailboats than pivoting windmills in that organizations require continuing cooperation based on mutual trust to make best use of irresistible forces. This chapter focuses on that critical difference in creating and maintaining your irresistible growth organization through outstanding teamwork. If you want to see organizational poetry in action, watch an on-board video of an America's Cup-winning yacht competing in shifting winds. That's what your organization needs to look like to get the most benefit from irresistible forces. You need to create a championship irresistible-force-pursuing team by adding mutually supportive people, capability, and incentives to create the ability to capture the perpetual fair wind.

Checking Your Skill Box to See What's Missing

Few organizations have been successful in consciously and deliberately adapting to changed irresistible forces. Exceptions include GE's refocus onto financial services, VISA's growth in credit cards, and Shell's adjustment to a changing petroleum market. Most success has come from simply being the beneficiary of forces that happen by chance to be helpful to the organization. This situation is like the sailboat that is always going in the same direction with its sails set in the same way. Often, the wind will blow in more or less the right direction and good progress will occur. However, whenever that wind shifts towards the bow, the progress will quickly slow or stall. If you and your organization can be prepared with the necessary skills to take advantage of whichever way the winds blow, you'll avoid those delays and stalls, and achieve breakthrough gains instead.

Essential Skills of Effective Organizations

To identify the skills missing from your organization in order for you to get the most benefit from irresistible force management, you first need to determine what new tasks will have to be implemented to achieve that benefit. Here are some areas to consider where you may need additional skills:

- Developing a statistical capability to aid in the identification of new and shifting irresistible forces.

- Spotting the causes of new irresistible forces with which your organization is now unfamiliar.

- Developing a strong ability to anticipate continuing shifts in irresistible forces.

- Interpreting when changes become unstoppable trends.

- Deciding what skills are needed to make the best use of shifting irresistible forces.

- Determining how to acquire the necessary skills that your organization is missing.

- Integrating new employees, skills, suppliers, and partners effectively into key task areas.

- Improving coordination among those sensing and needing to adapt to irresistible forces.

- Designing compensation and recognition programs to match the shifting needs of the organization in order to fully benefit from the irresistible force trends.

- Improving communications about and response time to changed irresistible forces.

- Adapting to rapid changes in growth rates smoothly and effectively.

Of particular interest is that some of these skills (and others) will be in short supply until more organizations become highly effective at adapting to irresistible force shifts. For example, executives frequently report that there are few people who are experienced in designing computer-based systems that provide lasting competitive advantages, as measured by continuing gains in market share and profit margin. Yet few of the organizations that do adapt well to shifting irresistible forces lack such capabilities. You should assume that you will probably have to find this talent in other organizations, and that you will have to help high-potential people in your organization learn to fill partial or total gaps that cannot be handled better by hiring and partnering. To be effective in this search inside and outside your organization, be sure to check whether the people you find can solve the kinds of problems you plan to throw at them, that they are excited by the purposes of your organization's activities, that they are self-motivated to do the kind of work you need them to pursue, and that they enjoy working with others.

Once you've determined the tasks, you then need to assess your skill levels and effectiveness in these areas. Many organizations will make mistakes in this assessment process. One mistake is to try to do the evaluation solely through interviewing and having forms filled out. A far better approach is to search for case histories of your organization's performance in the context of shifting irresistible forces, and to provide assessments that test capabilities in these areas instead. (This is described more fully in the next two sections.) Another common error is to look at how well people executed fixed assignments and focus primarily on narrowly defined results rather than on adaptation to irresistible forces.

Easier Essentials

Understanding the complexity of irresistible forces can overwhelm the skills and experience of almost anyone. Break the same issue down into smaller and smaller pieces, and more and more people will have, or can learn, the skills to provide useful perspectives. Then, the pieces can be assembled in the most attractive way by one of your better generalist thinkers. This approach works best, naturally, if all of those working with the pieces stay in contact with each other, and share information and insights.

Imagine that your organization is growing rapidly around the world from a small base. Initially, your sales organization is headed by one person. As your business grows, you decide to split that job into two jobs, one for domestic sales and one for international sales. As time passes, the international sales job will be broken down by continent or end markets served. Eventually there will be a head of sales for each country of any size. Finally, there will be heads of sales for large individual customers in individual countries. As you can see, the need to coordinate increases greatly, but the skill set that each person must have becomes much smaller. Many organizations err in not specializing rapidly enough so that they can provide their people with an appropriate scope of responsibility to match their existing skills and experiences.

Completing Your Skill Box

To be sure that your initial skill assessment is adequate, you should rely on people who are widely regarded as being very effective in these activities in your own and other organizations to help you design appropriate assessments. In addition, you can work with academics, consultants, and trainers in this process, but *not to transfer their own skills.* You should use these intermediaries solely to help you identify what skills need to be transferred, if any, from those who have them in comparable organizations to your own organization's people.

Unless your organization is very small or unusual, you already have someone who has at least one of all the essential skills you've determined you need. However, many people currently lack all the skills they need to be effective. Relax. This latter circumstance can be changed fairly rapidly through hands-on learning, outsourcing, partnering and hiring.

Help Wanted

You should investigate how partnering, outsourcing, and hiring compare to internal learning to supplement your existing capabilities. Hiring is usually thought of first, but will often be the poorest alternative because of the expense, time delays, and risks involved.

As an example, let's consider a case where changes in technology represent shifting irresistible forces. You may find that partnering with academic institutions in evolving technology areas is a much better solution to understanding and tracking those technologies than trying to hire permanently for such a position. The academic institution will tend to attract knowledge within the field more effectively than any one outside organization can hope to do. However, assigning people from your organization to work as liaisons with academic partners (who are sharing their knowledge) will probably be more effective than only hiring outside organizations to play this continuing role. The internal liaison person will have much more knowledge of how to apply the new knowledge to your organization than any outside person could have.

Partnering with noncompeting organizations that are implementing adjustments to the same forces you face has a major advantage: You can get additional perspectives on what needs to be done in your organization. The partner, in this case, can be a coach for your organization in helping you customize the perspective that both of you end up sharing.

Outsourcing is best reserved for circumstances where the other organization can free your people to work on more valuable tasks, where using this organization's work will be simple and error free, and where you can trust the other organization to look out for your interests. Obviously, if this is also a less expensive solution, the lower cost will be an added benefit.

Hiring provides the important benefit of keeping scarce talent away from your competitors. Done properly, you may actually preempt the competition's potential progress by attracting those whom your competitors are most likely to need in order to threaten your enterprise. Obviously, you should have a significant role for these people. Keep in mind that there is a disproportionate benefit from creating the longest lead time over the competitors' responses. Your lead time expands the size and duration of your benefits from each shift in irresistible forces. If you can deny resource access to your competitors in several areas, the size and duration of your potential benefits may grow exponentially.

Hands-On Apprenticeships

Once you have identified the skills and determined who in your organization already has them, you now need a way to create a continuing expansion of those important skills. The best way to accomplish this expansion is to share the skills you have with those who need them. With the proper approach, you can rapidly multiply how many people are involved in learning so that almost everyone can learn in a relatively short period of time.

Begin by converting your most effective skilled people into learning facilitators. Then encourage them to stay involved with those they have helped, both as mentors and as experts. Here's how to start the process: For at least an hour a day over a month's time, have a skilled person work on a variety of your irresistible force issues with someone who needs this skill. For the first learners, choose people who are highly admired in the organization and who are good at working with others to expand skills. Their high emotional intelligence and esteem will help offset any weaknesses in people skills among those with specific skills to share. The purpose of the hour or more together is for the experienced person with the skills to coach, advise, counsel and provide relevant exercises to the person who is learning. The learner should first focus on getting the necessary background from the skilled person, and then on applying the knowledge to current issues. The learners should be assigned to this task full-time for the month. Whenever possible, rotate these learners to work with two or three skilled people in the same area during the same month. This rotation allows the learner to get the benefit of being exposed to different communication styles, which will facilitate learning. During the following month, continue the process with two or three other skilled people for the same learner, continuing to work on different irresistible force shift issues. Continue this process until the learner has developed all of the necessary skills.

Your next step is critical: These first learners become coaches and get together to create a one- or two-month learning experience that can be provided to everyone else in the organization. This work, too, should be a full-time learning assignment for each person. The difference for this second tier of learners is that each person will learn all the skills he or she needs during the same assignment with one skilled person. Also, instead of having many coaches, each learner will have only one. This setup allows each coach to work with three or four people (or three or four work groups) simultaneously. This shift is possible since the first learners were chosen because others already respect them and find it easier to learn with their help. The first learners will be very helpful in improving the learning experience for everyone else, based on their own recent apprenticeships.

After the second group of learners has finished the process, they, too, become coaches, keeping their original coach for up to an hour a day to work with them on how to coach others. Much of this time together will be used for going over problems that individual learners are having. Then the third group of learners becomes coaches for a fourth set of learners. The third group of learners retains the second set of learners as coaches for their coaching efforts, and so on.

Essentially, you are creating an apprenticeship system for irresistible force skills. Like an apprenticeship, the emphasis should be on the effectiveness of the learners rather than on meeting a rigid timetable. Some learners will require more time, and some will require less. Be sure to be flexible in providing the right length of time and amount of learning assistance. Try to provide a lot of freedom in letting coaches and learners select each other.

Many organizations have learned that they can gain a great deal by having all employees involved in constant learning activities. The time required to pursue this process can simply come from using the regular allotment for learning. Otherwise, an explicit time commitment for learning will have to be made by the organization's leaders.

This process may seem slow to you compared to traditional training methods, but it will actually increase your organization's benefits the fastest. The first learners will get tremendous experience in the skills needed as well as in helping others to learn. They should eventually be able to improve the process enormously, especially if your most effective initial practitioners of the skills are diverted as little as possible from exercising those skills, serving primarily as expert resources. The second and subsequent learners will also be serving their apprenticeship as they coach others, and can be included in direct assignments related to irresistible forces after they develop the necessary skills.

You'll have created a waterfall that cascades from expert to learner, who becomes coach to new learners, who will, in turn, eventually become coaches, and so forth, driving the learning deeper and more broadly across the organization. Using this process, you should be able to expand skills through the organization in less than two years (for all but the largest organizations where it will probably take three to four years). In addition, you'll create a lot of adjustments to irresistible forces along the way as you practice the new skills.

Creating the Incentives to Use the Skill Box Well

While it's easy to define an incentive as simply what motivates someone to focus on the right things at the right time and in the right way, determining the best ways to motivate people to accomplish a task has become an eternal debate among those who study motivation. Some focus on freedom of scope and action. Others emphasize money. Still others mention recognition (awards and prizes, for example) or promotion. Another perspective includes the balance of risk and reward as perceived by the person receiving the incentives. Other experts point to the relevance of what the incentive is being applied to, focusing on the right causes to get the right effects. In addition, having work that has personal meaning is becoming ever more important. The newest line of argument builds on the idea of trust-based relationships.

This debate has never been settled because there is some important truth in each point of view. The real challenge lies in determining how and when to combine elements from the various viewpoints.

One Size Doesn't Fit All

From the earliest research on this subject by experts such as Elton Mayo and his famous studies of the Hawthorne Works in Illinois, it has been clear that each person is somewhat differently motivated from the next person.* If you ask people, they'll tell you what motivates them. In fact, in complex situations, they can tell you what combinations of factors are the most meaningful incentives. To get candid answers, however, requires trust because the person you are asking may fear that the result will be to reduce her or his incentives. And in some cases, people may not be aware of what would motivate them in situations they haven't experienced before. You can experiment using simulated environments to find out. You should especially find out if what your organization is trying to do is inspiring to each person. Few companies meet the potential of their peoples' need to be inspired with the organization's purpose, and inspiration is certainly a powerful incentive. Those who are not inspired by the company's purpose, work, and goals might be happier elsewhere where they can be more inspired.

Many companies are now proud to offer so-called cafeteria benefit programs that allow employees to pick and choose from among many benefits the combination that is most valuable to them. The same kind of approach would be useful regarding incentives.

---

*See *The Human Problems of an Industrial Civilization* (Macmillan, 1933).

One Size Doesn't Fit Anybody

Having decided to change direction, many organizations are so excited about pursuing the opportunity that they forget to consider how incentives need to be shifted as well. Or the compensation system is managed with all the delicacy of a dinosaur eating lunch, and so people may be afraid to ask about changing incentives. For example, in one of the most highly regarded high technology companies in the country, a manager was charged with creating a multi-billion-dollar business in only three years. He was provided with the help and financial resources he needed to succeed. He was concerned that this was going to be a high-risk assignment, and that his colleagues would perform poorly unless the financial incentives were matched to the risk profile.

Soon, the manager was so concerned that he could think about nothing else. But because the corporate compensation people were viewed with fear, he was reluctant to contact them. Finally, a consultant insisted that he make a telephone call. The executive was astonished to learn that the company already had a program that he could use to do just exactly what he wanted to do. He had simply been too intimidated to ask about it. Months of time had been wasted unnecessarily because of the poor level of trust about compensation in that company. The compensation people, in this case, could have helped by making more information available about their philosophy about incentives so that managers would be less reluctant to approach them with questions. Keep this lesson in mind when making your irresistible force management plans.

In addition, be sure to remember that the type of incentives often have to be shifted over time to be effective. New people in an organization may be very concerned about recognition, as feedback that they belong and fit in with the others. After they become convinced that they are accepted and fit in, they may want more in the way of promotion and compensation incentives. Further along in their careers, they may be concerned about building financial security, and, prior to retiring, they may want as many pension benefits as possible.

It's also possible that a person may have a life-changing experience and thereafter see things differently. For example, following a heart attack many people look for more balance in their lives rather than more professional challenge. Or after losing a loved one or having a baby, personal responsibilities for relatives, home, or family may dramatically change and cause a new outlook on work.

To be most effective, then, your incentive program has to be a work in progress in general, as well as highly adaptable on a personal level.

Stallbusting

The following activities and questions can help you pinpoint your organization's strengths and weaknesses regarding the skills, learning environment, and incentives it needs to succeed in surpassing the future best practice and approaching the ideal best practice of locating, anticipating, and adapting to changing irresistible forces.

Create and Use Scenarios to Reveal Your Level of Capability

Most organizations can address three or four scenarios successfully at the same time. In testing for skills, learning environment, and incentives, these scenarios can give you a dry run on the kind of actual changes you may face in the future. Operating the scenarios will help reveal the strengths and weaknesses of your current skills and experience.

What scenario can you study that will be the most challenging for your organization to adapt to? Think of this approach as a variation on the Nth-degree test that we discussed in chapters 15 and 16. Try to identify the most recalcitrant aspects of organizational resistance to change, a particularly knotty irresistible force.

What scenario can you study that will create the most potential confusion in implementing a new direction? Many organizations unknowingly select strategies that depend on a certain business environment, such as the growth of one channel of distribution at the expense of another. Should these trends reverse for some reason, a lot of organizational thinking quickly becomes obsolete. For example, the old rules of thumb for one part of the market may be a disaster for the other market. Value-added resellers of computers need a high selling price on their equipment to make money after covering their substantial costs. Direct sellers of computers need a low selling price to offset their lower value-added and to help reduce marketing costs on a per unit basis. If you suddenly choose to compete in both channels, how do you price your computers and be successful in both channels?

What scenario can you examine that will be most dangerous to your organization's health and vitality? Developing such scenarios is helpful in focusing people's minds on survival, something that they are usually very interested in. In that context, concerns will become more realistic about where changes are required in skill levels and incentives. Such a scenario could be one whereby your company's reputation was harmed in some fundamental way such that customers were inclined to shun your products and services.

What scenario would cost you the largest number of your critically skilled people? For many companies today, such a circumstance could be triggered by a continuing collapse of their own stock price while the stocks of competitors stayed high. Highly capable executives and technical people would see that they could earn vastly more money from the same efforts elsewhere, often in a more interesting environment. Many organizations suddenly collapse because of the loss of one or two key people. Creating a scenario that causes widespread loss of skills helps focus attention on the need to back up skills in other people, and on what may be currently lacking in the learning environment.

After you have worked through each of these scenarios, review the results to determine what skills were missing, what experience was missing, where coordination was weak, and where skills and experience were strong and effective. Use what you find out to devise the first steps in your learning plans, following the process described in Hands-On Apprenticeships.

Consider the Competitive Implications of Differential Skills, Learning Environments, and Incentives

Competitive gaming is a planning activity that many organizations have found to be useful for understanding which paths offer more promise than others. In this activity, different individuals or teams assume the role of a competing company and consider how best to undo your organization's situation. In doing this work, it's important to consider both current and potential competitors. This work is also valuable for planning how to have an advantage in effectiveness for your organization.

What skills and incentives could you add that would create the most competitive differential in the future? For example, in the on-line book selling business, this differential first appeared as Web-site design, but it quickly changed to include helping customers find books they would like but didn't yet know about. Later, providing an easy purchasing experience for nonbook items became important. Over time, the necessary skills to excel will certainly shift again, and that's why it's important for you to continually ask and answer this question. You need to be sure that incentives encourage finding, developing, and using those skills at the optimal times.

What skills and incentives could you expand throughout your organization that would create the most competitive advantage? Many organizations are constrained by an elitist view that only a chosen few can know and work on certain key issues. However, it's more often true that the more people who work on the problem, the more potential insights will be developed. In the case of on-line book selling, for example, anyone can buy a book on-line and have an opinion about what their unmet needs are, now and in the future. Having people learn how to elicit those opinions and use them to find simple, effective, inexpensive solutions would be a great skill to have.

In light of the skills and incentives that would help your organization prosper the most competitively, what learning environment would work best for you? This chapter provides a detailed learning environment model that you should modify to reflect the preferences and needs of your organization. To help you in this regard, have the people in your organization who need to learn read this book, paying special attention to this chapter. Then ask them to comment on how the learning process should be customized for your organization. Finally, track how you do with the learning approach and modify it through measured experiments to better adapt the process to each person's particular learning style. Some people will benefit from more written materials. Others need a lot of dialogue. Some will be helped by focusing on feelings. You need to accommodate any way that works well to access a person's ability to appreciate and successfully use the new knowledge.

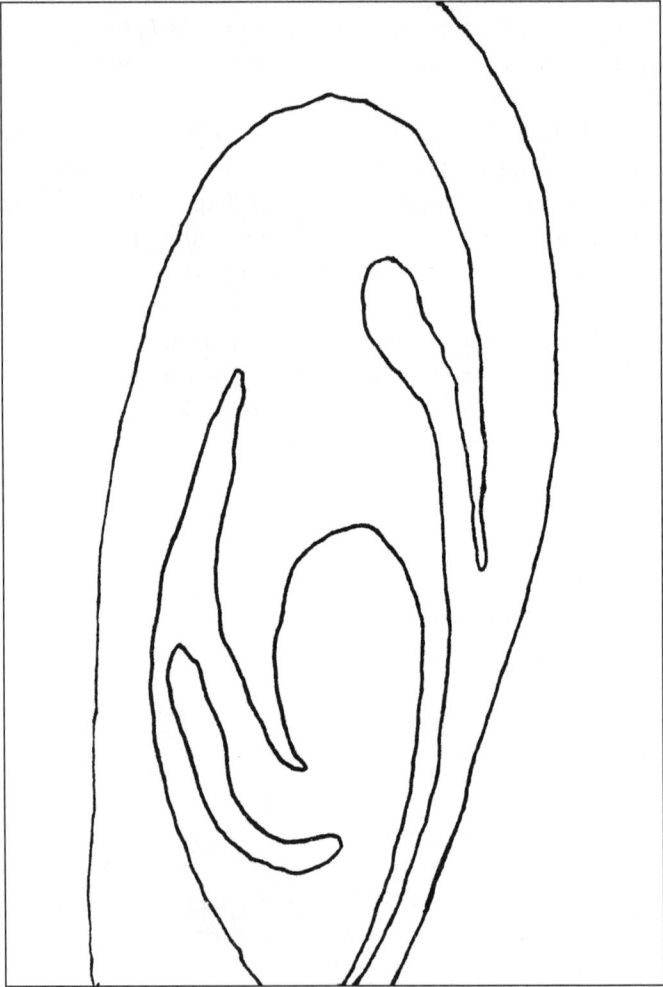

Repeating the first seven steps of irresistible force management will help you create even better solutions each time you repeat.

18

CONTINUALLY CHECK OUT THE NEWEST FASHIONS

STEP EIGHT: REPEAT STEPS ONE THROUGH SEVEN FOR IMPROVED EFFECTIVENESS IN USING THE IRRESISTIBLE FORCE MANAGEMENT PROCESS

Few things are impossible to diligence and skill . . .
Great works are performed not by strength, but perseverance.

—Samuel Johnson

To become most successful at locating, anticipating, adapting to, and creating changes in irresistible forces, you and your enterprise must repeat indefinitely the steps outlined in chapters 11 through 17. This chapter shows you the importance of continually reevaluating your use of the irresistible force management process. You will also learn how increased skill with the process can help you to locate even better opportunities and ways to capitalize on them. The process can also help you to build new capabilities and relationships that will permit you to pursue additional directions more successfully.

Is There an M.D. in the House?

Many businesses enjoy one smashing success but are then unable to repeat that breakthrough in the future. As the world changes around them, the benefits of the initial advantage erode and performance lags. Consider Xerox, for example. The company's Palo Alto Research Center (PARC) invented the software that made possible the connected personal computers of the early twenty-first century. PARC also created the practical model for user software conventions that Microsoft and Apple Computer have built upon. Yet Xerox reaped little benefit from this remarkable work, in part because the company had a limited understanding of the irresistible forces that would shape the personal computer business.

In contrast, consider Dell Computer. While just a teenager, Michael Dell spotted an important irresistible force: Personal computers are far more attractive to customers when the machines are reliable, easy-to-use, quickly available, work faster, have more capabilities, and cost less. Dell thought first of all like a customer, and he soon found ways to improve off-the-shelf machines to run faster by adding relatively inexpensive components. He bought excess and discontinued IBM personal computers from computer stores at a discount, improved their performance, and sold them directly to customers at a lower price than a computer store could charge. Dell was off and running.

When customers began demanding faster service than could be provided by sending the machines back to the company, Dell responded by finding service providers who could come to the customer's place of business or home and make repairs on the spot. Because such service calls are expensive, Dell quickly designed ways to help customers solve their own problems. Soon, fewer than 10 percent of the problems reported to Dell required a service visit. This approach also provided Dell with faster feedback about faulty components. Dell could replace the bad parts in newly built machines much sooner, which meant that few customers would have problems.

By continuing to examine why breakdowns occur, Dell determined that reduced component handling could help. Suppliers did the inspections at their facilities so that Dell didn't have to. This solution further reduced handling that could damage components, and problems rapidly declined.

A few years after Dell started up, IBM responded to the challenge presented by Dell and others by changing the pricing on its newest computers. The result was that Dell's upgrading of the performance of new IBM machines would provide little profit. This irresistible force made Dell realize that the company needed to manufacture its own personal computers, using standard components in high-performance designs. Direct selling continued to provide a large cost advantage. Dell was soon able to produce custom-built-to-spec computers in a short period of time. Sales again soared, as did profits.

Continued success soon brought Dell Computer to a crisis point. The company was growing so fast that it could not both meet the immediate demand and add the personnel, systems, and coordination needed to keep up with the market's irresistible forces. Like a sailboat in a hurricane, sometimes you have to reef many of your sails to avoid being overwhelmed by the force of the winds. Dell learned the lesson of pursuing controlled, profitable growth rather than maximum growth.

As corporate intranets expanded, customers wanted thousands of machines delivered simultaneously around the world in compatible configurations for easy installation, communications, and maintenance. Dell found that it could underprice rivals by preloading the customer's own data and software on the machines at the factory. This innovation reduced the customers' costs by more than $200 per machine.

Understanding the customers' needs required a new approach to direct selling, so Dell began assigning salespeople to work on-site with customers to help them plan for their future needs. Dell beefed up its worldwide shipping and service capabilities to back up this expanded market opportunity. Soon the company was growing at an enormous rate in countries it had only begun serving a few months or years earlier. With its newly created worldwide scope, multinational corporate accounts became Dell's mainstay in the mid- to late 1990s. Since these customers also wanted to have a single supplier for the whole network, Dell began offering an expanded product line. Servers became an important part of its capabilities in attracting these accounts.

With greater volumes, the time from order to shipment continued to drop. By 2000, most of these custom-built computers left the shipping dock within 30 hours of being ordered. This speed also provided Dell with another important advantage: The company didn't need much capital in order to grow. Its use of working capital was very small. Customers usually paid Dell before Dell had to pay component suppliers. By using standard components and largely unautomated factories (to provide maximum flexibility), the company also was not very fixed-asset intensive.

During the late 1990s, Dell was able to use excess cash flow to repurchase shares at a time when other fast growing companies had to either borrow large sums or sell more common stock. As a result, Dell's stock price soared even faster than its market share, revenue, and profit gains. Because the stock was growing so rapidly, the company soon began making a tidy profit selling put options to buy back its stock at lower prices. In such a favorable environment for employee stock options, Dell found itself able to attract and retain many of the most talented people in the personal computer industry.

Observers and executives at Dell have been unanimous in ascribing this excellent adaptability to irresistible forces to Michael Dell's thorough understanding of and unstinting attention to the irresistible forces. Many have wondered how this precocious teenage leader could have emerged into the longest-serving CEO in this very demanding industry. Clearly, Michael Dell believes in repeating the search for locating, anticipating, and adapting to irresistible forces. That repetition has kept him ahead of the competition in personal computers. The company faces new challenges in the 21st century as growth of personal computers inevitably slows.

To repeat outstanding success, you must continually reapply what you have learned in Part Two of this book. That lesson is your ultimate 2,000 percent solution.

Repeating the Process Improves the Results from Subsequent Repetitions of the Process

The first time you go through the irresistible force management process, you'll find that unfamiliarity with the process will slow your progress at various stages. As you repeat the process, familiarity and the reuse of information that you have developed in the past will allow you to proceed more rapidly.

Learn, People, Learn

You can expand on and improve your existing thinking by having those who are learning irresistible force management examine irresistible forces that you have already considered. This reconsideration allows those who are learning the process to offer new perspectives that fill previously missed gaps in understanding. These new perspectives are especially valuable to those who used the process earlier. This sharing will help the others to expand their understanding of how to use and benefit from the process. The more people you involve, and the more heterogeneous their backgrounds and ways of thinking, the more you will learn about irresistible forces to benefit your enterprise.

You need to create integrated ways to exchange the new information about irresistible forces. If your company has an intranet, you can create a work site on it. You can post questions and solicit reactions to the responses from everyone. Posting research on future best practices helps as well. This communication will reduce some of the work involved for others. If you don't have an intranet, you can circulate working papers along with reply forms to get answers and reactions to questions. You will need someone to administer this process.

To involve even more people, expand your use of the process to include other stakeholders such as users, suppliers, customers, partners, distributors, shareholders, and the communities you serve. However, for reasons of confidentiality, you may have to limit their access to some of your thinking. You'll probably find that these stakeholders have important perspectives on the irresistible forces you face and how to adapt to them that will be very helpful to you. Be sure to involve them as much as you possibly can. And, while confidentiality should always be a concern, you should be equally careful to test the conclusions you reach with these stakeholders before committing yourself to an approach for an irresistible force. Otherwise, your perspective could wander off in a direction that is comfortable for employees, but is not really going to be effective in the marketplace.

A Second Chance (and a Third, and. . . .)

Use repeating the process to reconsider how well you and your operation have located, anticipated, adapted to, and created irresistible forces. You'll locate patterns of success, missed opportunities, and failure in how your organization uses the process. Then you can benefit from thinking about how you could use the process differently to get better results. In this evaluation, as in the use of the process itself, remember that you'll benefit from involving as many people and as many different perspectives as possible.

If you are still unsure why you were less successful than you would like to have been, bring in an outside expert in process redesign to suggest improvements. You'll often find that the problem is that your people lack certain experience, background, or skills in order to have produced the best possible results. These shortcomings, when they occur, will be difficult for your own people to perceive and overcome. In the near-term, you may find it useful to simply add some people to the process who do have these particular attributes, even if they aren't employees.

Repeating the Process Expands Its Scope

When you first use the process, you'll probably look primarily at areas where large, obvious forces are operating. You may also limit your consideration of these forces to the impacts on immediate stakeholders. Many of the most valuable insights will come from moving beyond these initial perspectives.

Did You Feel Something?

In your initial applications of irresistible force management, you'll tend to locate irresistible forces that are already in place in such strength that you immediately have to adapt more effectively to them. As you use the process longer, important benefits will arise from beginning to anticipate the arrival of new forces and shifts in current ones. These new arrivals and shifts will normally appear first as subtle changes in parts of the current environment.

A good way to find these subtle influences is to look at the parts of your existing environment that should first feel the effects of new trends. For example, weather forecasters concerned about the eastern seaboard of the United States find it productive to watch minor disturbances forming off the western coast of Africa during hurricane season. Although no one at Cape Hatteras needs to begin evacuating when a storm initially forms off the African coast, monitoring the progress of such weather systems from that time helps everyone to prepare an appropriate and timely response before a storm arrives at that vulnerable North Carolina coastline.

For a business, you may have particular customers who will experience the effects first. For example, many new trends in consumer products can be first detected in Hawaii, California, and Florida. These states have more exposure to foreign countries, and their people frequently try new products and experiences. Concerning government regulation, Wisconsin, Minnesota, and the Canadian province of Ontario can provide advance insights because new trends in regulation often begin in these socially conscious locales.

Like Links in a Chain

As repeated trips through the process expand the scope of its application, you'll want to look at the effects on those linked to your stakeholders. For example, your customers may have customers, who in turn may have customers, and so forth. In many industries, these relationships forward to the ultimate consumer can involve numerous links. The same may be true of suppliers, who in turn have suppliers, who also have suppliers, and so forth. Partners also present complex relationships because they have an additional full universe of customers, distributors, suppliers, partners, employees, and communities that they interact with and depend on. Most people limit themselves to considering one level of these relationships and end up missing the most important points as a result. Don't let that happen to you!

Your first reaction may be to feel a little overwhelmed by the potential complexity of this investigation. But bear in mind that your competitors and those with whom you must compete for resources are probably not yet looking this far afield. If you expand your scope now, you can greatly increase your likelihood of developing skills in adapting that will be superior and preemptive. For example, if your competitors are focusing on making products less expensive to produce, they may miss the opportunity to focus on an irresistible force that will make the ultimate consumer more sensitive to some proprietary product or service attribute than to price.

Repeating the Process Focuses Competitive Thinking

Consider your management of irresistible forces as a competitive tool for creating product and service differentiating strategies. Early in the use of this process, your competitive thinking will tend to be fairly primitive. You'll probably only consider the opportunity to arrive first with a better solution to the irresistible force circumstance. By continually working through the irresistible force management process, you can expand your success through preemptive adaptations. As a result, other organizations delay their response or even take the wrong path, increasing the likelihood that they become confused and misdirected in responding.

What About the Other Guy?

After several passes through the irresistible force management process have helped improve your enterprise's thinking and approach to irresistible forces, you can turn your attention to analyzing how forces are affecting your competition. You'll discover that some forces work better to your advantage than to others, and vice versa.

Consider that today companies in many industries subscribe to the strategy that they should consolidate to achieve cost advantages in reducing overheads and in purchasing. In actuality, it's rare that two or more diverse organizations can combine to create one that is more effective with irresistible forces. By recognizing this circumstance, you are likely to be able to circumvent such a narrowly preoccupied set of competitors as they grapple with the very significant problems of mismatched organizations consolidating.

For example, in 1998 Compaq, the personal computer industry leader, acquired Digital Equipment, the minicomputer industry leader. Compaq's concept was to use Digital's established relationships with companies and software vendors to add more value through retail channels and through value-added resellers. Dell meanwhile pursued its focus on direct selling effectiveness and value-added for customers. Before the Compaq-Digital combination, the irresistible force of consolidation among large companies in all industries favored Dell more than Compaq. Dell could respond much faster and at a much lower price to the need for creating a uniform computing environment within the constantly consolidating large companies. Compaq could only gain an advantage if Dell failed to expand its service and flexibility to the full world scale of these customer organizations.

After Compaq acquired Digital Equipment, the impact of this consolidation irresistible force directly benefited Dell in another way. Many computer consulting organizations and accounting firms favored working with a personal computer supplier who didn't compete with them in systems solutions as Digital Equipment did. Consequently, Dell used its relationships with these consulting organizations to expand its ability to adapt to the emerging worldwide needs of these consolidating computer customers. Dell's market share gains accelerated.

One on One

A great weakness of many competitive strategies is to assume that all customers have the same needs. Similarly, a grave error in considering irresistible forces is to assume that all customers will be equally affected by the same forces. That error often shows itself as having a single strategy applied in the same way with each customer. When you repeat the irresistible force management process, you'll discover ways to fine-tune your competitive analysis of irresistible force impacts to include an account-by-account consideration of opportunities.

For example, in a small account where there are few special and emerging needs for personal computers, Dell may have little or no advantage from forces versus a competitor like Gateway (that also does direct selling of built-to-order computers). As previously mentioned, if two enormous financial services companies suddenly merge with operations in over 100 countries, only IBM, Compaq, and Dell may be able to provide what the merged customer needs. The fleet-footed Dell should have a large opportunity in this situation unless it has failed to establish a meaningful service presence in some of these countries. If that weakness exists, Compaq will probably have the edge, unless IBM has established a CEO-to-CEO relationship with the customer company.

From such head-to-head comparisons can come a sense of the size of different opportunities, now and in the future, and what actions will be most likely to create a positive result for your enterprise.

Stallbusting

The following questions will keep your business focused on repeating the irresistible force management process. This perspective can also help you to see that you obtain more benefit from using the process, the more frequently, broadly, and pervasively you employ it.

Improve Effectiveness Through Repetition

Many forces may conspire to retard your company's repetitive use to create better results. If you allow that slowdown to occur, you increase the likelihood of having one breakthrough that you cannot follow promptly with another. You'll be tempted, in particular, to shorten up your learning efforts in order to get more gains from your early insights. However, you need to follow Dell's example and choose controlled growth. Moving forward more slowly will allow you to continue to develop and exploit new irresistible forces and shifts in old ones, plus add insights into how to create proprietary advantages for yourselves.

What concrete incentives for repeating the process of irresistible force management does your organization need? Since you would like to extend the benefit of repeating the process in many different ways, you'll probably have to provide financial incentives for each person to learn and expand the use of irresistible force management. You can use the context of a management-by-objectives approach and link the recognition and financial incentives to the effectiveness of each person in particular, the teams each person is on specifically, and the entire business in general.

Another approach is to make promotions and raises contingent, at least in part, on the individual's performance in learning and supporting others in learning how best to use and repeat irresistible force management.

How can you create a structure to make it easy for your company to repeat the process and learn from the experience? As we mention earlier in the chapter, a company intranet or formal, paper-based sharing method will facilitate communication, appreciation of insights, and learning from past experiences. An important element for establishing and maintaining this structure is seeking constant feedback on how to make this sharing more helpful, faster and easier to use, and less expensive.

How can you best involve those who are nonemployee stakeholders? In some cases, you may already have a way of communicating and sharing ideas with these individuals and organizations. You'll usually find that these mechanisms are too simple and infrequent to accommodate the opportunities of working together on irresistible force management. A good way to begin finding a better mechanism is by describing your organization's experiences with the process to these stakeholders. At the same time, you can propose some initial experiments for working together in areas of obvious common interest. For example, Dell, in the wake of the Compaq acquisition of Digital Equipment, could have teamed with the computer consultants it provides equipment to for bidding situations. The teams could have created one-on-one case studies of how best to serve the newly consolidating customer companies, following their acquisitions and mergers. Based on such experiments, you'll need to propose expanded involvement with your stakeholders. With experience, you can build on what worked well and improve on what did not.

How should you measure how well your enterprise has done in locating, anticipating, adapting to, and creating changed irresistible forces? You should certainly set up an internal capability to monitor and evaluate your effectiveness. But you should also set up a more objective third-party-based mechanism to track how you have done. To the extent possible, you should base such measurements on independently testable information, rather than on subjective impressions. Almost everyone feels that he or she is doing an outstanding job, so this bias can trip you up if you are not careful.

Improve Effectiveness Through an Expanded Focus

Your initial use of the irresistible force management process will probably find you looking in all the usual places, which will limit your ability to anticipate new forces and changes in existing ones. By looking in more unusual places, your insights into exponential success will grow much more rapidly. You will learn less by only reexamining the ground you covered in your first uses of the process.

Which customers have changed their behavior most recently? Although these customers won't necessarily be subject to new or changed forces, this is a good place to be looking for such shifts in conditions. You are most likely to have found something significant if those who are behaving differently have a common element such as the same location, similar business strategies, or early exposure to new influences.

In the past, which customers have been first to signal new irresistible forces and changed irresistible forces? You'll want to monitor these customers as a way to locate early influences. Then you can test your changed responses before all your customers feel the effects.

How are those who are connected to your stakeholders changing their behavior? When looking for the answer to this question, be sure to consider the following groups:

- Customers' customers

- Customers' customers' customers

- Customers' customers' customers' customers (and so on, for as long as the linkages go)

- Suppliers' suppliers

- Suppliers' suppliers' suppliers

- Suppliers' suppliers' suppliers' suppliers (and so on, for as long as the linkages go)

- Partners' customers, distributors, and suppliers (and so on, as for customers and suppliers)

- Employees' families

- Families in the communities in which you operate

- Other organizations in the communities in which you operate

Frequently, the forces that affect these people and groups will change the behavior they exhibit toward your firm. This situation is like watching a stone fall into a pond. Based on seeing where it lands, you can predict the timing of when the ripples will arrive where you are standing. You may find it more advantageous to focus your actions first on helping the stakeholders closest to you. Prepare them to adjust to the shifting force trends in ways that will benefit both them and your company.

Improve Effectiveness Through a Competitive Focus

Adding irresistible forces and their shifts as factors in analyzing potential competitive interactions can help you to create circumstances in which you have the playing field to yourself. This happens when competitors are unwilling or unable to respond. As a result, you can gain more advantage sooner and for a sustained period of time.

Which irresistible forces are affecting each of your competitors more or less than they are affecting you? Differential effect is a keystone in creating competitive advantages that last. For example, all those forces that have stronger effects on you than on the competitor can be most easily turned into advantages. Where the effect is weaker on you, you have a potential vulnerability if the competitor shifts to take advantage of the forces.

To which irresistible forces are each of your competitors most misaligned? Even better than having a differential effect is to have a competitor resisting a force that you are using to your advantage. This circumstance is like being in a sailing race with the wind comfortably from the side while the competitor's boat is facing headwinds because the boat is being sailed incorrectly. Until the competitor tacks in the right way to capture the winds, you can make enormous progress. However, you need to be sure that you don't allow yourself to be swamped by excess demand for your products and services in such circumstances.

How do these match-ups of differential effect, alignment, and misalignment look on an account-by-account customer basis? Answering this question will not only make you even more effective, it will make the thinking process more practical and easier to understand. This simplification is a great help to those who will be implementing based on what you have discovered. Such a specific way of thinking will be critical in markets where there are few customers. However, it will become an even larger advantage in markets where there are many customers because your competitors are unlikely to take their analysis to this individualized level. That oversight will allow you to easily maneuver around them using the irresistible forces to your advantage.

EMBRACE THE FORCES

Why You Should Seek Out Irresistible Forces and How to Start Taking Action Now

If there is no struggle, there is no progress.

—Frederick Douglass

The Benefits of Exposure to Challenge

During the development of our previous book, *The 2,000 Percent Solution,* many outstanding executives, academics, and journalists shared helpful ideas and comments. Interestingly, only one person commented on that book's epilogue, which included a story about some lizards. However, that one person happened to be Arie de Geus, a former Royal Dutch/Shell executive cited in this book, who is one of the finest business thinkers ever.

The above-mentioned lizards were part of an experiment designed to cause extinction. Scientists placed the lizards on islands with habitats ill suited for them so that more could be understood about the process of a species dying out. Regardless of the ethics (which seem questionable at best) of the experiment, the unintended lesson was profound. Typically, the lizards didn't become extinct. Instead, they overcame the adverse conditions of their new habitats. To survive, the lizards evolved at more than 2 billion times the normal rate (as suggested by what normally occurs from looking at fossil records) in both behavior and physical characteristics in a single generation. Rapid behavioral and physical changes continued in succeeding generations of lizards, until they were soon quite at home in their new environments. The lesson of the lizards' phenomenal evolution, as de Geus pointed out in his feedback, is a most important clue to how irresistible forces can unleash humanity's full potential.

Let's consider outer space for a moment. Many people question the wisdom of the substantial sums spent by the United States and others on manned space exploration. These critics see few advantages to these efforts, and point out other uses for the funds that would have more obvious benefits. Defenders passionately and optimistically point out the potential for new scientific discoveries.

What both sides of the debate miss is that the harsh and limitless dimensions of outer space are the perfect environment for encouraging humanity's most rapid physical, behavioral, and organizational development. For example, when exposed to weightlessness, human bodies degenerate in a number of subtle, but threatening, ways similar to aging. One such reaction is to lose calcium from bones. Evolving our bodies in outer space might provide important benefits for earth-bound people in learning how to retard similar degenerative effects. And if humans make mistakes while operating in outer space, the errors become life-threatening more rapidly, which suggests the necessity of learning how to operate closer to the ideal best practice. Finally, manned space exploration is so difficult and expensive that the nations of the world have little choice but to pool resources, providing models of cooperation and alliances to be applied in other areas.

An aggressive commitment to manned space exploration could cause a rate of human evolution far in excess of what happened with the lizards. Rapid physical changes in response to new environments may be just as possible for humans as for lizards. Although humans and lizards look very different, the DNA of each is similarly subject to change. Understanding genetics increasingly allows people choices for changing their own bodies, as in using gene therapy to overcome hereditary diseases. Scientists now predict that we will eventually be able to grow replacement parts for ourselves.

And people have advantages over lizards. In particular, humans can use techniques and tools to think in new and more valuable ways. These tools include asking new questions, abandoning old ways of thinking, and using powerful machines such as computers to extend the physical limits of the human mind. This improved thinking, in turn, can create both more tools and more physical changes that are beneficial. People probably have more psychological ability to adapt than lizards do, also, by being more cognizant of the full extent and implications of our environments.

Astronauts operating in outer space create the potential for faster human progress. This is a good analogy to the advantages provided by an irresistible growth enterprise taking on greater irresistible forces to accelerate its progress. (© CORBIS)

As a result, we truly may be living at a new dawn of human creativity, at the threshold of a time when more evolution occurs than in the entire period since mammals developed. And it is possible that all of this could occur in only one century (three to five generations)!

In the context of this book, then, you should see by now that the potential for human organizations to improve can be greatly aided by thoughtful exposure to the rapidity and severity of irresistible forces and their changes. Such forces are, in fact, the environmental cause of almost all improvement. Therefore, you should seek out controlled exposure for your organization to additional large, overwhelming, and unpredictable irresistible forces to create the most valuable learning experiences.

You needn't risk extinction for your enterprise to get the improvements; care should be taken to avoid risk beyond what is prudent. You need only expose part of your organization to strong forces that can cause extinction for that activity if you don't adapt in time. To make this exposure less risky, tie that part of the organization to a safety harness (like the ones that trapeze artists use for very dangerous stunts). Such a safety harness can simply be continuous monitoring to determine whether to terminate an experiment that is too challenging (whether for an organization or for an individual in that organization).

An Action Plan for Irresistible Force Management

Shed your complacency about irresistible forces, think about how you relate to irresistible forces now, and start using all irresistible forces as proprietary advantages. To help you get started, here is a list of things to do now:

1. Write down where your company is good at locating and preparing for tomorrow's irresistible forces.

2. Write down where your firm needs to improve now to respond effectively to tomorrow's irresistible forces.

3. Write down those areas where your business must change in order to perform close to its future potential for irresistible force management, and set deadlines for when those changes need to happen.

4. Share what you have written with those who will have to make the changes. Give them this book, and set a time limit for them to review their plans with you for how they are going to meet these deadlines for change.

5. Begin helping everyone in your enterprise learn how to identify the stalls described in Part One of this book, how to overcome them through stallbusting, and how to create many 2,000 percent solutions by using the eight-step irresistible force management process described in Part Two.

6. Put measurements in place for each key activity to track the effectiveness of your response to irresistible forces affecting your company.

7. Begin experimenting with exposing parts of your operations to severe environments in order to create greater ability to work with these forces.

8. Review your progress monthly against what you found initially.

9. Reread this book frequently.

Make two copies of the preceding list of tasks and put one somewhere near your office telephone and the other near your computer. You will see it every time you make or receive a call, or write or read an e-mail. It will remind you to communicate these critical points.

If you would like free copies of the eight-step process list and this list of tasks to post in your office, go to this book's Web site <www.irresistibleforces.com>. On the home page, click on the buttons for those materials and print two sets for yourself. If you don't have access to the Internet, call (781) 466-9500 in the United States, 24 hours a day and leave your name and address. We will mail complimentary copies to you.

The book's Web site also has several chapters available for free browsing. You can send your colleagues there for information instead of always loaning them your copy of the book.

If you have questions about anything in this book, please send them to <mitchell@mitchellandco.com>. We enjoy hearing from you and helping you get the most benefit from this book. Feel free to use us as your safety harness.

PERSONAL IRRESISTIBLE FORCE MANAGEMENT LESSONS

The life which is unexamined is not worth living.

—Plato

This appendix is for those who want to learn how irresistible force management can be most useful outside of an enterprise. It covers some topics to suggest how to apply the new thinking habits proposed in this book to your personal and family lives.

Irresistible forces affect your personal life as well as the lives of your family's members and, indeed, the lives of everyone with whom you come in contact. As examples to spur your thinking, consider the following things that are especially apt to be created or influenced by irresistible forces:

- Sources of frustration and anger
- Time wasters
- Joyless tasks
- Continuing disagreements with others
- Health problems
- Loss of loved ones
- Loss of job

- Limited effectiveness
- Financial problems

If you are struggling against personal irresistible forces rather than using them to your and your family's advantage, you'll be draining lots of energy from your life and feeling a fair amount of frustration. By consciously thinking about how to turn these forces to your advantage, you'll overcome personal stalls and create 2,000 percent solutions where they will be the most satisfying to you and those you care most about.

Be Practical and Look for the Silver Lining

One of the lessons of irresistible force management is that all irresistible forces can be used to your benefit. Thus, when life seems to have hit you with a hard blow, the lesson is that a potential benefit exists from the blow that can be used to make your life much better. But you have to take the time to look for the silver lining. Rather than seeing this idea as part of some mantra to always think positively, think of it instead as intensely practical advice.

In our career-obsessed age, hard blows can come from either being passed over for a promotion or losing your job. Few will be immune from these events over the course of a working life. Even entrepreneurs who start their own businesses may face the equivalent challenges to their role in the company. Rather than living optimistically in the vague hope that neither negative job event will happen to you, you should always be prepared to see the events for what they are—opportunities for you to flourish. If you are passed over for promotion, take it as an indication that you have some improving to do to make yourself the most appealing candidate and then do something positive along those lines. You can choose to nurse your wounds or you can choose to find out how you need to improve. The latter action will help you a lot more than the former.

How about losing a job? How can that have a silver lining? That occurrence is one of the most severe emotional wounds that many people experience in their lives, right up there with the death of loved ones and divorce. However, losing that job can provide you with the impetus to reconsider how well your work really used to fit you. Now that you have to look around for something else, you may be able to find a better job fit. You may find a new job that has more free time associated with it so you can pursue more time with your family and your personal interests. Or you may be able to learn what you need to do differently to avoid being at risk for losing another job. Then you can use those lessons to be more successful in the next job. We all learn a lot faster from things that don't work out as we had hoped than we do from our successes. In addition, there may be irresistible forces at work that were affecting your last employer that you need to adapt to in future employment. That realization, too, can be a very valuable lesson. (For other ideas on how to overcome stalled thinking about getting a new job, be sure to visit our Web site <www.2000percentsolution.com> and click on the "job search" button.)

Apply New Thinking Habits in Choosing a Career

Choosing a career is one of the key ways that you select which irresistible forces you will be subject to, and what resources you will then have available for dealing with them. Like analyzing the circumstances to choose which irresistible forces can provide the most benefit to your organization, you should use similar analytical thinking in choosing a profession. You can thrive if you have work that has great personal meaning for you, helps you learn and grow as a person, provides you with a sense of accomplishment and competency, and makes you feel appreciated and valuable. Most people pursue their life's work in terms that are too limited to be fully rewarding for them. What they miss is that the fit is a highly personal one, like custom-made clothing that fits only you well.

Consider that many people pick a profession from choices that were highly visible when they were quite young, without knowing what else is around. As you can imagine, a lot of great jobs have no visibility at all to children. You need to actually try different types of work before you can know how well they fit you. That approach is the best way to learn. Screening tools, such as tests that match your personality to different types of work, can help you come up with ideas that you might not have considered on your own. Try some of them on for size.

Some people may not be able to find paid work that gives their lives the fullest meaning they would like. Don't give up. You may be able to do volunteer work to provide that meaning. Volunteerism is on the rise, and the meaningfulness of the work is the primary benefit that many volunteers report. In addition, volunteering can make you a better person to work with all the time. You'll improve your understanding of how to help make work meaningful for others, as well as how to help others find the right work for themselves. Becoming good at understanding this perspective will help not only you, but it will also help you counsel others you care about who face these same issues.

Seek the Benefits of Coaching or Teaching Children

As we point out in the book, simulations (especially playful ones) are great ways to develop a lot of experience with irresistible forces. What could be better than to have fun, meaningful ways to test your mettle? Coaching and teaching children provide excellent opportunities of this sort.

Prior to having a paid job, most people learn very little about the realities of working for and with others. On the job, most initially assume that the problem they should focus on is simply how to get power. They often think that with power others can be ordered to do the right thing, and great results will occur. Many people never outgrow this mistaken perspective, and so they are doomed to being surrounded by rebellious people (whether children, spouses, or coworkers), who resent their attempt to dominate situations.

To avoid this perspective's pitfall, you can quickly learn that progress stems from thoughtful examples, cooperation, and mutual assistance when you work with children. You will find this experience works particularly well with those who are not your own so that you have some emotional distance. Children who are on a sports team, for example (whether they are girls or boys), usually come out for the fun of it. If you don't believe it, ask each child at the start of the season. But the adults are usually slow to catch on. Adults think about skills and winning. It's true that winning can be more fun than losing. But how can you make the entire experience fun for everyone even when you're not winning?

You'll soon find that letting the children play in ways they want to is a lot more fun for them than anything else. For example, in team sports let them play the positions they like. You simply have to find lots of ways for them to play that both can be fun and develop their effectiveness. That solution means they'll have a better chance of enjoying the experience of increased competence as well. But be sure not to sacrifice the fun. That's the core. Even when they don't learn very much, give them as much play time as you can. You will then have served them well.

The lessons of this experience can easily carry over into being a parent. Children don't usually just decide to have a bad relationship with their parents. They usually degrade the relationship as a way to get the parents' attention. The children know what the parents' hot buttons are, and how to push them. If supportive parental attention is not forthcoming, then worse behavior will follow. Being children, they would also like to have fun at home as well as on the sports field. Play with them. You'll be glad you did. Everyone can have fun!

Now return to thinking about the workplace. Believe it or not, adults have many of the same perspectives as children do. They want to have fun, too.

They want to have a supportive relationship with the others in the organization. And they want to have meaning in their lives, as you do in yours. To be an effective leader in this environment, you need only remember the words of retired general Norman Schwarzkopf, "Be the leader you would like to have." Follow that advice and you can be more successful in your role as an organizational person, as well as a parent, coach, or a volunteer.

Adopt an Ageless Perspective

An irresistible force that creates stalls for many people is viewing one's life solely through the perspective of one's current chronological age. Ask yourself: Do you want to have wonderful experiences, or only age-stereotyped ones?

The psychology of human experience for most of us is heavily influenced by our age. What you thought important as a teenager will differ greatly from the thoughts you'll have when you become a retiree. The libraries are full of research that shows what issues and ways of thinking are predominant at different ages. For example, people in their twenties don't feel secure yet as adults and are constantly seeking reassurance that they are competent. Immediately after retirement, many people who have closely identified with their work wonder who they really are. And so forth.

One of the personal irresistible forces that you need to be careful about, then, is thinking and acting as though you will always be the same age you are today, or were yesterday, and that you'll have exactly the same concerns. While being active, idealistic, and open-minded like young people can do a lot for you, taken to an extreme these characteristics can also make you feel insecure and lead you to ignore the benefits of more age and experience.

You should instead adopt an ageless perspective, one that combines the best of the questions and concerns of each age in a person's life. Among other things, this perspective will make you more mature and understanding when you are young, and more interesting and outgoing when you're older. You can obtain these perspectives by having plenty of friends, family, and acquaintances in all age categories so that you can see the world through their eyes as well as yours.

By achieving and maintaining an ageless perspective you can acquire sooner the benefits that usually only accrue later in life and thus be able to use those benefits for a longer time. Such benefits include a practical and well-considered approach for dealing with the personal and family challenges that you'll encounter, like saving for your child's higher education and for your own retirement plans.

Another advantage to having an ageless perspective is realizing that each age has its unique pleasures and joys but that these can also be carried into other times of your life. Almost everyone enjoys being with young children, and that experience doesn't have to be limited to being a young parent. At any age, you can volunteer to help with youngsters in other parts of your family or community. Indeed, the world is full of children who want and need more attention from caring people. You can be one of those caring people, and everyone will benefit from your participation.

Be a Role Model of Irresistible Force Management

One of your greatest contributions to yourself and your family is to serve as a role model of how to locate, anticipate, and adapt to irresistible forces. You'll also be helping yourself to improve your irresistible force management skills.

Although people learn best by doing, they can learn even faster when they also have a role model. Think about how foreign the irresistible force concept will be at first to your family members. They'll see the world as mostly unchanging and hard to fathom. Share with them your ideas about how irresistible forces, especially the ones that seem threatening, can be helpful to you and your family. Encourage them to share their own ideas about what these forces mean. Ask questions to guide their thinking into more productive lines of inquiry.

For example, if a child is having trouble at school with a teacher, the child may feel totally helpless in the situation. The teacher can be a very formidable irresistible force to a child. Your child may not know that teachers like supportive attention as well as the child does. Help your child to see that having a problem with this teacher is an opportunity to learn how to get along better with adults. Encourage the child to visit privately with the teacher to ask the teacher's help in overcoming the trouble. People, and especially teachers, feel good about being asked for help, unless you catch them at a busy moment. To ask for help means you respect them, want to be with them, and want to have a better relationship. What can be more flattering?

Concerning your spouse, irresistible forces present wonderful opportunities for intimacy. Most of the irresistible forces will be ones that affect both of you and the family. By jointly considering how you can best take advantage of the energy and direction of these irresistible forces, you can forge a greater closeness and sense of cooperation that is loving and mutually rewarding.

❖ ❖ ❖

After you have considered these thoughts for improving your relationship to irresistible forces in your personal life, you'll probably come up with your own ideas on the subject. We'd like to ask that you share those ideas and any personal experiences with irresistible forces with others through us. You can send e-mail to us at <mitchell@mitchellandco.com>, and telephone us at (781) 466-9500 in the United States.

INTERNET IRRESISTIBLE
FORCE LESSONS

There's something thrilling about the Internet.

—Brian Eno (rock musician)

This appendix focuses on ideal best practices for using the Internet, a subject about which nothing has been written before. By viewing the lessons from the perspective of dealing with the unfamiliar in general, you can reap the most benefit.

What's All the Fuss About?

As this book is being written, many people see the Internet's future as an irresistible force that will change the shape of all organizations forever. Outlining the best ways to locate, anticipate, and adapt to the Internet's elements is beyond the scope of this book. But the fast-changing face of this electronic connection provides a fitting context for how you can apply one of the book's most important concepts, locating the ideal best practice.

As you recall from chapter 15, the ideal best practice for dealing with irresistible forces doesn't mean you have to forecast forces perfectly and prepare advance plans totally aligned with those forces. Rather, you should identify ways of working with these forces that will give you close to a perfect flexibility that creates advantages from every change in the irresistible forces, whether anticipated or not. As models, think of the pivoting windmill that can use the wind from any direction equally well, or the football fan prepared to enjoy a Packer's playoff game in Green Bay, Wisconsin, during January, regardless of the weather.

Let's begin with an examination of the Internet as an irresistible force. First consider the cause-and-effect question: Is the Internet an irresistible force causing changes in your organization's environment, or is the Internet the result of more fundamental irresistible forces? At first glance, many would say that the Internet is an enormous irresistible force. Just look at the extent to which companies have been helped (like Cisco and Dell) or hurt (like Encyclopedia Britannica and some primarily bricks-and-mortar retailers).

But the Internet's effects on an organization are much more complicated than its simply being used as a new marketing channel. A wide variety of organizations are helped by e-mail and group software communications, by being able to purchase goods and services less expensively, and by being better able to gauge demand. Others are hurt by the high costs of starting e-commerce unsuccessfully, greater pressure on their products' selling prices, and increased service demands from customers. In fact, the Internet's influence is pervasive, and the combined effects on an organization cannot be easily isolated and measured.

The broad scale of its impact should tell you that something more fundamental must be going on than electronically wiring the world together with common software protocols. The Internet, in fact, would change nothing for your company unless a variety of other irresistible forces were already in place. Here are some of the more important ones:

- People like to communicate with each other.
- Almost everyone likes to be able to get information more easily.
- Many people like to shop.
- Everyone likes a bargain.
- Everyone likes better service.
- Almost everyone wants their needs fulfilled now!
- The cost in time and money of using the Internet is dropping.
- The usefulness of the Internet's services is growing.
- The computer-literate population is growing rapidly.

Interestingly, most of this list relates to constant characteristics of human nature, rather than to technology. The Internet is simply one way of satisfying these fundamental human desires and needs. The increased need to provide these satisfactions relates to both the expanded expectations and improved choices that the Internet brings.

The Nth-Degree Connection

Estimates of the Internet's future size and impact vary widely. For the sake of argument, let's simply multiply where the Internet's influence is today by a large factor in order to describe circumstances that may happen in the future (but that may not happen at all). Applying the Nth-degree concept from chapter 15, let's assume that at some point 5 billion people have easy, free access to the Internet. We'll also assume that every computer on the planet can communicate with every other computer without human intervention, except for repairs. Add to the scenario any other assumptions that help you think about what organizations will look like in the future as the Internet expands and develops. For example, you may want to assume that Internet communications will include realistic holograms to make conversing from a distance much more like actually being with the other person. The idea is to make assumptions that clarify the potential of the future for you, regardless of the ultimate precision of those assumptions.

Who will be the organizational winners in such an environment? Which enterprises will be outstripping all others? Consider that satisfying the fundamental, unchanging human needs from the preceding list will be as essential to success then as now. All that will change from now is that your enterprise will have more ways to provide for those needs.

Let's focus on peoples' desire to communicate. When your company's products or services facilitate communication better than anyone else does (or is likely to do) in a way that people enjoy, you'll be on the road toward an ideal best practice regarding use of the Internet. Similarly, if your business makes it easier and more fun to shop than ever before, you will also prosper. You get the idea. Anyone who thinks of today's e-mail, Web surfing, and e-shopping as the ultimate has a limited imagination.

But what about all of those technical things that are so hard for an enterprise to provide on the Internet now? Actually, the Internet will probably turn them into inexpensive commodities. Already, thousands of organizations are springing up that can give any technical support aspect you could possibly want for providing services and products over the Internet. Consider the evolution of earlier communications technologies. Do you have to be a telecommunications engineer to have a working telephone system for your organization? The Internet's technical side in the future will at some point be like the telephone's technical side now. IBM and others are already providing "one-stop shop" Internet services and technical support for everyone from the biggest to the smallest organizations. For many small organizations, the cost of that support is already less than the charge for their payroll service.

If having an advantage in serving one basic human need is an ideal best practice, imagine what you can do when you can deliver several of these in a superior way. As an example, let's explore the opportunities that the Internet could open up for a theme park enterprise. Suppose the theme park people decide that they want to add customer benefits by providing more communications and faster, more individually appropriate service. How might the Internet come into play? Perhaps it could deliver a preview of the park experience. Visitors could then decide in advance which attractions to visit. They might even then be able to map out how to minimize the time spent traveling to and from the desirable attractions and standing in lines. Internet chat groups could be set up for sharing ideas and experiences, such as entertaining and interesting things to do while standing in lines. The park could also forecast the size of the crowds and duration of lines so that customers could select the best times to make their visits. You can see that the possibilities are many and varied, and can probably think of others yourself.

Why should the park's owners want to do these things? By improving the experience that people have when they come to the park, attendance should rise. Also, this information will tend to increase attendance when the park has the most capacity for more guests. Further, being able to plan ahead will increase the pleasure for a lot of people and put them in a better mood to spend when they do arrive.

Interestingly, all of these things can be accomplished without using the Internet. For example, the company could offer a guidebook and an 800 number to call for ideas. But what is new is that the Internet allows these services to be provided on an individualized basis. Solving problems with the Internet seems so daunting in some cases because important opportunities to serve these same basic human needs better in the past have been overlooked. So your enterprise, whether new or old, is probably trying to catch up with many years of missed opportunities to serve these needs in a brief period of time.

To help you begin, think about what couldn't have been done before that can now be done through the Internet. For a service organization like a theme park, you can immediately see that there is an opportunity to provide a virtual theme park visit over the Internet. Although you can't exactly duplicate the thrill rides, you could create games having the feel of the park that people would want to buy and play at home. As holograms become universal, these games could become more and more realistic. Tying into the Internet, these games could be played competitively to simulate some of the shared adventure of a theme park. In fact, you could even have some of the games interact with the people enjoying the attractions at the park.

Half of the fun of some of these experiences is talking about them with others. You could set up chat groups so people who had just finished playing the same game could talk about their experiences, or for people who wanted to learn how to play the games better. Imagine the potential income from selling this service.

In pursuing the ideal best practices with the Internet, it should be obvious that the key factor will be having people in your enterprise who are good fundamental thinkers about the customer's perspective and how to devise improved ways to serve these fundamental human needs on the Internet. It will be fairly easy to find the technical people to implement any customer-driven vision, but real innovation comes in conceptualizing large numbers of desirable outcomes that can be inexpensively developed and tested to see how people react to them.

By expanding irresistible force management knowledge and using the Nth-degree test within your enterprise, you can reap the benefits of developing a large number of people with skill and experience in conceiving ideal best practices on the Internet as well as in other environments and circumstances.

The Always-Win, No-Lose Option at the Speed of Light

One big problem with creating so many wonderful ideas is having to choose among them. Pick wrong and you may miss an opportunity to create a gigantic success. For this reason, looking for the best always-win, no-lose options makes a difference.

Returning to the theme park business, it could probably find a large number of potential partners to develop these new services. If the partners would pay for all of the development and the initial implementation of the services as well as the time the park's employees spent working on the tasks, the park could pursue a large number of alternatives. Not wanting to inundate its customers with new services, the company could then simply pick those that did best in tests. Partners would probably be amenable to such arrangements if they felt that there was a good chance of succeeding. How hard would it be, for example, to fund an Internet start-up that had a development contract with a theme park operation like Disney? The experience of Pixar in providing animation for Disney movies suggests that it would be easy.

What if you don't have the appeal of Disney? How can you find always-win, no lose options? Partners usually won't be willing to fund your development and start-up costs, but you can certainly emphasize projects where those costs will be quite small. Once you find many low-cost projects, you can then evaluate them for how hard it would be to recover your expenses. Some will pay off in a few days, others in decades. Go for those with the fastest benefits, then compare the choices for the size of the long-term benefit, net of any on-going costs you will have.

Here are some categories that should emerge. Anything that builds the recognition of, and reputation for, your enterprise should be near the top. Existing customers will be more attracted (making them easier to retain), and you'll get new customers. Anything that enhances your proprietary advantages in knowledge about your customers should also be attractive. Eventually, marketing, products, and service will be totally unique to each customer, but you can't create the right individual solution unless you know what is specifically attractive and useful to the customer. A third category is self-service, where the customer can provide the service they want better for themselves and at lower cost to both of you than you can provide it to them. An example is the tracking of packages by overnight delivery companies. You can usually get the information faster, better, and cheaper on the companies' Web sites than by calling the toll-free lines.

Good luck with your search, and be sure to share your questions and ideas with us at <mitchell@mitchellandco.com>. We'll be sure the information is shared on our web site <www.irresistibleforces.com> and in future editions of this book so that all of our readers benefit.

BIBLIOGRAPHY

Amabile, Teresa, "How to Kill Creativity," *Harvard Business Review,* September/October 1998.

Augustine, Norman R., *Augustine's Laws* (Viking Penguin, 1986).

Bonner, John Tyler, *The Cellular Structure of Slime Molds* (Princeton University Press, 1959, revised edition 1967).

Bonner, John Tyler, "The Society of Amoebas," *Science '84,* December 1984.

Byrne, Harlan S., "Facing Up to Asia," *Barron's,* November 9, 1998.

Cialdini, Robert, *Influence: Science and Practice,* 3rd ed. (HarperCollins College Publishers, 1993).

de Geus, Arie, *The Living Company* (Harvard Business School Press, 1997).

de Geus, Arie, "Planning as Learning," *Harvard Business Review,* March/April 1988.

Dell, Michael, *Direct from Dell* (Harper Business, 1999).

Drucker, Peter F., *Management Challenges for the 21st Century* (HarperCollins, 1999).

Gardner, Howard, *Multiple Intelligences* (HarperCollins, 1993).

Hammond, John S., Ralph L. Kenney, and Howard Raiffa, *Smart Choices* (Harvard Business School Press, 1999).

Huang, Kuang-Tsae; Yang W. Lee, and Richard Y. Wang, *Quality Information and Knowledge* (Prentice-Hall PTR, 1999).

Kanter, Rosabeth Moss, *World Class* (Simon and Schuster, 1995).

Kroll, Luisa, "Denim Disaster," *Forbes,* November 29, 1999.

Magretta, Joan, "The Power of Virtual Integration," *Harvard Business Review,* March/April 1998.

Maremont, Mark, "Gillette Won't Meet Profit-Growth Goal While Emerging Markets Face Turmoil," *The Wall Street Journal,* November 9, 1998.

Mayo, Elton, *The Human Problems of an Industrial Civilization* (Macmillan, 1933).

Mitchell, Donald W., "Become a Master of Capital Management," *Directors & Boards,* Summer 1998.

Mitchell, Donald, Carol Coles, and Robert Metz, *The 2,000 Percent Solution* (AMACOM Books, 1999).

Robinson, Alan G. and Sam Stern, *Corporate Creativity* (Berrett-Koehler, 1997).